1. Introduction

The financial services profession in developed countries is a major contributor to their economies. This is particularly true in long-standing financial centres, such as New York, London and Tokyo, the increasingly significant Chinese cities of Shanghai and Hong Kong, and the European hub of Frankfurt among others. The financial services profession provides considerable employment and overseas earnings, as well as vital functions that enable businesses to raise finance, grow and prosper.

Fundamentally, the financial services profession provides the link between organisations needing capital and those with capital available for investment. For example, an organisation needing capital may be a growing company and the capital may be provided by individuals saving for their retirement in a pension fund. It is the financial services profession that channels money invested to those organisations that need it, and provides execution, payment, advisory and management services.

The financial services profession is constantly evolving and it is vital for anyone working in it, or aspiring to work in it, to keep pace with changes and developments. At the time of writing (June 2017), there are major political developments, such as the Trump administration in the US and the decision made by the UK to leave the European Union (EU) (Brexit), and these will inevitably alter some aspects of financial services. In the US, there may be increased government spending with the inevitable impact on borrowing, and some rules that currently restrict the activities of banks may be relaxed. Brexit may result in some financial services activities moving away from London, spurring the growth of the main financial centres within the EU, such as Paris and Frankfurt.

Stock markets and investment instruments are not unique to one country, and there is increasing similarity in the instruments that are traded on all world markets and in the way that trading and settlement systems operate and are developing.

With this background, therefore, it is important to understand the core role that the financial services profession undertakes within the economy and the key institutions that make up the global financial services sector. However, the basic building blocks need to be clarified first – in particular, **equities** and bonds.

1.1 Equities and Bonds

Learning Objective

1.1.4 Know the basic differences between equities and bonds

Traditionally, the assets available in the financial markets focused on the two major types of securities – equities and bonds. In essence, equities are shares that represent an ownership stake in a company, and bonds are similar to an IOU (I owe you) – an issuer, such as a company or government, receives a sum of money in exchange for a bond. The bond is typically a contractual agreement to pay the bondholder a regular amount of interest and then to repay the bond at a set date in the future.

As global markets have developed, participants have started to look at, and invest in, other asset classes in addition to equities and bonds. These include different currencies – for example a European-based investor may benefit from buying US dollars using euros, holding them for a period, and then selling the dollars and potentially receiving more euros in return. Clearly, this will only happen if the US dollar has strengthened relative to the euro over the investor's holding period.

This workbook will provide further detail on equities, bonds and currencies, as well as introducing additional instruments and sub-classes, such as money market instruments and collective investment funds.

However, before moving forward, it is useful to explain some terminology and outline the essential differences between the two major types of securities.

Investors in bonds essentially hold an IOU from another organisation, such as a government or company. Bond investors:

- loan money to the issuing organisation in return for an agreed rate of interest
- have an agreed date on which they get their money back
- may have legal recourse against the issuer of the bond if the interest on the bond is not paid
- may have legal recourse against the issuer of the bond if repayment does not occur.

Investors in equities hold a stake in a company. The way equities are described varies in different parts of the world. For example, in the US, equities are typically described as stocks, while in many other parts of the world, equities are described as shares.

Equity investors:

- purchase a small piece, or share, of a company
- cannot be certain that they will receive a regular return in the form of dividend payments
- cannot be certain of the amount of dividend payments that they will receive
- can suffer a total loss of investment if the company collapses.

Securities, like equities and bonds, take one of two main forms – registered or bearer – and the form determines how an investor proves ownership of a particular investment. Bearer certificates, as their name suggests, mean that the person that bears (or holds) them has title to them, like banknotes. In comparison, registered certificates require that the holder's ownership is recorded in a register as the owner (or title-holder) of the investment. The certificate itself is less important.

Example

An investor owns 100 shares in a global retailer in registered form. If a burglar breaks into the investor's house and steals their share certificates, can the burglar pretend that they own the shares and sell them?

Fortunately, the answer is no.

The answer to the above example is no because most shares around the world are held in registered form. This means that the certificate is simply evidence of ownership. Furthermore, with the advent of technology, share certificates are usually held electronically rather than physically. Either way, the proof that really counts is the name and address held on the company's stockholder register.

Some securities come in bearer form and, unlike registered securities, the physical possession of the certificate is the proof of ownership. **Bearer securities** are easier to transfer as there is no register and they can simply be handed over. However, this does raise some issues including the following:

- It is difficult for the authorities to monitor ownership, making them attractive investments for money launderers.
- The issuing organisation has difficulty knowing to whom **dividends** or interest payments are to be sent.
- Physical security of the certificates is of greater importance and can increase the cost of holding the investment. If, in the example above, the shares stolen were in bearer form, then the burglar would be able to sell them

It is important to note that many bearer securities are held in central securities depositories (CSDs), such as Euroclear and Clearstream, and are technically referred to as 'immobilised'. This removes the worry about physical security, makes it easier for the issuer to pay any income due and also lessens the risk of inappropriate use because the CSDs will be communicating with financial services regulators.

Examples of securities that are usually held in bearer form are **eurobonds** and **American depositary receipts (ADRs)**.

2. Professional and Retail Business

Learning Objective

1.1.1 Know the differences between retail and professional businesses, including: their clients; equity markets; bond markets; foreign exchange markets

Within the financial services profession, there are two distinct areas – the wholesale sector and the retail sector. The wholesale sector is also often referred to as the professional sector or institutional sector. It is the business-to-business (B2B) part of the profession where both sides of a transaction are businesses, not individuals.

The activities that make up the wholesale sector include:

- **equity markets** – the trading of shares
- **bond markets** – the trading of government, supranational or corporate debt
- **foreign exchange** – the trading of currencies
- **derivatives** – the trading of **options**, **swaps**, **futures** and **forwards**
- **insurance markets** – major corporate insurance (including professional indemnity), **reinsurance**, **captive insurance** and risk-sharing insurance
- **fund management** – managing the investment portfolios of **collective investment schemes (CISs)**, pension funds and insurance funds

- **investment banking** – banking services tailored to organisations, such as undertaking mergers and acquisitions, equity trading, fixed-income trading and private equity
- **custodian banking** – providing services to asset managers involving the safekeeping of assets, the administration of the underlying investments, settlement, corporate actions and other specialised activities.

By contrast, the retail sector focuses on services provided to personal customers/individuals. It is business-to-consumer (B2C) and includes:

- **retail banking** – the traditional range of current accounts, deposit accounts, lending and credit cards
- **insurance** – the provision of a range of life assurance and protection solutions for areas such as medical insurance, critical illness cover, motor insurance, property insurance, income protection and mortgage protection
- **pensions** – the provision of investment accounts specifically designed to capture savings during a person's working life and provide benefits on retirement
- **investment services** – a range of investment products and vehicles ranging from execution-only stockbroking to full wealth management services and private banking
- **financial planning and financial advice** – helping individuals to understand and plan for their financial future.

2.1   Equity Markets

Equity markets are the best known financial markets and facilitate the trading of shares in quoted companies. The participants in equity markets include investors, many of which are institutional investors such as asset managers, trading the shares held in their clients' funds and insurance companies. The trades they undertake are arranged by stockbrokers (often simply referred to as brokers). The arranged trade will often involve purchasing from, or selling to, a bank which is acting as a dealer or, in some cases, a **market maker**. As larger banks provide their clients with the capacity to both arrange and to buy equities from them, or sell equities to them, the banks are often termed broker/dealers.

The World Federation of Exchanges provides data from the global stock exchanges. As illustrated in the following graph, global **market capitalisation** was over US$67 trillion at the end of 2016 (note that not all stock exchanges provide data to the World Federation of Exchanges so actual figures will be higher). Global market capitalisation is the total value of shares quoted on the world's stock exchanges.

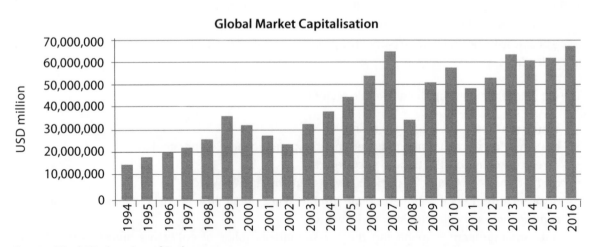

Source: World Federation of Exchanges

- The New York Stock Exchange (NYSE) is the largest exchange in the world and had a domestic market capitalisation of US$18.8 trillion as at September 2016 (domestic market capitalisation is the value of shares listed on an individual exchange).
- The other major US market, Nasdaq, was ranked as the second largest, with a domestic market capitalisation of over US$7.6 trillion, meaning that the two New York exchanges account for around one third of all exchange business.
- Japan Exchange Group, which includes the Tokyo Stock Exchange (TSE), is the world's third largest market and had a domestic market capitalisation of over US$5 trillion.
- In Europe, the largest exchanges are the **London Stock Exchange (LSE)**, **Euronext**, Deutsche Börse, the Frankfurt Stock Exchange (FSE) and the SIX Swiss Exchange.
- The Toronto Stock Exchange (TSX) in Canada is one of the ten largest exchanges in the world, and the Bombay, Australian and Korean exchanges are in the top 15. The Bombay Stock Exchange (BSE), although not largest in terms of market capitalisation, has the most companies listed on it compared to any other exchange in the world.
- Many African countries have stock exchanges; the largest include South Africa's Johannesburg Stock Exchange (JSE), Morocco's Bourse de Casablanca, the Egyptian Exchange and the Nigerian Stock Exchange (NSE).

Rivals to traditional stock exchanges have also arisen with the development of technology and communication networks known as multilateral trading facilities (MTFs) in Europe and alternative trading systems (ATSs) in the US. MTFs and ATSs are systems that bring together multiple parties that are interested in buying and selling financial instruments such as shares. These systems are also known as crossing networks or matching engines, and are provided by either an investment firm or another market operator.

2.2   Bond Markets

Although less frequently reported on than equity markets, bond markets are larger both in size and value of trading. As with equities, the major participants include the investors (particularly the institutions such as the funds run by asset managers and insurers) generally undertaking deals with the dealers (or traders) at the large banks. However, in contrast to equities, little dealing is done via stock exchange systems, with the majority of trades taking place away from the exchanges in over-the-counter (OTC) trades. Furthermore, the volume of bond trading is lower, as most trades tend to be very large when compared to equity market trades. The amounts outstanding on the global bond market are close to US$100 trillion. Domestic bond markets account for around three quarters of the total and international bonds for the remainder.

The instruments traded range from domestic bonds issued by companies and governments, to international bonds issued by companies, governments and supranational agencies such as the World Bank. Although the US has the largest bond market, trading in international bonds is predominantly undertaken in European markets.

2.3   Foreign Exchange (FX) Markets

Foreign exchange (FX) markets are the largest of all financial markets, with average daily turnover in excess of US$5 trillion.

The rate at which one currency is exchanged for another is set by supply and demand and by the strength of one currency in relation to another. For example, if there is strong demand from Japanese investors for US assets, such as property, bonds or shares, the US dollar will rise in value.

There is an active FX market that enables governments, companies and individuals to deal with their cash inflows and outflows denominated in overseas currencies. Historically, most FX deals were arranged over the telephone. The market was provided by the major banks who each provided rates of exchange at which they were willing to buy or sell currencies. However, with advances in technology and stricter banking regulation, electronic trading is becoming increasingly prevalent which, in turn, has prompted a growth in remittance companies alongside established banks.

As FX is an OTC market, meaning one where brokers/dealers negotiate directly with one another, there is no central exchange or clearing house. Instead, FX trading is distributed among major financial centres.

The Bank for International Settlements (BIS) releases figures on the composition of the FX market every three years. The latest report for 2016 shows that market activity has become ever more concentrated in a handful of global centres. As you can see in the chart below, FX transactions are concentrated in five countries/regions, with the UK as the main global centre:

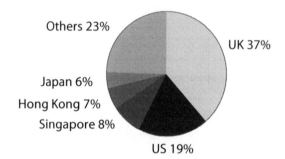

Source: *Bank for International Settlements*

3.   Participants – Retail Sector

Learning Objective

1.1.2   Know the role of the following within the retail sector of the financial services markets: banks; pension funds; insurance companies; investment services; financial planning and advice

The following sections provide descriptions and roles of some of the main participants in the financial services industry that serve retail customers.

3.1   Retail Banks

Retail banks provide services such as taking deposits from, and lending funds to, retail customers, as well as providing payment and money transmission services. They may also provide similar services to business customers.

Historically, these banks have tended to operate predominantly through a network of branches located in towns and cities but, increasingly, they are moving to telephone and internet-based services.

CHARTERED INSTITUTE FOR
SECURITIES & INVESTMENT

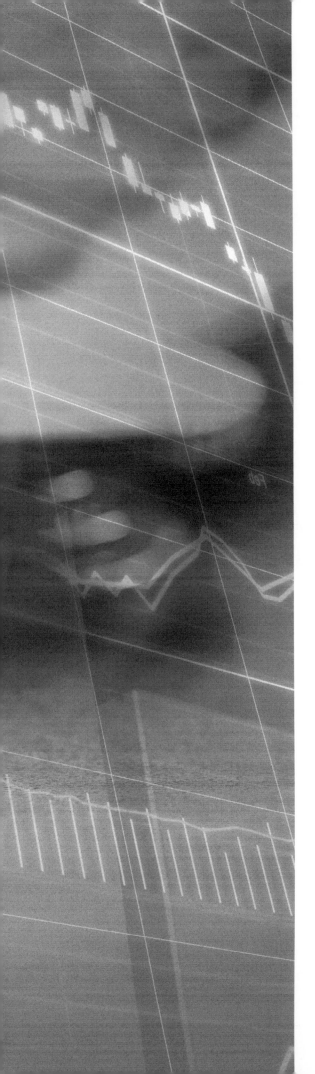

Capital Markets Programme

Securities

Edition 13, October 2017

This workbook relates to syllabus
version 17.0 and will cover examinations from
22 March 2018 to 21 March 2019

APPROVED WORKBOOK

Welcome to the Chartered Institute for Securities & Investment's Securities study material.

This workbook has been written to prepare you for the Chartered Institute for Securities & Investment's Securities examination.

Published by:
Chartered Institute for Securities & Investment
© Chartered Institute for Securities & Investment 2017
20 Fenchurch Street
London
EC3M 3BY
Tel: +44 20 7645 0600
Fax: +44 20 7645 0601

Email: customersupport@cisi.org
www.cisi.org/qualifications

Author:
Martin Mitchell FCSI

Reviewers:
Kevin Rothwell, Chartered MCSI
Julie Petrera, MBA (FS)

This is an educational workbook only and the Chartered Institute for Securities & Investment accepts no responsibility for persons undertaking trading or investments in whatever form.

While every effort has been made to ensure its accuracy, no responsibility for loss occasioned to any person acting or refraining from action as a result of any material in this publication can be accepted by the publisher or authors.

A learning map, which contains the full syllabus, appears at the end of this workbook. The syllabus can also be viewed on cisi.org and is also available by contacting the Customer Support Centre on +44 20 7645 0777. Please note that the examination is based upon the syllabus. Candidates are reminded to check the Candidate Update area details (cisi.org/candidateupdate) on a regular basis for updates as a result of industry change(s) that could affect their examination.

The questions contained in this workbook are designed as an aid to revision of different areas of the syllabus and to help you consolidate your learning chapter by chapter.

Workbook version: 13.1 (October 2017)

Learning and Professional Development with the CISI

The Chartered Institute for Securities & Investment is the leading professional body for those who work in, or aspire to work in, the investment sector, and we are passionately committed to enhancing knowledge, skills and integrity – the three pillars of professionalism at the heart of our Chartered body.

CISI examinations are used extensively by firms to meet the requirements of government regulators. Besides the regulators in the UK, where the CISI head office is based, CISI examinations are recognised by a wide range of governments and their regulators, from Singapore to Dubai and the US. Around 50,000 examinations are taken each year, and it is compulsory for candidates to use CISI workbooks to prepare for CISI examinations so that they have the best chance of success. Our workbooks are normally revised every year by experts who themselves work in the profession and also by our Accredited Training Partners, who offer training and elearning to help prepare candidates for the examinations. Information for candidates is also posted on a special area of our website: cisi.org/candidateupdate.

This workbook not only provides a thorough preparation for the examination it refers to, it is also a valuable desktop reference for practitioners, and studying from it counts towards your Continuing Professional Development (CPD). Mock examination papers, for most of our titles, will be made available on our website, as an additional revision tool.

CISI examination candidates are automatically registered, without additional charge, as student members for one year (should they not be members of the CISI already), and this enables you to use a vast range of online resources, including CISI TV, free of any additional charge. The CISI has more than 40,000 members, and nearly half of them have already completed relevant qualifications and transferred to a core membership grade. You will find more information about the next steps for this at the end of this workbook.

The Financial Services Profession 1

Asset Classes 15

Primary Markets 81

Secondary Markets 107

Corporate Actions 137

Clearing and Settlement 167

Accounting Analysis 193

Risk and Reward 227

Glossary 257

Multiple Choice Questions 267

Syllabus Learning Map 299

1

2

3

4

5

6

7

8

It is estimated that this workbook will require approximately 100 hours of study time.

What next?
See the back of this book for details of CISI membership.

Need more support to pass your exam?
See our section on Accredited Training Providers.

Want to leave feedback?
Please email your comments to learningresources@cisi.org

Chapter One
The Financial Services Profession

1. Introduction   3

2. Professional and Retail Business   5

3. Participants – Retail Sector   8

4. Participants – Wholesale Sector   10

This syllabus area will provide approximately 3 of the 100 examination questions

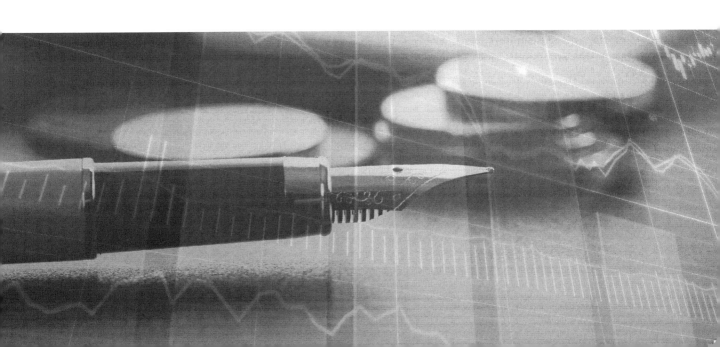

As well as providing traditional banking services, larger retail banks also offer other financial products to their clients, such as investments, pensions and insurance.

3.2   Pension Funds

Pension funds are one of the key methods by which individuals can make provision for retirement. There are a variety of pension schemes available, ranging from those provided by employers to self-directed schemes.

Pension funds are large, long-term investors in shares, bonds and cash. Some also invest in physical assets, like property. To meet their aim of providing a pension on retirement, the sums of money invested in pension funds are substantial.

3.3   Insurance Companies

One of the key functions of the financial services profession is to ensure risks are managed effectively. The insurance industry provides solutions for much more than the standard areas of life and general insurance cover.

Protection planning is a key area of financial advice, and the insurance industry offers a wide range of products to suit many potential scenarios and clients. These products range from payment protection policies, designed to pay out in the event that an individual is unable to meet repayments on loans and mortgages, to fleet insurance against the risk of an airline's planes crashing.

Insurance companies collect premiums in exchange for the cover provided. This premium income is used to buy investments, such as shares and bonds, and as a result, the insurance industry is a major player in the stock market. Insurance companies will subsequently realise these investments to pay any claims that may arise on the various policies.

3.4   Investment Services

Individuals may want to deploy their savings in financial assets, such as shares and bonds, however, investing savings can be complex and time-consuming. Specialists, therefore, have emerged to provide services around the investments for customers, generally for a fee.

When the customers are individuals (retail), the typical investment services will help them select the right investments, arrange their purchase (and subsequent sale), keep the investments under review and collect any income from them. These activities need to be reported to the customers on a regular basis.

The providers of these services include the retail banks as well as stockbrokers. Stockbrokers traditionally arranged trades in financial instruments on behalf of their clients, which include investment institutions, **fund managers** and private clients. Today, many of these are institutional brokers operating in the wholesale or professional market and making their money by using their discretion and skill to execute large trades for their clients. Others are execution-only brokers who give no advice, but simply offer trading services to retail clients. These firms earn their profits by charging **commissions** on transactions.

3.5   Financial Planning and Wealth Management

Stockbrokers also traditionally advised investors about which shares, bonds or funds they should buy and the services they offered expanded to include investment management and wealth management services. As a result, many stockbrokers now offer wealth management services to their clients and so are referred to as wealth managers. These wealth management firms can be independent companies, but some are divisions of larger entities, such as banks. They earn their profits by charging fees for their advice and commissions on transactions. They may also look after client assets and charge custody and portfolio management fees.

In a similar fashion, financial planning is a professional service available to individuals, their families and businesses who need objective assistance in organising their financial affairs to achieve their financial and lifestyle objectives more easily.

Financial planning is clearly about financial matters, so it deals with money and assets that have monetary value. Invariably this will involve looking at the current value of clients' bank balances, any loans, investments and other assets. It is also about planning, ie, defining, quantifying and qualifying goals and objectives and then working out how those goals and objectives can be achieved. In order to do this, it is vital that a client's current financial status is known in detail.

Financial planning is ultimately about meeting a client's financial and lifestyle objectives, not the adviser's objectives. Any advice should be relevant to the goals and objectives agreed. Financial planning plays a significant role in helping individuals get the most out of their money. Careful planning can help individuals define their goals and objectives, and work out how these may be achieved in the future using available resources. Financial planning can look at all aspects of an individual's financial situation and may include tax planning, both during lifetime and on death, asset management, debt management, retirement planning and personal risk management – protecting income and capital in the event of illness and providing for dependants on death.

4.   Participants – Wholesale Sector

Learning Objective

1.1.3   Know the role of the following within the wholesale sector of the financial services markets: investment banks; fund managers; stockbrokers; custodians

The following sections provide descriptions and outline the roles of some of the main participants in the financial services profession that specialise in providing services to the professional/wholesale sector.

4.1   Investment Banks

Investment banks provide advice and arrange finance for companies that want to float on a stock market, raise additional finance by issuing shares or bonds, or assist companies in carrying out mergers and acquisitions. They also provide services for those who might want to invest in shares and bonds, for example, pension funds and asset managers.

Typically, an investment banking group provides some or all of the following services, either in divisions of the bank or in associated companies within the group:

- Corporate finance and advisory work, normally in connection with new issues of securities for raising finance, takeovers, mergers and acquisitions.
- Banking, for governments, institutions and companies.
- Treasury dealing for corporate clients in foreign currencies, with financial engineering services to protect them from interest rate and **exchange rate** fluctuations.
- Investment management for sizeable investors, such as corporate pension funds, charities and private clients. This may be either via direct investment for the wealthier, or by way of CISs (or investment funds). In larger firms, the value of funds under management runs into many billions of pounds.
- Securities trading in equities, bonds and derivatives, and the provision of broking and distribution facilities.

Only a few investment banks provide services in all these areas. Most others tend to specialise to some degree and concentrate on only a few product lines. A number of banks have diversified their range of activities by developing businesses such as proprietary trading, servicing hedge funds, or making private equity investments.

4.2   Fund Managers

Fund management is the professional management of investment portfolios for a variety of institutions and private investors.

The US is the largest centre globally for fund management, followed by the UK, which is the biggest in Europe.

Fund managers, also known as investment or asset managers, run portfolios of investments for others. They invest money held by institutions, such as pension funds and insurance companies, as well as for CISs, such as US mutual funds and Europe's **unit trusts** and investment companies with variable capital (ICVCs), and portfolios for wealthier individuals. Some are organisations that focus solely on this activity; others are divisions of larger entities, such as insurance companies or banks.

Investment managers who buy and sell shares, bonds and other assets in order to increase the value of their clients' portfolios can conveniently be subdivided into institutional and private client fund managers. Institutional fund managers work on behalf of institutions in the wholesale/professional sector, for example, investing money for a company's pension fund or an insurance company's fund. Private client fund managers invest the money of relatively wealthy individuals in the retail sector. Institutional portfolios are usually larger than those of regular private clients.

Fund managers charge their clients for managing their money; these charges are often based on a small percentage of the value of the fund being managed.

Other areas of fund management include the provision of investment management services to institutional entities, such as companies, charities and local government authorities.

4.3   Stockbrokers

As already seen in the previous section, stockbrokers arrange trades in financial instruments on behalf of their clients, which include institutional brokers operating in the wholesale or professional market and making their money by using their discretion and skill to execute large trades for their clients. A number of these stockbroking activities are undertaken by divisions of large investment banks rather than independent entities and, like retail stockbrokers, they earn revenue by charging commissions on the transactions they arrange.

4.4   Custodian Banks

Custodians are banks that specialise in safe custody services, looking after portfolios of shares and bonds on behalf of others, such as fund managers, pension funds and insurance companies.

The core activities they undertake include:

*   holding assets in safekeeping, such as equities and bonds
*   arranging settlement of any purchases and sales of securities
*   processing corporate actions, including collecting income from assets, namely dividends in the case of equities and **coupons** in the case of bonds
*   providing information on the underlying companies and their **annual general meetings (AGMs)**
*   managing cash transactions
*   performing FX transactions when required
*   providing regular reporting on all their activities to their clients.

Competition has driven down the charges that a custodian can make for its traditional custody services and has resulted in consolidation within the profession. The custody business is now dominated by a small number of global custodians, which are often divisions of large banks.

End of Chapter Questions

1. List the essential differences between equities and bonds.
   Answer reference: Section 1.1

2. What is a bearer certificate?
   Answer reference: Section 1.1

3. What is the professional sector?
   Answer reference: Section 2

4. What is considered the largest of the financial markets?
   Answer reference: Section 2.3

5. Which of the following are considered to be active primarily in the retail sector or the wholesale sector?

   • Insurance companies
   • Investment banks
   • Stockbrokers
   • Pension funds
   • Financial planners

   Answer reference: Sections 3 and 4

Chapter Two
Asset Classes

1. Equities	17
2. Debt Instruments	20
3. Government Debt	33
4. Corporate Debt	41
5. Cash Assets	49
6. Eurobonds	54
7. Other Securities	55
8. Foreign Exchange (FX)	61
9. Collective Investment Schemes (CISs)	68

This syllabus area will provide approximately 24 of the 100 examination questions

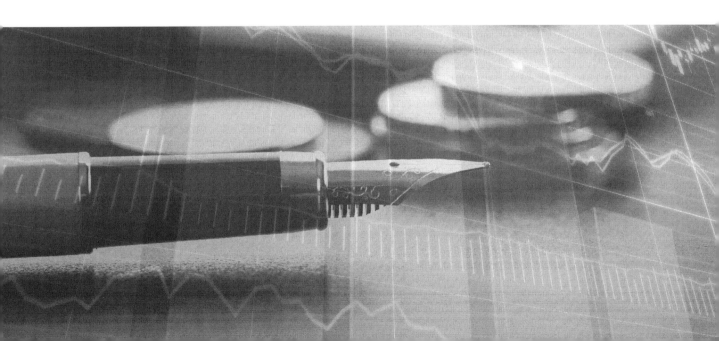

1. Equities

Learning Objective

2.2.1 Understand the advantages and disadvantages to issuers and investors of the following investments and their principal features and characteristics: ordinary shares; non-voting shares; redeemable shares; partly paid shares and calls; and in respect of these, the generally accepted practice regarding ranking for dividends and voting rights

Equities can be divided into two categories – ordinary shares and **preference shares**. In the US, the first category – ordinary shares – is termed common stock, and the second – preference shares – is termed preferred stock. This workbook will generally use the terms ordinary shares and preference shares, although concepts mentioned in relation to ordinary shares can be considered to apply to what the US would describe as common stock, and concepts mentioned in relation to preference shares can be considered to apply to preferred stock.

Every company has ordinary shares in issue. In addition to the ordinary shares, some companies also issue preference shares.

The performance of ordinary shares is closely tied to the fortunes of the company. Holders of ordinary shares have the right to vote on key decisions and receive dividends. Some companies issue more than one class of ordinary shares (perhaps distinguished as A ordinary shares and B ordinary shares) and one class may have more voting rights than the other. Occasionally, one class of shares may not have any voting rights at all; these shares are described as non-voting shares.

Example

Alphabet Inc is one of the world's largest companies and owns Google. At the time of writing (June 2017), Alphabet has three classes of shares in issue:

- 296,992 shares of Class A Common Stock – each share has one vote
- 47,437 shares of Class B Common Stock – each share has ten votes (these shares are mostly owned by the Google founders and enable them to retain control)
- 346,864 shares of Class C Capital Stock – each share has no voting rights at all.

Redeemable shares are relatively unusual. They are shares offered by a company to shareholders that may be bought back by the company at its election. Companies are permitted to issue ordinary shares that can be redeemed, as long as conventional non-redeemable ordinary shares are also in issue.

Preference shares are usually less risky than ordinary shares of the same company and, therefore, potentially less profitable to invest in. They carry less risk due to the dividend policy and they rank above ordinary shares in the event of bankruptcy. Holders of preference shares generally do not have the right to vote on company affairs, but they are entitled to receive a fixed dividend each year (as long as the company feels it has sufficient profits). These dividends must be paid before any dividends are paid to ordinary shareholders, hence the term preference or preferred. Although preference shares tend to be non-voting, it is common for preference shareholders to become entitled to vote in the event of no dividend being paid for a substantial period of time. Precisely how long the period needs to be to make it substantial will be detailed in the company's constitution. Preference shares are sometimes referred to as 'hybrid' securities as they have some characteristics like bonds (a fixed amount of payment each year) and some like equities (they are shares).

As stated, companies have an obligation to pay dividends to preference shareholders before they pay a dividend, if any, to the ordinary shareholders.

In the case of a liquidation, priority would be given first to debtholders. Once the obligations to debtholders have been discharged, preference shareholders take priority over the ordinary shareholders.

1.1   Features of Ordinary Shares

It is the common stockholders or ordinary shareholders of a company that face the greatest risk. If the company is liquidated, they will only receive any payout if there is money remaining after satisfying all of the other claims from creditors, bondholders and preference shareholders.

However, if the company is sufficiently profitable, the ordinary shareholders may receive dividends. Dividends for ordinary shareholders are proposed by the directors and generally ratified by the shareholders at the annual meeting (often referred to as the annual general meeting (AGM)). However, the ordinary shareholders will only receive a dividend after any preference dividends have been paid.

Each ordinary share is typically given the right to vote at AGMs and extraordinary general meetings (EGMs), although sometimes voting rights are restricted to certain classes of ordinary shares. Such different classes of shares (often called A and B ordinary shares) are created to separate ownership and control, such as with Google/Alphabet, where the founders retain control, and as illustrated in the following example where the founders cede control.

Example

ABC plc is a small, successful, privately owned company with two founding directors, each holding 500 of its total issue of 1,000 ordinary shares. ABC needs more investment for expansion and the company agrees to issue 200 new shares to venture capitalists. However, the venture capitalists require control over the company as a condition of their investment.

This is achieved by creating a second class of ordinary shares. The founding directors' shares become non-voting A shares and the venture capitalists hold voting B shares. The result is that, although the founding directors hold non-voting A shares, they still own most of the company (1,000 shares of the total 1,200 shares), but control is now exercised by the venture capitalists since it is their B shares that have votes.

If they do have voting shares, each shareholder may, if they so wish, appoint a third party, or **proxy**, to vote on their behalf. A proxy may be an individual or group of individuals appointed by the board of directors of the company to represent the shareholders who send in proxy requests, to vote the represented shares in accordance with the shareholders' instructions.

In many jurisdictions, each ordinary share has a **nominal value** (also known as par value or face value) which represents the minimum amount that the company must receive from subscribers on the issue of the shares. Occasionally, the company may not demand all of the nominal value at issue, with the shares then referred to as being partly paid. At some later date, the company will call on the shareholders to pay the remaining nominal value and make the shares fully paid.

Most ordinary shares are registered, meaning that the issuing company maintains a register of who holds the shares. This contrasts with bearer instruments when the issuer does not maintain a register – they can be transferred to other investors by simply handing over the certificate. For registered shares, a transfer requires a change of entry in the shareholders' register.

1.2   Types of Preference Share

Learning Objective

2.2.2   Understand the advantages and disadvantages to issuers and investors of the following classes of preference/preferred shares and their principal characteristics: cumulative; participating; redeemable; convertible

Preference shares can come in a variety of forms.

- **Cumulative** – a cumulative preference shareholder will not only be paid this year's dividend before any ordinary shareholders' dividends are paid, but also any unpaid dividends from previous years. Non-cumulative shares, on the other hand, would forfeit dividends not paid in the previous period.
- **Participating** – one drawback of preference shares when compared to ordinary shares is that, if the company starts to generate large profits, the ordinary shareholders will often see their dividends rise, whereas the preference shareholders still get a fixed level of dividend. To counter this, some preference shares offer the opportunity to participate in higher distributions.
- **Redeemable** – these are preference shares that enable the company to buy back the shares from the shareholder at an agreed price in the future. The shares, from the company's perspective, are similar to debt. The money provided by the preference shareholders can be repaid, removing any obligation the firm has to them.
- **Convertible** – in this case, the preference shareholder has the right, but not the obligation, to convert the preference shares into a predetermined number of ordinary shares, eg, perhaps one preference share may be converted into two ordinary shares. This is another method of avoiding the lack of upside potential in the preference shares, compared to ordinary shares.

Note that a particular preference share may exhibit more than one of these features.

2. Debt Instruments

2.1 Features and Characteristics

Learning Objective

2.3.1 Know the principal features and characteristics of debt instruments

As outlined in chapter 1, a bond is essentially an I owe you (IOU) issued by an organisation (the borrower, or issuer), in return for money lent to it.

The nominal value (or par value) of a bond is the amount that the borrower will pay back to the holder of the bond on **maturity**.

The issuer of a bond is important in determining the return the buyer will demand. If the company or government issuing a bond is considered high-risk – being more likely to fail to make the contractual coupon payments or principal repayment – it will need to offer a high rate of interest on the bond to attract investors. Some of the most significant issuers of bonds are governments; examples include the US Government's Treasuries, Japanese Government bonds (JGBs), Germany's bunds and the UK Government's gilts.

The redemption date of a bond is the date on which the borrower agrees to pay back the nominal value of the bond. It is also referred to as the date on which the bond matures, ie, the maturity date.

A bond's coupon is the interest rate that the borrower pays to the bondholder, expressed as a percentage of the nominal value. In diagrammatic form:

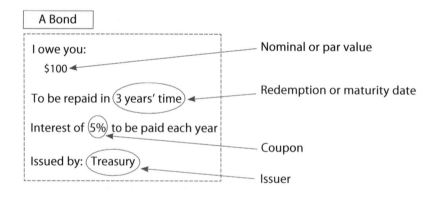

2.2 Yields

Learning Objective

2.3.2   Understand the uses and limitations of the following: flat yield; gross redemption yield (using internal rate of return); net redemption yield; modified duration in the calculation of price change

The **yield** is a measure of the percentage return that an investment provides. For a bond, there are three potential ways yields can be calculated: the flat yield (also known as the interest or running yield), the **gross redemption yield (GRY)** that is commonly also referred to as the yield to maturity (YTM), and the **net redemption yield (NRY)**.

2.2.1   Flat Yield

The flat yield only considers the coupon and ignores the existence of any capital gain (or loss) if the bond is held through to **redemption**. As such, it is best suited to short-term investors, rather than those investors who might hold the bond through to its maturity and benefit from the gain (or suffer from the loss) at maturity.

The calculation of the flat yield is as follows:

$$\text{Flat yield} = (\text{annual coupon}/\text{price}) \times 100$$

For example, the flat yield on a 5% gilt, redeeming in six years and priced at £104.40, is:

$$(5/104.40) \times 100 = 4.79\%$$

Exercise 1

a.   Calculate the flat yield on a 4% gilt, redeeming in eight years and priced at £98.90
b.   Calculate the flat yield on a 7% gilt, redeeming in three years and priced at £108.60

The answers can be found at the end of this chapter.

Using the flat yield, it is simple to see how a change in interest rates will impact bond prices. If interest rates increase, investors will want an equivalent increase in the yield on their bonds. However, because the coupon is fixed for most bonds, the only way that the yield can increase is for the price to fall. This causes the inverse relationship between interest rates and bond prices. When interest rates rise, bond prices fall and vice versa.

2.2.2 Gross Redemption Yield (GRY)

The GRY is a fuller measure of yield than the flat yield, because it takes both the coupons and any gain (or loss) through to maturity into account – hence its alternative name 'yield to maturity' or just YTM. Because it considers the gain or loss if the bond is held until it matures, it is more appropriate for long-term investors than the flat yield. However it does ignore the impact of any taxation (hence the 'gross' in GRY), so this measure of return is especially useful for non-tax-paying long-term investors such as pension funds and charities.

The calculation of the GRY utilises the approach covered in Section 2.6 of this chapter to arrive at the present value of a bond. It is the internal rate of return (IRR) of the bond. The IRR is simply the discount rate that, when applied to the future cash flows of the bond, produces the current price of that bond.

Example

Assume that there is a US Government bond known as a 5% Treasury Note and that it will be repaid in exactly five years' time. Its current price is $115, and so if an investor buys $10,000 nominal of the bond today, it will cost $11,500, excluding brokers' costs. The annual interest payments will amount to $500, so its flat yield [(500/11,500) x 100] is currently 4.35%.

In five years' time, however, the investor is only going to receive $10,000 when the bond is redeemed, and so will make a loss of $1,500 over the period. If an investor were simply to look at the flat yield, it would give a misleading indication of the true return that they were earning. The true yield needs to take account of this loss to redemption and this is the purpose of the redemption yield.

Very simply, the investor needs to write off that loss over the five-year period of the bond, let us say at the approximate rate of $300 per annum, so the annual return that the investor is receiving is actually closer to $200 – the annual interest of $500 less the $300 written off. If you recalculate the flat yield using this $200 as the interest, the return reduces to 1.74%.

The GRY, then, gives a more accurate indication of the return that the investor receives, and can be used to compare the yields from different bonds to identify which is offering the best return.

Example

The following data gives the prices of two US Government bonds that are both due to be repaid in 2027. Consider the data and identify which is producing the best overall return assuming that the investor will hold the bonds until redemption.

Stock Name	Redemption	Price	Flat Yield	GRY
7.625% Treasury	2027	150.04	5.08%	2.139%
6.875% Treasury	2027	144.46	4.76%	2.191%

As can be seen, although the first stock appears to be the more attractive on the basis of flat yield, the GRY shows it will in fact produce a poorer overall return to the investor. An investor concerned with maximising their overall return will clearly pick the second.

2.2.3 Net Redemption Yield (NRY)

The NRY is similar to the GRY in that it takes both the annual coupons and the profit (or loss) made through to maturity into account. However, it looks at the after-tax cash flows rather than the gross cash flows and, as a result, is a useful measure for tax-paying, long-term investors.

2.2.4 Modified Duration

It is clear that, if interest rates rise, the price of fixed-rate debt instruments (eg, most government bonds, including gilts and many corporate debt issues) falls, and vice versa.

If an investor thinks that interest rates are going to fall in the future, then investing in **fixed-interest securities** is a good idea because, if the investor is correct, their price will rise.

However, some fixed-interest securities will be more responsive to a movement in interest rates than others. They will all rise in value when interest rates fall, but some will probably rise by more than others. The ones that rise the most are the more volatile securities.

All other things being equal, a lower-coupon bond will be more volatile to a change in interest rates than a higher-coupon bond. Similarly, all other things being equal, a longer-dated bond will be more responsive than a shorter-dated bond.

To identify which bonds are more volatile, volatility measures can be used.

The one measure of volatility required for this examination is modified duration.

The modified duration of a particular debt instrument shows the expected change in its price, given a specified change in interest rates. The higher the modified duration, the more the price of that instrument will move. The modified duration is the approximate percentage change in the price of a bond brought about by a 1% change in the interest rate.

Example

If a government bond is priced at $95.84, and its modified duration is 1.02, what is the effect on the price after an increase in interest rates by one percentage point?

If interest rates rise by one percentage point, the bond's price will fall by 1.02/100 x $95.84 = $0.98.

If interest rates rise by one half of a percentage point, the bond's price will fall by 1.02/100 x $95.84 x 0.5 = $0.49.

2.3 Interest and Conversion Premium Calculations

Learning Objective

2.3.3 Be able to calculate: simple interest income on corporate debt; conversion premiums on convertible bonds and whether it is worth converting; flat yield; accrued interest (given details of the day count conventions)

2.3.1 Interest on Corporate Debt

Corporate debt – the borrowing of a company – requires servicing by making regular interest payments. Interest on bonds is calculated by reference to the coupon rate, coupon frequency and nominal value. The flat yield is calculated using the coupon rate and the bond's price.

Example

XYZ Inc has issued bonds paying an annual 8% coupon and maturing in 2020. The bonds are currently priced at 106, meaning investors have to pay $106 for each $100 of nominal value.

If an investor buys $5,000 nominal value, the bonds will cost $5,300 ($5,000 x 106/100).

The interest income for the investor each year will be the nominal value multiplied by the coupon rate – $5,000 x 8% = $400. If the interest was paid semi-annually, then the annual payment would be split into two portions.

The flat yield for the investor is the coupon divided by the price expressed as a percentage, ie, (8/106) x 100 = 7.55%.

2.3.2 Convertible Bonds

Some corporates issue bonds with conversion rights, known as **convertible bonds**. Convertible bonds give the holder of the bond the right, but not the obligation, to convert the bond into a predetermined number of ordinary shares of the issuer. Given this choice, the holder will choose to convert into shares if, at maturity, the value of the shares they can convert into exceeds the redemption value of the bond.

Because there is this potential advantage to the value of a convertible bond if the share price rises, and the downside protection provided by the redemption value if the shares do not perform well, convertible bonds generally trade at a **premium** to their share value. The calculation of the premium is shown by the following example.

Example

A convertible bond issued by XYZ Inc is trading at $142.5. It offers the holder the option of converting $1,000 nominal into three shares. The shares of XYZ Inc are currently trading at $380.

To calculate the premium, first work out the share value of the conversion choice.

For $1,000 nominal value, that is $380 x 3 shares = $1,140.

The bond is trading at $142.5 ($1,000 nominal costs $1,425), and so the premium in absolute terms is 1,425 − 1,140 = $285 per $1,000 nominal.

It is more usual to express it as a percentage of the conversion value:

$$(285/1,140) \times 100 = 25\%$$

Exercise 2

The convertible bonds issued by ABC plc are trading at £110. Each £100 nominal value offers the holder the option of converting into 15 ordinary ABC shares. The ordinary shares of ABC are currently trading at £6.40. What is the conversion premium, expressed in percentage terms?

The answer can be found at the end of this chapter.

Convertible bonds enable the holder to exploit the growth potential in the equity, while retaining the safety net of the bond. It is for this reason that convertible bonds trade at a premium to the value of the shares they can convert into. If there were no premium, there would be an **arbitrage** opportunity for investors to buy the shares more cheaply via the convertible than in the equity market.

Usually, convertible bonds are issued where the price of each share is set at the outset, and that price will be adjusted to take into account any subsequent bonus or **rights issues**. Given the share price, it is simple to calculate the conversion ratio – the number of shares that each £100 of nominal value of the bonds can convert into.

$$\text{Conversion ratio} = \frac{\text{Nominal value}}{\text{Conversion price of shares}}$$

Example

£100 nominal value of a convertible bond is able to convert into shares at £4.46 each.

The conversion ratio is £100/£4.46 = 22.42 shares

If the issuing company had a 1-for-1 **bonus issue**, then the conversion price would halve and the conversion ratio would double.

2.3.3 Flat Yield Calculation

The simplest measure of the return used in the market is the flat (interest or running) yield. You will recall that the flat yield looks at the annual cash return (coupon) generated by an investment as a percentage of the cash price. In simple terms, it is the regular annual return that is generated on the money invested.

The calculation of the flat or running yield is provided by the formula:

$$\text{Flat Yield (\%)} = \frac{\text{Annual Coupon Rate}}{\text{Market Price}} \times 100$$

The flat yield only considers the coupon and ignores the existence of any capital gain (or loss) through to redemption. As such, it is best suited to short-term investors in the bond, rather than those investors that might hold the bond through to its maturity and benefit from the gain (or suffer from the loss) at maturity.

Limitations of Flat Yield

There are three key drawbacks for using flat yield as a robust measure in assessing bond returns:

- Since it only measures the coupon flows and ignores the redemption flows, it often gives an incomplete picture of the actual returns from the bond. A bond that has been purchased at a price that is below the redemption value will be significantly undervalued because the redemption gain is excluded from the calculation. The opposite is also true when a bond is purchased at a price above the redemption value.
- The calculation completely ignores the timing of any cash flows and, because there is no discounted cash flow analysis, the time value of money is completely overlooked.
- If the bond is a **floating-rate note**, the return in any one period will vary with interest rates. If the coupon is not a constant, using a flat-yield basis for measuring returns becomes an arbitrary matter of selecting which coupon amount among many possible values to use for the calculation.

2.3.4 Accrued Interest

Listed bond prices are flat prices, which do not include accrued interest. The flat price is alternatively referred to as the **clean price**. Most bonds pay interest semi-annually. For settlement dates when interest is paid, the bond price is equal to the flat price. Between payment dates, however, the actual price paid for the bond will be the flat price plus the accrued interest.

Accrued interest is the interest that has been earned, but not paid, and is calculated by the following formula:

$$\text{Accrued interest} = \text{Coupon payment} \times \frac{\text{Number of days since last payment}}{\text{Number of days between payments}}$$

The following graphic shows how the **dirty price** (ie, the clean price plus accrued interest) of a bond fluctuates over the lifetime of the bond, in this case two years. The assumption made is that the flat price remains constant over the two years; however, in reality, it will probably fluctuate with interest rates and because of other factors. The flat price is what is listed in bond tables for prices. The accrued interest must be calculated according to the formula above. Note that the bond price steadily increases each day until reaching a peak the day before an interest payment, then drops to minimum immediately following the payment.

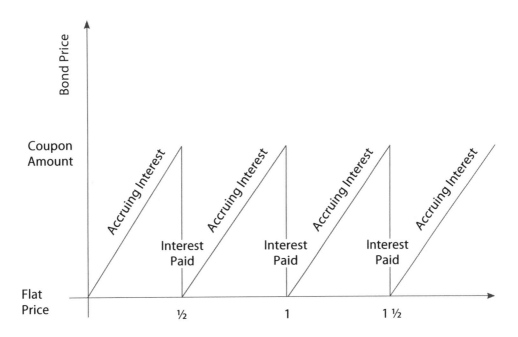

Calculating the Purchase Price for a Bond with Accrued Interest

Example

An investor purchases a corporate bond with a settlement date on 15 September with a face value of $1,000 and a nominal yield of 8%, which has a listed price of 100.25, and which pays interest semi-annually on 15 February and 15 August. How much should the investor pay for the bond, or in other words what is its dirty price?

The semi-annual interest payment is $40 and there were 31 days since the last interest payment on 15 August. Assuming the settlement date fell on an interest payment date, the bond price would equal the listed price: 100.25 x $1,000.00 = $1,002.50.

Since the settlement date was 31 days after the last payment date, accrued interest must be added. Using the above formula, with 184 days between coupon payments, we find that:

$$\text{Accrued Interest} = \$40 \times \frac{31}{184} = \$6.74$$

Therefore, the actual purchase price for the bond will be $1,002.50 + $6.74 = $1,009.24.

Day Count Conventions

Historically, different day count conventions have evolved in calculating accrued interest to take into account the fact that fixed-income securities have different coupon payment date characteristics, and to address issues related to the vagaries of the calendar system. The Julian calendar has uneven-length months and also has leap years, when once every four years there are 366 days to a year rather than 365. This has given rise to a number of different ways of counting the intervals between payments and even the length in days of the year assumed in the calculations.

There is no central authority defining day count conventions, so there is no standard terminology. Certain terms, such as 30/360, actual/actual (ACT/ACT), and money market basis must be understood in the context of the particular market. There has also been a move towards convergence in the marketplace, which has resulted in the number of conventions in use being reduced.

In the example just cited, the day count is what can be called actual/actual, since the exact number of days between coupons and the actual days since the last payment have been used.

Common day count conventions that affect the accrued interest calculation are:

- **ACT/360 (days per month, days per year)** – each month is treated normally and the year is assumed to be 360 days, eg, in a period from 1 February 2017 to 1 April 2017, T is considered to be 59 days divided by 360.
- **30/360** – each month is treated as having 30 days, so a period from 1 February 2017 to 1 April 2017 is considered to be 60 days. The year is considered to have 360 days. This convention is frequently chosen for ease of calculation: the payments tend to be regular and at predictable amounts.
- **ACT/365** – each month is treated normally, and the year is assumed to have 365 days, regardless of leap year status, eg, a period from 1 February 2017 to 1 April 2017 is considered to be 59 days. This convention results in periods having slightly different lengths.
- **ACT/ACT – (1)** – each month is treated normally, and the year has the usual number of days, eg, a period from 1 February 2017 to 1 April 2017 is considered to be 59 days and the year is 365 days in length. In this convention leap years do affect the final result.
- **ACT/ACT – (2)** – each month is treated normally, and the year is the number of days in the current coupon period multiplied by the number of coupons in a year, eg, if the coupon is payable 1 February and 1 August then on 1 April 2017 the number of days in the year is 362, ie, 181 (the number of days between 1 February and 1 August 2017) x 2 (semi-annual).

2.4 Spreads and Pricing Benchmarks

Learning Objective

2.3.4 Understand the concept of spreads: spread over a government bond benchmark; spread over/ under swap

Commentators often refer to spreads in the bond markets. A spread is simply the difference between the yield available on one instrument and the yield available elsewhere. It is usually expressed in basis points, with each basis point representing 1/100 of 1%.

The comparison tends to be against one of two yields:

1. **Government bond yields** – benchmarks for corporate bonds are generally selected according to market convention; typically, the most recently issued government bond closest to the maturity of the corporate bond is selected as a benchmark. Gilts, bunds and US Treasuries are the reference securities in the UK, Europe and the US, respectively.
2. **Swap rates** – there is a very active market in exchanging floating rates for fixed rates in the so-called swaps market. The rates available on swaps are also used as benchmarks against which to judge yields.

The spreads on a particular instrument could be above or below benchmarks as shown in the following example:

Example

UBX Inc is a well-established and highly rated company. It has bonds in issue that expire in approximately ten years and are currently yielding 5.40%. Comparative government bonds (based on the ten-year Treasury bond) are yielding 5.15%, and the ten-year swaps rate is 5.20%. Three month LIBOR (London Interbank Offered Rate) is 5.54%.

The spreads can be summarised as follows:

- UBX bonds spread above government bonds = 25 basis points (5.40%–5.15%).
- UBX spread under LIBOR = 14 basis points (5.40%–5.54%).
- UBX bonds spread over swap rates = 20 basis points (5.40%–5.20%).

Spreads will vary, mainly as a result of the relative risk of the corporate bond compared to the government or the financial institutions providing the swaps. For a more risky corporate issuer, the spread will be greater.

2.5 The Yield Curve

Learning Objective

2.3.5   Understand the role of the yield curve and the relationship between price and yield with reference to the yield curve (normal and inverted)

In many government bond markets there are a range of government bonds available with various periods until maturity. By plotting the GRYs of these gilts on a graph, with yields on the Y axis and time to maturity on the X axis, a pattern emerges. The line of best fit across these points is the **yield curve**. It shows the yields available to investors in government bonds over different time horizons. The yield curve is a visual representation of what is known as the term structure of interest rates – the relationship between yields on financial instruments from the same issuer, but with different periods (terms) to maturity.

The yield curve provides a useful tool for comparison – eg, if ten-year gilts yield 4%, then a ten-year corporate bond should provide a higher yield to compensate investors for the additional default risk they face.

2.5.1 The Normal Yield Curve

Typically, the shape of the yield curve is upward-sloping to the right, as shown in the following diagram:

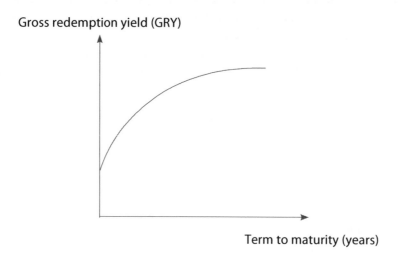

This is known as the normal yield curve, and its shape captures the fact that investors have a **liquidity** preference: they prefer more rather than less liquidity. As a result of this, they are willing to accept a lower yield on more liquid, short-dated government bonds, and demand a higher yield on less liquid, longer-dated government bonds. In other words, given the same coupon rate, the price of a short-dated government bond will be higher than that of a longer-dated government bond, resulting in a higher yield for the longer-dated instrument than the equivalent shorter-dated instrument.

2.5.2 The Inverted Yield Curve

Occasionally, the yield curve may not exhibit its normal, upward-sloping to the right shape. Instead, it might be downward-sloping to the right, known as the 'inverted yield curve'.

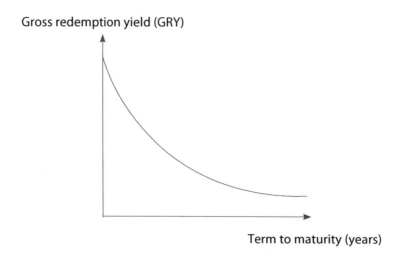

Clearly, in an inverted yield curve scenario, yields available on short-term government bonds exceed those available on long-term government bonds. This occurs when there is an expectation of a significant reduction in interest rates at some stage in the future. The consequence of this is that, when investing in longer-term instruments that will be outstanding when the interest rates fall, the investor is willing to accept a lower yield. For shorter-term instruments that will not be outstanding when the interest rate falls, the investor is demanding a higher yield.

The existence of an inverted yield curve does not remove any liquidity preference, but the impact of the anticipated interest rate fall outweighs the effect of the liquidity preference.

2.5.3 Inflation and the Yield Curve

Nominal yields are drawn from conventional debt instruments and include investors' anticipation of **inflation**. However, in addition to nominal yield curves, real yield curves can be observed from the yields on instruments that already include an uplift for inflation within their returns, such as the UK's index-linked gilts and the US Treasury Inflation Protected Securities (TIPS). The difference between nominal yields and real yields reveals the term structure of inflation – the expectations for inflation in the future that are currently captured within bond prices.

Generally, if inflation is expected to increase, then the yields demanded by investors need to reward them for the anticipated inflation – so yields and the yield curve would be expected to rise. However, when the **central bank**, such as the US Federal Reserve or the UK's Bank of England (BoE), is concerned about inflationary pressures and increases short-term interest rates to counter the danger, the impact on medium- and long-dated bonds can be that the yields fall. This is because the investors have confidence that, in the medium term, inflationary pressures will be removed by the pre-emptive actions of the central bank.

2.6 The Present Value of a Bond

Learning Objective

2.3.6   Be able to calculate the present value of a bond (maximum two years) with annual coupon and interest income

---

Money has a time value. That is, money deposited today will attract a rate of interest over the term it is invested. For example, $100 invested today, at an annual rate of interest of 5%, becomes $105 in one year's time. The addition of this interest to the original sum invested acts as compensation to the depositor for forgoing $100 of consumption for one year.

The time value of money can also be illustrated by expressing the value of a sum receivable in the future in terms of its value today, again by taking account of the prevailing rate of interest. This is known as the sum's present value. So, $100 receivable in one year's time, given an interest rate of 5%, will be worth $100/1.05 = $95.24 today, in present value terms. This process of establishing present values is known as discounting, the interest rate in the calculation acting as the discount rate.

In other words, the value today, or the present value, of a lump sum due to be received on a specified future date can be established by discounting this amount by the prevailing rate of interest.

To arrive at the present value of a single sum, receivable after n years, when the prevailing rate of interest is r, simply multiply the lump sum by the following:

$$1/(1 + r)^n$$

Referring back to the earlier example, $100 receivable in one year's time, given an interest rate of 5%, will have a present value of:

$$\$100 \times 1/(1+r)^n = \$100 \times 1/(1+0.05)^1 = \$100 \times 1/1.05 = \$100 \times 0.9524 = \$95.24$$

If $100 was due to be received in two years' time, then the present value will be:

$$\$100 \times 1/(1+r)^2 = \$100 \times 1/(1.05)^2 = \$100 \times 1/1.1025 = \$100 \times 0.907 = \$90.70$$

Present value calculations can also be used to derive the price of a bond, given the appropriate rate of interest and the cash flows.

Example

Imagine $1,000 nominal of a two-year bond paying annual coupons of 10%. Given an appropriate rate of interest, the sum of the present values will provide the logical price for the bond.

Using an interest rate of 5% per annum, the following present values emerge:

Time	Cash flow	Discount factor	Present value
End of year one	$100	$1/1.05$	95.24
End of year two	$1,100	$1/1.05^2$	997.73
Sum of the individual present values = price of the bond			$1,092.97

Exercise 3

What is the price of the same two-year 10% coupon-paying bond if interest rates are:

a. 6%?

b. 4%?

The answers can be found at the end of this chapter.

3. Government Debt

Most developed countries have active markets for bonds issued by their government, eg, Treasury bonds issued by the US Government and gilts issued by the UK Government. They are issued to cover the government's borrowing needs through the Bureau of the Fiscal Service in the US and the **Debt Management Office (DMO)** in the UK, respectively.

As with other bonds, government bonds are issued with a given nominal value that will be repaid at the bond's redemption date, and a coupon rate representing the percentage of the nominal value that will be paid to the holder of the bond each year. Obviously different government bonds can have different redemption dates, and the coupon is payable at different points of the year (although it is generally at semi-annual intervals).

Example

Government bonds are denoted by their coupon rate and their redemption date, for example, the US 3% Treasury Bond 2047. The coupon indicates the cash payment per $100 nominal value that the holder will receive each year. This payment is made in two equal semi-annual payments on fixed dates, six months apart. An investor holding $1,000 nominal of 3% Treasury Bond 2047 will receive two coupon payments of $30 each, on 15 May and 15 November each year, until the repayment of the $1,000 on 15 May 2047.

3.1 Interest Rates and Accrued Interest

Learning Objective

2.4.1 Understand the following features and characteristics of conventional government debt: redemption price; interest payable; accrued interest; effect of changes in interest rates; concept of risk-free

All government bonds specify a redemption value (the nominal value of the bond) that will be repaid at the end of the bond's life and a coupon. The coupon is the amount of interest paid to the holder of the bond each year.

Government bonds are typically quoted on the basis of the price a buyer would pay for 100 units of the currency's nominal value.

Example

For example, 6% Treasury 2028 might be trading at 108, so a buyer will have to pay £108 for each £100 nominal value. Why would the buyer be willing to pay more than £100? The answer lies in the available interest rate across the financial markets. If the interest rate available on deposited funds is lower than the coupon rate on the gilt, then that gilt will be a relatively attractive investment and its price will be pushed upwards until the return it offers is in line with other investments.

This is an example of the inverse relationship between interest rates and bond prices.

As interest rates across the financial markets decrease, the quoted price of government bonds will increase. Conversely, if interest rates increase, the quoted price of government bonds will decrease. In summary, there is an inverse relationship between government bond prices and interest rates.

The coupons on government bonds are paid to the registered holder of the gilt at each coupon payment date. However, because of the possibility of ownership changes just before the coupon payment date, there is a period prior to each coupon payment date when a bond is dealt without entitlement to the impending coupon payment. Despite the instrument being a bond, this is known as the **ex-dividend** period. This period is short, for example for most gilts it is seven working days prior to the coupon payment date. For the remainder of the time the gilt is described as trading **cum-dividend**.

The government bond markets are the facilities that enable investors to buy and sell bonds issued by the relevant government. They are important as they are the benchmark bonds on which the return provided by other bonds is judged.

For example, the yield available on US Treasuries is considered the risk-free rate for dollar-denominated bonds. After all, it is the US Government that ultimately controls the printing of dollars, and so US Treasuries are effectively credit risk-free. The risk-free rate represents the minimum amount an investor would accept to invest any money and the investor would always want compensation of an amount greater than the risk-free rate when accepting any risk at all. If a 15-year Treasury bond was trading at a price to produce a 5% yield, a 15-year dollar-denominated corporate bond would be expected to yield 5% plus a margin to cover the increased credit risk that the corporate borrower presents.

3.2   Inflation-Protected Securities

Learning Objective

2.4.2   Understand the following features and characteristics of index-linked debt: inflation – effects and measurement; index-linking; effect of the index on price, interest and redemption; return during a period of zero inflation and, in some economies, deflation

3.2.1   Inflation

Inflation can be one of the most significant obstacles to successful investing because the real value of the income flow from investments, such as bonds and equities, as well as the long-term value of capital, is eroded by the effects of inflation and the decline in the purchasing power of the wealth that is created.

Controlling inflation is the prime focus of economic policy in most countries, as the economic costs inflation imposes on society are far-reaching. While there are many negative consequences, the two which are most pertinent for the typical investor are that:

- inflation reduces the spending power of those dependent on fixed incomes, such as pensions or fixed-coupon investments, including conventional bonds
- individuals may not be rewarded for saving; this occurs when the inflation rate exceeds the nominal interest rate, ie, when the real interest rate is negative.

Real interest rates are calculated as follows:

$$\text{Real interest rate} = [(1 + \text{nominal interest rate}) / (1 + \text{inflation rate})] - 1$$

So, the real return takes into account the inflation rate and in times of excessive inflation the real returns available may well become negative.

In addition to the specific impact of inflation on returns mentioned, the broader macroeconomic problems associated with periods of high inflation are well illustrated by the difficulties faced by investors during the 1970s. This was a period of extremely high inflation, fuelled by surging **commodity prices**, especially crude oil, which led to demands from organised labour for higher wages. This pushed up the costs for producers of goods and services who, in turn, pushed on these additional costs to end-consumers in the form of higher prices. A vicious circle was created which required very drastic increases in short-term interest rates at the end of the 1970s – the base rates in the US and UK were approximately 20% as the 1980s began – and this caused widespread distress for asset prices. The 1970s was one of the worst periods on record for global stock market returns.

Inflation will also have negative implications for holders of bonds and fixed-income instruments. A major driver of bond prices is the prevailing interest rate and expectations of interest rates to come. Yields required by bond investors are a reflection of their interest rate expectations, which, in turn, will be largely influenced by expectations about inflation. For example, if inflation and interest rates are expected to rise, bond prices will fall to bring the yields up to appropriate levels to reflect the interest rate increases. To remain competitive, equities prices would also suffer.

3.2.2 Consumer Price Indices

Index-linked bonds are ones where the coupon and the redemption amount are increased by the amount of inflation over the life of the bond. The amount of inflation uplift is determined by changes in the index that reflects the rate at which prices faced by individuals (consumers) are increasing – generally referred to as consumer price indices.

The markets pay attention to consumer price indices because they are good indicators of the level of inflation and, consequently, government reaction to it. These indices also signal the need for increases in the yield paid on bonds in order to compensate for the erosion of real returns.

Example – Inflation Measures in the UK

Historically, the measure used in the UK has been the retail prices index (RPI). It is calculated by looking at the prices of a basket of over 300 goods. The prices are then weighted to reflect the average household's consumption patterns, so those important items on which a lot of money is spent receive a higher weighting than peripheral items. The index itself is based on movements in prices since a base period.

In 2003, the Chancellor of the Exchequer began using a new target for inflation, the **harmonised index of consumer prices (HICP)**, which was renamed the **consumer prices index (CPI)**. The level of the new CPI-based inflation target for the BoE's **Monetary Policy Committee (MPC)** was set at 2% from 10 December 2003.

The CPI is calculated each month by looking at the goods and services that a typical household might buy, including food, heating, household goods and travel costs.

As already mentioned, the CPI was known as the harmonised index of consumer prices (HICP). HICPs were originally developed in the European Union (EU) to assess whether prospective members of European Monetary Union (EMU) would pass the required inflation convergence criterion, and then used as the measure of inflation to assess price stability in the euro area by the European Central Bank (ECB).

Producer prices indices (PPIs) measure inflationary pressures at an earlier stage in the production process. PPIs include input price indices that measure the change in prices going into the production process, including raw materials and other inputs. Changes in commodity prices will directly affect this number. There are also output or factory gate indices that measure the changes in the price of goods as they leave the production process and enter the retail sector. There is obviously a very strong relationship with input price variation.

Historically, any changes in raw material prices had tended to pass on through the production process and result in higher retail prices. However, in recent years, the generally low level of inflation, coupled with the more competitive nature of the labour market, has made it increasingly difficult for producers to pass on price increases. Consumers have grown used to stable prices, and appear to be unable to force their wages up in order to compensate for the higher prices.

Summary of Inflation Measures in the UK

The main measures of inflation used in the UK are:

- **CPI** – based on an EU-wide formula that was originally called the harmonised index of consumer prices (HICP), allowing direct comparison of the inflation rate in the UK against that in the rest of Europe. CPI at 2% is the current target for the BoE's MPC.
- **RPI** – an average measure of change in the prices of goods and services. Once published, it is never revised.
- **PPI** – this is based on measuring inflation further up the supply chain at the wholesale level, including 'factory gate' inflation.

3.2.3 Index-Linking

Index-linked bonds, such as the UK's **index-linked gilts** and the US TIPS, differ from conventional bonds in that the coupon payments and the principal are adjusted in line with a published index of price inflation, such as the RPI or CPI. This means that both the coupons and the principal on redemption paid by these bonds are adjusted to take account of inflation since the bond's issue. Assuming inflation is positive, the nominal amount outstanding of an index-linked bond is less than the redemption value the government will pay on maturity.

Example

Index-linking US TIPS

With US TIPS, the index-linking is achieved by adjusting the principal outstanding on the bond using the CPI. If the CPI is positive, there is inflation and the principal increases. If the CPI is negative, there is deflation and the principal decreases. The coupon paid on the US TIPS is based on the fixed coupon set at issue multiplied by the adjusted principal. When TIPS mature, the investor is paid the greater of the adjusted principal and the original principal.

Example

UK Index-Linked Gilts

It should be noted that the older RPI inflation measure is still being used for UK gilts as it was contained in the prospectuses of older index-linked issues and consultation with the industry indicated a preference for its continued use.

To calculate the inflation adjustment for a coupon payment, two index figures are required: that applicable to the bond when it was originally issued, and that relating to the point at which interest is paid. For UK gilts, the RPI figures used were originally those applicable eight months before the relevant dates (eg, for a December coupon, the previous April RPI data was used). This indexation lag was shortened for index-linked gilts issued after 2005 to just three months and it is this method for index-linking gilts that is explained below.

An index ratio is used to calculate the coupon payments and the redemption payment. The index ratio for each index-linked gilt measures the growth in the RPI since the gilt was first issued. For a given date, it is the ratio of the reference RPI applicable to that date divided by the reference RPI applicable to the original issue date of the gilt.

The reference RPI for the first calendar day of any month is the RPI for the month three months earlier (so the reference RPI for 1 June is the RPI for March, for the 1 July it is the RPI for April, etc). The reference RPI for any other day in the month is calculated by linear interpolation between the reference RPI applicable to the first calendar day of the month in which the day falls and the reference RPI applicable to the first calendar day of the month immediately following.

The nominal amount of the index-linked gilt is uplifted by the index ratio to give an updated principal. This principal is then used to generate the coupon payable by multiplying by the coupon percentage. The coupon payments on an index-linked gilt that pays coupons half-yearly are based on the stated coupon divided by two and multiplied by the nominal value uplifted by the relevant index ratio. The redemption payment is based on the nominal value uplifted by the index ratio that applies at the point of redemption, namely the RPI three months prior to redemption divided by the RPI three months prior to the gilt's issue date.

For example, a 2% Index-Linked Gilt 2035 pays semi-annual coupons on 26 January and 26 June each year. An investor holding £20,000 nominal will receive 2% x 6/12 of £20,000 x index ratio each half-year. At the redemption date in 2035, the investor will receive £20,000 uplifted by the index ratio that captures the RPI increases since issue.

Because these bonds are uplifted by increases in the relevant price index, they are effectively inflation-proof. In times of inflation, they will increase in price and preserve the purchasing power of the investment.

In a period of zero inflation, index-linked bonds will pay the nominal coupon rate with no uplift and simply pay back the nominal value at maturity.

In periods of deflation (negative inflation, with prices persistently falling), some sovereign index-linked bonds (eg, in the US and France) have a 'deflation floor', with the issuer guaranteeing that the redemption payment will not be less than the original par value. However, there is no deflation floor for the UK's index-linked gilts, where the possibility exists of returning less than the nominal value at redemption.

3.3 Separate Trading of Registered Interest and Principal of Securities (STRIPS)

Learning Objective

2.4.3 Understand the purpose and characteristics of the strip market: advantages, disadvantages and uses; result of stripping a bond; zero coupon securities

Zero coupon bonds (ZCBs) pay no interest; instead, they promise to pay just the nominal value at redemption. As there is no other possible form of return, investors will pay less than the nominal value when they buy ZCBs, with their return coming in the form of the difference between the price they pay for the bond and the amount they receive when the bond is redeemed. The bond is said to be issued at a discount to its face value, with the discount providing all of the return on a ZCB.

STRIPS is an acronym of Separate Trading of Registered Interest and Principal of Securities. Stripping a bond involves trading the interest (each individual coupon) and the principal (the nominal value) separately. Each individual strip forms the equivalent of a ZCB. Each strip will trade at a discount to its face value, with the size of the discount being determined by prevailing interest rates and time.

To illustrate how STRIPS work, a ten-year US Treasury note (T-note) can be stripped to make 21 separate securities: 20 STRIPS based on the coupons, which are entitled to just one of the half-yearly interest payments; and one strip entitled to the redemption payment at the end of the ten years. Similarly, a two-year, semi-annual coupon-paying UK gilt could be used to create five individual securities, one for each of the four remaining coupon payments and one for the principal payment to be paid in two years.

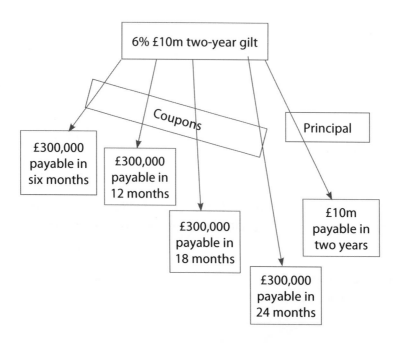

STRIPS markets have been developed in US Treasuries and in the UK gilts market. US financial institutions are able to create STRIPS from US T-notes and bonds, including TIPS. In the UK, only those gilts that have been designated by the DMO as strippable are eligible for the STRIPS market, not all gilts. Those gilts that are stripped have separate registered entries for each of the individual cash flows that enable different owners to hold each individual strip, and facilitate the trading of the individual STRIPS. It is only gilt-edged market makers (GEMMs), the BoE or the UK Treasury that are able to strip gilts.

The key advantage of STRIPS is that investors can precisely match their liabilities, removing any reinvestment risk.

Example

An investor wants to fund the repayment of the principal on a $5 million mortgage, due to be paid in five years' time. Using US Treasuries, there are three major choices:

1. The investor could buy a $5 million nominal coupon-paying Treasury with five years remaining to maturity, but the coupons on this will mean that it will generate more than $5 million.
2. The investor could buy less than $5 million nominal, attempting to arrive at $5 million in five years. However, the investor will have to estimate how the coupons over the life of the bond can be reinvested and what rate of return they will provide – the estimate could well be wrong.
3. The investor could buy a $5 million strip. This would precisely meet the need.

As seen in the example above, STRIPS can meet the liabilities of the investor precisely, removing any reinvestment risk that is normally faced when covering liabilities with coupon-paying bonds. Furthermore, investors in government bond STRIPS have few worries about the risk that the issuer of the bonds will default – for example, liabilities of the US and UK Governments are generally considered to be virtually free of any default risk (also known as credit risk).

3.4 International Government Bonds

Learning Objective

2.4.4 Understand the characteristics and purpose of government bonds in developed, undeveloped and emerging markets: settlement periods; coupon payment frequency; terms and maturities; currency, credit and inflation risks

The following table highlights the way government bonds are referred to and classified across the major economies of the world, and the settlement period for any market transactions that may take place after the bonds are issued.

The coupon payment is the periodic payment that is made by the bond issuer to the bondholder, and the maturity represents the time period during which the coupon payments will be paid, at the conclusion of which the principal amount of the bond will be repaid to the holder.

Country	Name	Coupon Frequency	Maturity	Settlement Period
US	Treasury bonds (T-bonds)	Semi-annual	Over 10 years The longest maturity is for 30 years and is known as the long bond.	T+1
	Treasury notes (T-notes)	Semi-annual	2–10 years	T+1
	Treasury bills (T-bills)	No coupon paid	Less than 1 year	Trade date
UK	Gilts	Semi-annual	0–7 years remaining – 'short-dated' 7–15 years remaining – 'medium-dated' 15 years and over remaining – 'long-dated'	T+1
France	OAT	Annual	7–30 years	T+2
	BTAN	Annual	2–5 years	
Germany	Bund	Annual	Over 10 years	T+2
	Bobl	Annual	5 years	
	Schatz	Annual	Up to 2 years	
Japan	Japanese Government Bond (JGB)	Semi-annual	Long (10 years, most common), super-long (20 years)	T+2

Outside of the developed markets, many sovereign states are considered undeveloped in relation to government bonds. Examples include much of sub-Saharan Africa and South America. It is argued that well-functioning bond markets would help sustain economic stability, in particular, the ability to weather financial crises by providing funding sources for these countries to finance fiscal stimulus packages.

Additionally, the development of bond markets can improve the intermediation of savings. Government bond markets are an effective way to intermediate capital savers with capital users, particularly if they also spur the development of a corporate bond market.

The last 30 years or so have also seen major increases in the issuance of government bonds by emerging markets, both in US dollar denominations and each government's currency. Traditionally, the emerging markets were captured in the acronym BRIC – Brazil, Russia, India and China – and it has since been broadened to include countries such as South Africa, Indonesia, Mexico, Turkey and Malaysia.

The risks of investing in emerging market government bonds include the standard risks that accompany all debt issues, such as the variables of the issuer's economic or financial performance and the ability of the issuer to meet payment obligations. These risks are heightened due to the potential political and economic volatility of these developing nations which could increase the risk of default (credit risk) and also allow inflation to take hold.

Emerging market government bonds also pose other cross-border risks, as a result of exchange rate fluctuations and currency devaluations. If a bond is issued in the local currency, the exchange rate of the investor's home currency versus that currency can positively or negatively affect yield. Investors that do not want to reduce this currency risk need to avoid bonds that are denominated in the local currency and select dollar-denominated bonds, or issued only in US dollars.

4.   Corporate Debt

Corporate debt is simply money that is borrowed by a company that has to be repaid. Generally, corporate debt also requires servicing by making regular interest payments. Corporate debt can be subdivided into money borrowed from banks via loans and overdrafts, and money borrowed directly from investors in the form of IOU instruments, typically bonds.

Debt finance is less expensive than equity finance because investing in debt finance is less risky than investing in the equity of the same company. The interest on debt has to be paid before dividends, so there is more certainty for the lenders than the equity investors. Additionally, if the firm were to go into liquidation, the holders of debt finance would be paid back before the shareholders received anything.

For investors in bonds, firms like Standard & Poor's (S&P) capture the comparative riskiness of the issuer and the bond in their credit ratings.

However, raising money via debt finance does present dangers to the issuing company. The lenders are often able to claim some or all of the assets of the firm in the event of non-compliance with the terms of the loan – in the same way that a bank providing consumer mortgage finance would be able to claim the property as security against the loan.

4.1   Secured Debt

Learning Objective

2.5.1   Understand the principal features and uses of secured debt: fixed charges and floating charges; asset-backed securities; mortgage-backed securities; covered bonds; securitisation process; role of the trustee, when involved

Investors in corporate debt face the risk that the issuer will not be able to pay the interest and/or the principal amount. When this happens, it is known as default.

One way for the corporate borrower to lessen the risk of default is to issue secured debt, when the debt offers assets of the company as a guarantee. There are two ways of doing this:

- **fixed charge** – the debt carries a fixed charge over a particular company asset, eg, a building
- **floating charge** – the debt is secured against a group of the company's assets; in the event of default, a floating charge crystallises over the available assets.

Bonds issued with a fixed charge are generally referred to as debentures.

4.1.1 Asset-Backed Securities (ABSs)

Asset-backed securities (ABSs) are bonds that are backed by a particular pool of assets. These assets can take several forms, such as mortgage loans, credit card receivables and car loans. Major banks, such as Citigroup, Bank of America and JP Morgan Chase, commonly securitise the amounts owed by their customers on their credit cards.

The assets provide the bondholders' security, since the cash generated from them is used to service the bonds (pay the interest), and to repay the principal sum at maturity. Such arrangements are often referred to as the securitisation of assets. The name 'securitisation' reflects the fact that the resulting financial instruments used to obtain funds from the investors are considered, from a legal and trading point of view, as securities.

Diagrammatically:

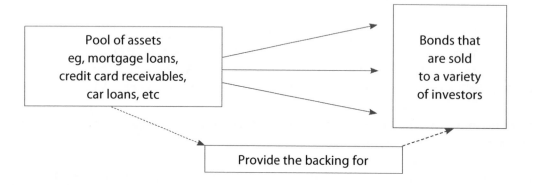

4.1.2 Mortgage-Backed Securities (MBSs)

Mortgage-backed securities (MBSs) are one example of ABSs. They are created from mortgage loans made by financial institutions like banks and building societies. MBSs are bonds that are created when a group of mortgage loans are packaged (or pooled) for sale to investors. As the underlying mortgage loans are paid off by the homeowners, the investors receive payments of interest and principal.

The MBS market began in the US, where the majority of issues are made (or guaranteed) by an agency of the US government. The Government National Mortgage Association (commonly referred to as Ginnie Mae), the Federal National Mortgage Association (Fannie Mae) and the Federal Home Loan Mortgage Corporation (Freddie Mac) are the major issuers. These agencies buy qualifying mortgage loans, or guarantee pools of such loans originated by financial institutions, then they securitise the loans and issue bonds. Some private institutions, such as financial institutions and housebuilders, issue their own MBSs.

As with other ABSs, MBS issues are often subdivided into a variety of classes (or tranches), each tranche having a specific priority in relation to interest and principal payments. Typically, as the underlying payments on the mortgage loans are collected, the interest on all tranches of the bonds is paid first. As loans are repaid, the principal is first paid back to the first tranche of bondholders, then the second tranche, third tranche, and so on. Such arrangements will create different risk profiles and repayment schedules for each tranche, enabling the appropriate securities to be held according to the needs of the investor. Traditionally, the investors in such securities were institutional investors, like insurance companies and pension funds, although they now also include the more sophisticated individual investor.

4.1.3 Further Details in Relation to Asset-Backed Securities

The investors in ABSs have recourse to the pool of assets, although there may be an order of priority between investors in different tranches of the issue.

The precise payment dates for interest and principal are dependent on the anticipated and actual payment stream generated by the underlying assets and the needs of investors. ABSs based on a pool of mortgage loans are likely to be longer-dated than those based on a pool of credit card receivables. Within these constraints, the issuers of ABSs create a variety of tranches to appeal to the differing maturity and risk appetites of investors.

ABSs often utilise a **special purpose vehicle (SPV)** in order to lessen the default risk that investors face when investing in the securities. This SPV is often a trust, and the originator of the assets, such as the bank granting the mortgage loans, sells the loans to the SPV and the SPV issues the asset-backed bonds. This serves two purposes:

1. The SPV is a separate entity from the originator of the assets, so the assets leave the originator's financial statements to be replaced by the cash from the SPV. This is often described as an **off-balance-sheet arrangement** because the assets have left the originator's balance sheet.
2. The SPV is a stand-alone entity, so, if the originator of the assets suffers bankruptcy, the SPV still remains intact with the pool of assets available to service the bonds. This is often described as bankruptcy-remote and enhances the creditworthiness of ABSs, potentially giving them a **higher rating than the originator of the assets.**

Diagrammatically:

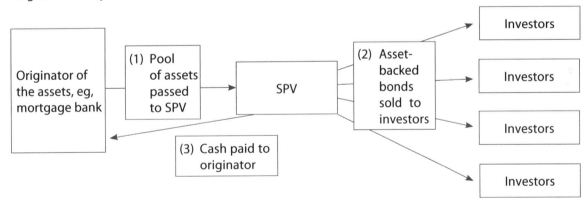

In instances when no SPV is created, the asset-backed bonds are simply referred to as 'covered bonds', referring to the pool of assets that provide the 'cover' to the bondholder. So, with covered bonds, the assets are retained on the balance sheet of the issuing entity, such as a bank, rather than transferred to an SPV. Indeed, when an SPV is used and the assets become distressed, or if there is no market for determining the value of the assets held in the SPV, as was the case during the sub-prime crisis of 2007–08, the originator of the securitisation instruments may decide to transfer the troubled assets back on to its balance sheet to become covered bonds.

4.1.4   Covered Bonds

Covered bonds are senior secured debt securities of a regulated financial institution, such as a bank. As with other forms of secured debt, if the issuing bank defaults, the collateral is used to cover any shortfall in payments due from the bank. An additional feature of covered bonds is that, as long as the collateral is sufficient, they continue to be paid according to their original schedule after default. Covered bonds are a form of asset-backed bond with the pool of assets providing the 'cover' to the bondholder.

With European covered bonds, the assets are typically retained on the balance sheet of the issuing entity, such as a bank, rather than transferred to an SPV. In other parts of the world, such as the US, an SPV structure is still used for covered bonds as existing legislation does not facilitate more direct issuance.

Interestingly, when an off-balance-sheet SPV has been used, and the assets become distressed, or if there is no market for determining the value of the assets held in the SPV (as was the case during the sub-prime crisis of 2007–08), some originators of the securitisation instruments decided to transfer the troubled assets back on to their balance sheets to become covered bonds.

4.1.5   The Role of the Trustee in Secured Debt

Trustee for Secured Debt Issues

The terminology for secured debt varies globally, in particular the term 'debenture'. In the UK, a secured debt transaction is called a debenture whereas in the US the term debenture generally refers to a loan agreement with no security at all. In the US, the term ABS is more commonly used for secured issues.

When a corporation either in the UK or US issues secured debt to a large number of persons, it is invariably the case that a trustee will be appointed.

The mechanics of this process are that, under the terms of the trust deed, the property of the company is mortgaged to the holders of the securities to secure the payment of the money owing. However, there is a contract or deed of trust put in place between the company and the trustees. The trustee holds the benefit of the covenant by the company to repay the monies on trust for the holders of the securities.

Under English law, the trustee has wide discretionary powers, whereas under US law its responsibilities are usually clearly defined. The main trustee roles for a UK debenture trustee are:

- **Note trustee** – is appointed to represent the interests of holders of the securities, while providing guidance to the issuer.
- **Security trustee** – for issues secured by a pledge of securities or other properties, the security is charged in favour of the trustee for the benefit of the various secured parties. The governing documents dictate the order of priority of payments among the entitled parties.
- **Share trustee** – holds the shares in an issuing SPV in order to ensure off-balance-sheet treatment for the originator of the transaction. Sometimes these SPVs are domiciled in offshore jurisdictions.
- **Successor trustee** – this role played by a trustee is provided for banks which need to resign because of conflicts of interest (especially in connection with defaulted or bankrupt issues) or when work requirements exceed the bank's capacity.

Benefits of a Trust Deed

The security and all enforcement powers in respect of the trust deed are vested in the trustee as a single entity acting on behalf of all the holders of securities. This enables a coherent enforcement procedure, rather than a series of disparate actions by different holders of securities. This is an advantage to the individual holders as it ensures organised action and parity of treatment. The trust deed would usually provide that all holders are paid proportionately, and a single action by the trustee prevents some holders recovering and not others. It is also an advantage to the company as it means it does not have to defend a series of actions for what might be a trifling breach of any one provision.

Costs

Administration and enforcement by the trustee will be less costly than numerous parties dealing with the company.

Representation of the Interests of the Bondholders

To make bonds a more marketable security, a trustee is assigned to represent the interests of the bondholders. The corporate trustee is usually a bank or a trust company, and, although the trustee is paid by the issuing corporation, it represents the interests of the bondholders.

Before marketing a bond, the issuer, often using the corporate trustee as its agent, will engage the services of a credit rating agency to assess the creditworthiness of the issuer and the likelihood that all of the terms of the securities offering are likely to be fulfilled. This engagement is to represent the interest of the bondholders, but there is cause for a potential conflict of interest, as the credit rating agency will be paid by the issuer, while its ratings are provided to advise the bondholders of the security risk of the offering. Credit ratings agencies will never specifically recommend any particular offering, but the ratings which are provided are relied upon by many investors.

The corporate trustee must keep track of all bonds sold, verifying that the amount issued is not greater than what is stated in the indenture and making sure that the corporation complies with all covenants – which are the terms of the indenture – while the bond issue is outstanding.

For instance, the indenture may stipulate that the corporation maintains a certain percentage of assets over liabilities, or that the corporation does not take on too much debt. Adherence to the covenants of the indenture is one of the principal roles of the trustee.

The trustee may either provide services for the payment of interest and the cash management function, or it may appoint a separate custodian for the purpose.

4.2 Unsecured Debt

Learning Objective

2.5.2 Understand the principal features and uses of unsecured debt: subordinated; guaranteed; convertible bonds

---

Unsecured debt is not secured against any of the company's assets, so the holder has no special protection against default. To compensate the holder for the additional risk, the coupon on an unsecured bond, or the interest on unsecured bank borrowing, will be higher than on equivalent secured borrowings.

Subordinated debt is not secured and the lenders have agreed that, if the company fails, they will only be repaid once other creditors have been repaid if there is enough money left over. Unsecured debtholders, however, would still be repaid prior to shareholders, as 'lenders' are always repaid before 'owners' in an insolvency. Interest payments on subordinated borrowings will be higher than those on equivalent unsecured borrowings that are not subordinated. This is simply because of the additional default risk faced by subordinated lenders.

Guaranteed debt is when a guarantee is provided by someone other than the issuer. The guarantor is typically the parent company, or another company in the same group of companies as the issuer.

Convertible bonds give the holder of the bond the right, but not the obligation, to convert into a predetermined number of ordinary shares of the issuer.

The following table summarises the characteristics of subordinated, guaranteed and convertible bonds as compared to an unsecured bond issued by the same company:

	Subordinated bond	Guaranteed bond	Convertible bond
Normal life	No difference: typically 7 to 30 years to maturity		
Ranking in a liquidation	Below unsecured bonds	Alongside other unsecured bonds	Alongside other unsecured bonds
Risk and rating	Greater risk of default, so a lower credit rating	Risk dependent upon the guarantor's own financial standing, so a higher credit rating	No difference from unsecured bonds
Coupon	Likely to be higher than unsecured bonds	Likely to be lower due to the guarantee	Potentially lower due to the upside potential of the share price
Benefits to the issuer	Attractive regulatory treatment for financial institution issuers	Guarantor is lowering the cost of the debt finance	Upside potential of the shares restricts the cost of the debt and the possibility of conversion lowers the risk of eventual repayment

Fixed-coupon bonds are issued with a fixed rate of coupon. If interest rates rise, the fixed coupon becomes less attractive and the price of the bond falls. The opposite is true of an interest rate fall. As for government bonds, the interest is always calculated by reference to the nominal value of the bond, so a $1,000 nominal 5% ABC corporate bond will pay $50 per annum to the holder.

Floating rate bonds or **notes** are bonds when the coupon rate varies. The rate is adjusted in line with published, market interest rates. The published interest rates that are normally used are based on the **London Interbank Offered Rate (LIBOR).** There are a number of LIBORs published each day for different currencies and different periods, such as three-month US dollar LIBOR and six-month sterling LIBOR. LIBORs reflect the average rates at which banks in London offer loans to other banks. Until 2014, LIBORs were published by the UK's British Bankers' Association (BBA), using quotes provided by a panel of banks; however, after regulatory investigations discovered that LIBORs were being manipulated by a number of those banks, the UK regulator, the Financial Conduct Authority (FCA), concluded that the administrator of LIBOR required regulatory authorisation. LIBORs are now calculated by Intercontinental Exchange Benchmark Administration ltd and are regulated by the FCA.

Floating rate notes typically add a margin to the LIBOR rate, measured in basis points, with each basis point representing one hundredth of 1%. A corporate issuer may offer floating-rate bonds to investors at three-month sterling LIBOR plus 75 basis points. If LIBOR is at 4%, the coupon paid will be 4.75%, with the additional 75 basis points compensating the investor for the higher risk of payment default.

4.3 Credit Ratings

Learning Objective

2.5.3 Understand the principal features and uses of credit ratings: rating agencies; impact on price; uses and risks of credit enhancements; difference between investment grade and sub-investment grade bonds; limitations

Bondholders face the risk that the issuer of the bond might default on their obligation to pay interest and the principal amount at redemption. This so-called credit risk or default risk – the probability of an issuer defaulting on their payment obligations and the extent of the resulting loss – can be assessed by reference to the independent credit ratings given to most bond issues.

There are a significant number of credit ratings agencies around the world, some of whom specialise in particular regions or particular types of company. However, the three most prominent agencies that provide these ratings are S&P, Moody's and Fitch Ratings Inc. Bond issues subject to credit ratings can be divided into two distinct categories: those accorded an investment grade rating and those categorised as non-investment grade or speculative. The latter are also known as high-yield or junk bonds. Investment grade issues offer the greatest liquidity and security, meaning the issuer is likely to meet both interest and principal repayments. In exchange for this assurance, however, they typically pay less interest. Bonds with lower credit ratings tend to pay higher coupons to compensate for the higher risk that investors take by investing in them. Further, if ratings change, the price of bonds that have already been issued will alter to reflect the fact that they have become more, or less, attractive to investors. The change in price will alter the effective return on the bond yields. The following table provides a comprehensive survey of the credit ratings available from the three agencies.

Although the three rating agencies use similar methods to rate issuers and individual bond issues, essentially by assessing whether the cash flow likely to be generated by the borrower will comfortably service, and ultimately repay, its debts, the rating each gives sometimes differs, though not usually significantly so.

Moody's		Standard and Poor's		Fitch		
Long-term	Short-term	Long-term	Short-term	Long-term	Short-term	
Aaa		AAA		AAA		Prime
Aa1		AA+		AA+		High grade
Aa2	P-1	AA	A-1+	AA	F1+	
Aa3		AA-		AA-		
A1		A+	A-1	A+	F1	Upper medium grade
A2		A		A		
A3	P-2	A-	A-2	A-	F2	Lower medium grade
Baa1		BBB+		BBB+		
Baa2	P-3	BBB	A-3	BBB	F3	
Baa3		BBB-		BBB-		
Ba1		BB+		BB+		Non-investment grade speculative
Ba2		BB		BB		
Ba3		BB-	B	BB-	B	
B1		B+		B+		Highly speculative
B2		B		B		
B3		B-		B-		
Caa1		CCC+				Substantial risks
Caa2	Not prime		C			Extremely speculative
Caa3		CCC-		CCC	C	In default with little prospect for recovery
Ca		CC				In default with little prospect for recovery
C			/	D		In default
/		D		D	/	
/				D		

Occasionally, issues such as ABSs are credit-enhanced in some way to gain a higher credit rating. The simplest method of achieving this is through some form of insurance scheme that will pay out should the pool of assets be insufficient to service or repay the debt.

In 2007–08, a financial crisis arose from ABSs such as MBSs. The credit rating agencies were criticised for the generous ratings they had attached to some of these securities. As a result, regulatory oversight of the credit ratings agencies has subsequently increased substantially.

5. Cash Assets

Cash assets embrace the market involving cash deposits and short-term instruments that are issued with less than one year to maturity. It is alternatively referred to as the money market. Over and above cash deposits, the two prime examples of money market instruments are T-bills issued by governments and **commercial paper (CP)** issued by companies.

5.1 Cash Deposits

Learning Objective

2.1.1   Understand the uses, advantages and disadvantages of holding cash deposits

Almost all investors keep at least part of their wealth in cash assets, which are often deposited with a bank or other savings institution to earn interest.

Cash deposits comprise accounts held with banks or other savings institutions. They are held by a wide variety of depositors – from retail investors through to companies, governments and financial institutions.

The main characteristics of cash deposits are:

- the return simply comprises interest income with no potential for capital growth, and
- the amount invested (the capital) is repaid in full at the end of the investment term.

The interest rate paid on deposits may vary between institutions, as well as with the amount of money deposited and the time for which the money is tied up.

- Large deposits are more economical for a bank to process and will earn a better rate.
- Fixed-term accounts involve the investor tying up their money for a fixed period of time, such as one, two or three years, or when a fixed period of notice has to be given, such as 30 days, 60 days or 90 days. In exchange for tying up their funds for these periods, the investor will demand a higher rate of interest than would be available on accounts that permit immediate access.
- Instant-access deposit accounts typically earn the lowest rates of interest of the various deposit accounts available.
- Current accounts (known in the US as checking accounts) will generate an even lower rate, and sometimes pay no interest at all.

Generally, interest received by an individual is subject to income tax. In many countries, tax is deducted at source – that is, by the deposit-taker before paying the interest to the depositor. The headline rate of interest quoted by deposit-takers, before deduction of tax, is referred to as gross interest, and the rate of interest after tax is deducted is referred to as net interest.

Advantages and Disadvantages

There are a number of advantages to investing in cash:

- One of the key reasons for holding money in the form of cash deposits is liquidity. Liquidity is the ease and speed with which an investment can be turned into cash to meet spending needs. Most investors are likely to have a need for cash at short notice and so should plan to hold some on deposit to meet possible needs and emergencies before considering other less liquid investments.
- The other main reasons for holding cash investments are as a savings vehicle and for the interest return that can be earned on them.
- A further advantage is the relative safety that cash investments have and the fact that they are not exposed to market volatility, as is the case with other types of assets.

Investing in cash does have some serious drawbacks, however, including the following:

- Banks and savings institutions are of varying creditworthiness and the risk that they may default needs to be assessed and taken into account.
- Inflation reduces the real return that is being earned on cash deposits and often the after-tax return can be negative.
- Interest rates vary, and so the returns from cash-based deposits will also vary.

Although banks and other savings institutions are licensed, monitored and regulated, it is still possible that such institutions might fail, as was seen in the aftermath of the financial crisis. Deposits are, therefore, often protected by a government-sponsored compensation scheme. This will repay any deposited money lost, typically up to a set maximum, due to the collapse of a bank or savings institution. The sum is generally fixed so as to be of meaningful protection to most retail investors, although it would be of less help to very substantial depositors.

When cash is deposited overseas, depositors should also consider:

- the costs of currency conversion and the potential exchange rate risks if the deposit is not made in the investor's home currency
- the creditworthiness of the banking system and the chosen deposit-taking institution, and whether a depositors' protection scheme exists and if non-residents are protected under it; not every country operates one, and so the onus is on the investor or their adviser to check
- the tax treatment applied to the interest on the deposit
- whether the deposit will be subject to any exchange controls that may restrict access to the money and its ultimate repatriation.

5.2 Treasury Bills (T-bills)

Learning Objective

2.1.2 Understand the features and characteristics of Treasury bills: issuer; purpose of issue; minimum denomination; normal life; no coupon and redemption at par

As well as issuing bonds to fund the government's long-term borrowing needs, developed countries also manage the liquidity needs of the government. This is done primarily through issuing short-term IOUs known as **Treasury bills** (T-bills).

T-bills are short-term loan instruments, issued and guaranteed by the government, with maturity dates ranging between one and 12 months. For example, the US issues T-bills weekly, with maturities of four weeks, 13 weeks, 26 weeks and 52 weeks. T-bills pay no coupon and, consequently, are issued at a discount to their nominal value, with the difference between the par value (maturity value) and the discount value (purchase price) representing the return to the investor.

Example

As in the US, the UK also issues T-bills weekly. These are at auctions known as tenders and are held by the DMO on the last business day of the week (usually a Friday). These tenders are open to bids from a group of eligible bidders which include all of the major banks. The bids are tendered competitively – only those bidding a high enough price will be allocated any T-bills and they will pay the price that they bid. The bids must be for a minimum of £500,000 nominal of the T-bills, and above this level bids must be made in multiples of £50,000. In subsequent trading, the minimum denomination of T-bills is £25,000.

Since they are guaranteed by the government, T-bills provide a very secure investment for market participants with short-term investment horizons, and this type of instrument often represents a risk-free investment. The return on a T-bill is wholly dependent upon the price paid.

Example

If a purchaser paid $990,000 for $1,000,000 nominal of a 13-week US T-bill, the return will be the gain made of $10,000. As a percentage of invested funds, the return is: $10,000/$990,000 x 100 = 1.01% over approximately three months.

5.3 Commercial Paper (CP)

Learning Objective

2.1.3 Know the principal features and uses of commercial paper: issuers, including CP programmes; investors; discount security; unsecured; asset-backed; rating; normal life, method of issuance; role of dealer

Commercial paper (CP) is an unsecured short-term promissory note issued primarily by corporations, although there are also municipal and sovereign issuers. It represents the largest segment of the money market through banks. CP is the corporate equivalent of a government's T-bill. It is issued at a discount to its nominal value and can have a maturity of up to one year in Europe and 270 days in the US; however, it is common to find in both territories that CP will be issued for three months.

Large companies issue CP to assist in the management of their liquidity. Rather than borrowing directly from banks, these large entities run CP programmes that are placed with institutional investors.

The various companies' CP is differentiated by credit ratings – when the large credit rating agencies assess the stability of the issuer.

Asset-backed CP is a short-term investment vehicle with a maturity that is typically between 90 and 180 days. The security itself will be issued by a bank or other financial institution, and the notes are backed by assets such as receivables. Finance companies will typically provide consumers with home loans, unsecured personal loans and retail automobile loans. These receivables are then used by the finance company as collateral for raising money in the CP market. Some finance companies are specialist firms that provide financing for purchases of another firm's products. For example, the major activity of Ally Financial Inc (formerly the General Motors Acceptance Corporation (GMAC)) is the financing of purchases and leases of General Motors' vehicles by dealers and consumers.

It is perhaps important to mention that a missed payment by an issuer of a CP for as little as one day can lead to bankruptcy proceedings. Issuers take great care to repay the principal on the due day.

5.3.1 Commercial Paper Issuance and the Role of Dealers

There are two methods of issuing CP. The issuer can market the securities directly to a buy-and-hold investor as with most money market funds. Alternatively, it can sell the paper to a dealer, who then sells the paper in the market. The dealer market for CP involves large **investment banks** and other financial services firms, such as bond dealers.

Unlike bonds or other forms of long-term indebtedness, a CP issuance is not all brought to market at once. Instead, an issuer will maintain an ongoing CP programme. It advertises the rates at which it is willing to issue paper for various terms, so buyers can purchase the paper whenever they have funds to invest. Programmes may be promoted by dealers, in which case the paper is called dealer paper. Larger issuers, especially finance companies, have the market presence to issue their paper directly to investors. Their paper is called direct paper.

Direct issuers of CP are usually financial companies that have frequent and sizeable borrowing needs and find it more economical to sell paper without the use of an intermediary. In the US, direct issuers save a dealer fee of approximately five basis points, or 0.05% annualised, which translates to $50,000 on every $100 million outstanding. This saving compensates for the cost of maintaining a permanent sales staff to market the paper. Dealer fees tend to be lower outside the US.

CP entails credit risk, and programmes are rated by the major rating agencies. Because CP is a rolling form of debt, with new issues generally funding the retirement of old issues, the main risk is that the issuer will not be able to issue new CP. This is called refinancing or rollover risk. Many issuers obtain credit enhancements for their programmes. These may include a line of credit or other alternative source of financing.

Since the banking crisis of 2008, the primary issuance of CP and the secondary market for CP have been severely curtailed, and it has been difficult to persuade dealers to make a market in it.

5.4 Repo Markets

Learning Objective

2.1.4 Understand the basic purpose and characteristics of the repo markets: repo; reverse repo; documentation; benefits of the repo market

A repo is a sale and repurchase agreement. It is legally binding for both buyer and seller. For example, a government bond repo is a contract in which the seller of government bonds agrees to buy them back at a future specified time and price. In effect, a government bond repo is a means of borrowing using the bond as security, as illustrated in the following diagram:

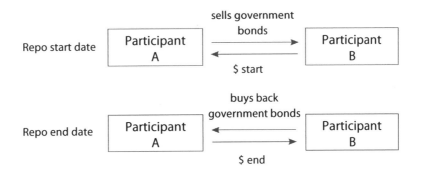

In the above diagram, both parts of the repo transaction are agreed between the participants at the outset: Participant A has entered into a repo transaction, Participant B has entered into a reverse repo agreement.

The amount of cash paid over by Participant B at the start of the repo will be less than the amount paid over to Participant B at the end of the repo period. The difference between the two amounts, expressed as a percentage, is the effective interest rate on the repo transaction. It is usually referred to as the repo rate.

The obvious benefit to Participant A is that they are able to raise finance against the security of the bonds that they hold – potentially a relatively cheap source of short-term finance. If Participant B is considered a conventional bank simply providing finance, then the benefit of using the repo is the security gained by holding the bonds. However, Participant B may be a market-making firm that has sold government bonds that it does not hold. The repo transaction enables the market-making firm to access the bonds that it requires to meet its settlement obligations. In this way, the government bond repo facilitates the smooth running of the secondary market in the bonds.

In the UK, the smooth running of the gilts market is further assisted by the DMO's standing repo facility. This enables any GEMM, or other DMO counterparty, to enter into a reverse repo arrangement with the DMO, perhaps to cover a **short position** in gilts. They must first sign the relevant documentation provided by the DMO and then are able to request any amount of a gilt above £5 million nominal. This facility is for next-day settlement, and the facility can be rolled forwards for up to two weeks. The DMO does charge a slightly higher than normal repo rate for firms accessing the standing repo facility.

Although the government bond and gilts market has been used as an example, it should be noted that the use of repos is an important liquidity provider for the debt markets as a whole.

6. Eurobonds

Learning Objective

2.6.1 Understand the principal features and uses of eurobonds: issued through syndicates of international banks; bearer; immobilised in depositories; accrued interest; ex-interest date; interest payments

Essentially, eurobonds are international bond issues. They are a way for an organisation to issue debt without being restricted to their own domestic market. The currency of issue does not need to be the euro; eurobonds can be issued in any currency as long as it is different to the currency of the place from which they are issued. So, if a eurobond was issued out of London, it would need to be in a currency other than pound sterling, such as the euro or the US dollar. If a eurobond was issued out of Frankfurt, it would need to be in a currency other than the euro, such as the US dollar or Japanese yen. Eurobonds are generally issued via a syndicate of international banks and it is unusual for eurobond issuers to keep a record of the holders of their bonds; the certificates themselves are all that is needed to prove ownership. This is the concept of bearer documents, when the holder of the certificates (the bearer) has all the rights attached to ownership. Eurobonds are issued in bearer form and, because they are issued internationally, they are largely free of national regulation. Eurobonds have been innovative in their structure to accommodate the needs of issuers and investors. There are plain vanilla, fixed-coupon bonds that normally pay the coupons once a year. Additionally, there are ZCBs and other forms of eurobond, such as floating-rate bonds and bonds with coupons that increase over time (stepped bonds).

An absence of national regulation means that eurobonds can pay interest gross, making the buyer responsible for paying their own tax and avoiding withholding tax (WHT) (tax being withheld in the country of origin). Initially, eurobonds were aimed at wealthy individuals, but as the market has grown they have increasingly become investments held by institutional investors.

As bearer documents, it is important that eurobonds are kept safe, and this is often achieved by holding the bonds in depositaries, particularly those maintained by Euroclear and Clearstream. When the bonds are deposited in these organisations they are described as being immobilised. Immobilisation does not mean that the bonds cannot be transferred in secondary market transactions, it simply means that the bonds are safely held within a reputable depositary and a buyer is likely to retain the bonds in their immobilised form.

As the eurobond market has grown, a self-regulatory organisation has been formed that oversees the market and its participants – the International Capital Market Association (ICMA).

Settlement and accrued interest conventions have been established for the secondary market. Settlement is on a T+2 basis and accrued interest is calculated on the basis of 30 days per month and 360 days per year (30/360 basis).

The following table highlights the major features of eurobonds:

Feature	Detail
Form	Bearer
Interest payments	Gross
Tax	Taxable but untaxed at source
Trades matched through	TRAX system
Trades settled through	Euroclear or Clearstream
Settlement period	Trade day plus two (T+2)
Trading mechanism	Over-the-counter (OTC)

7. Other Securities

7.1 Depositary Receipts (DRs)

Learning Objective

2.7.1 Know the principal features and characteristics of depositary receipts: American depositary receipts; global depositary receipts; means of creation including pre-release facility; registration; rights attached; dividends; transfer to underlying shares

Depositary receipts (DRs) come in two broad forms – American depositary receipts (ADRs) and global depositary receipts (GDRs).

The US is a huge pool of potential investment. Therefore, substantial non-US companies may want to attract US investors to raise funds. ADRs facilitate this process; indeed, they were created to make it easier for Americans to invest in overseas companies. GDRs are depositary receipts that are identical to ADRs, except that they are marketed to appeal to a broader base of investors, some of whom may be based outside the US.

Both ADRs and GDRs are negotiable certificates evidencing ownership of shares in a corporation from a country outside the US. Each DR has a particular number of underlying shares, or is represented by a fraction of an underlying share.

Examples

Volkswagen AG (the motor vehicle manufacturer) is listed in Frankfurt. It has two classes of shares listed – ordinary shares and preference shares. There are separate ADRs in existence for the ordinary shares and preference shares. Each ADR represents 0.2 individual Volkswagen shares.

The Indian consulting and IT services giant Infosys has ADRs traded on the New York Stock Exchange (NYSE) and each ADR represents a single share in Infosys ltd.

GDRs work in exactly the same way as ADRs, except that the target investors are not in the US, but in other parts of the world. For example, the Indian conglomerate Reliance Industries ltd is listed on the Bombay Stock Exchange in Mumbai, India, but also has GDRs available and traded in London – each Reliance GDR represents two underlying Reliance shares.

DRs are typically created (or sponsored) by the foreign corporation (Volkswagen and Infosys in the above examples). They will liaise with an investment bank regarding the precise structure of the DR, such as the number or fraction of shares represented by each DR. A depository bank will then accept a certain number of underlying shares from the issuer, create the DRs to represent the shares and make these DRs available to US, and potentially other, investors, probably via local brokers. This creation process for an ADR is illustrated by the following diagram:

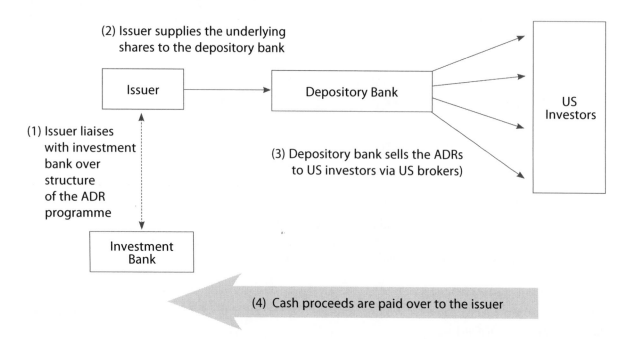

One characteristic of DRs that must also be considered is pre-release or **grey market trading**. When a DR is being created, the depository bank receives notification that, in the future, the shares will be placed on deposit. As long as it holds cash collateral, even though the shares are not yet on deposit, the depository bank can create and sell the receipt (the DR) at this time. Effectively, investors are buying a receipt that entitles them to all the benefits of a share that will, in the future, be held on deposit for them. The DR can be treated in this way for up to three months before the actual purchase of the underlying shares.

The shares underlying the DR are registered in the name of the depository bank, with the DRs themselves transferable as bearer securities. The DRs are typically quoted and traded in US dollars and are governed by the trading and settlement procedures of the market on which they are traded.

The depository bank acts as a go-between for the investor and the company. When the company pays a dividend, it is paid in the company's domestic currency to the depository bank. In an ADR, the bank will then convert the dividend into dollars and pass it on to the ADR holders. The US investors therefore need not concern themselves with currency movements. Furthermore, when an ADR holder decides to sell, the ADRs will be sold on in dollars. This removal of the need for any currency transactions for the US investor is a key attraction of the ADR.

DR holders are entitled to vote, just like ordinary shareholders, only the votes will be exercised via the depository bank.

If the DR represents a UK company's shares, there are tax ramifications. The UK tax authority, HM Revenue & Customs (HMRC) levies a tax known as stamp duty on share purchases, at 0.5% of the price paid to purchase shares.

However, because DRs may trade outside the UK, for example, in the US, no stamp duty is charged on the purchase of a DR. Instead, HMRC charges a one-off fee for stamp duty of 1.5%, when the DR is created.

If an investor wants to sell their DRs, they can do so either by selling them to another investor as a DR, or by selling the underlying shares in the home market of the company concerned. The latter route will involve cancelling the DR by delivering the certificates to the depository bank. The depository bank will then release the appropriate number of shares in accordance with the instructions received.

7.2 Warrants

Learning Objective

2.7.2 Know the rights, uses and differences between warrants and covered warrants

Traditionally, a warrant is an instrument issued by a company that allows the holder to subscribe for shares in that company at a fixed price over a fixed period. A typical warrant may have a life of several years.

Warrants are listed and traded on stock exchanges. If the holder decides to exercise, the company will issue new shares.

Example _____

Warrants are available in a (fictional) investment company, Cambridge Investment Trust plc. Cambridge Investment Trust shares are currently trading at 77p each, and warrants are available, giving the warrant owner the right, but not the obligation, to buy shares at £1 each, up until 2020. The warrants are trading at 4p each.

_____

In the above example, the warrant's expiry date is in 2020 and its exercise price is 100p.

What are the advantages to a company, such as the one encountered above, that persuade it to issue warrants? Clearly, the sale of warrants for cash will raise money for the company, and, if the warrants are exercised, then further capital will be raised by the company. As with call options, holding the warrant does not entitle the investor to receive dividends or to vote at company meetings, so the capital raised until the warrant is exercised could be considered as free.

Obviously warrants offer a highly geared investment opportunity for the investor, and they are often issued alongside other investments, rather than sold in their own right.

Example _____

CBC plc is attempting to raise finance by issuing bonds. Their advisers inform them that they could issue bonds paying a coupon of 6% pa, or lower it to 5% pa if they give away a single warrant with each £100 nominal of the bonds. The warrants are detachable from the bonds – in other words, the investors could decide to sell their warrants or keep them, regardless of whether they retain the bonds.

_____

Another type of warrant is a covered warrant. These are warrants issued by firms (usually investment banks), rather than the company whose shares the warrant enables the investor to buy. They are offered in the form of call warrants (giving the investor the right to buy), or put warrants (giving the investor the right to sell). In the UK, covered warrants are traded on the London Stock Exchange (LSE).

7.2.1 Warrant Price Behaviour

Warrants (including covered warrants) are highly geared investments. A modest outlay can result in a large gain, but the investor can lose the value of their entire stake in the warrant. Their value is driven by the length of time for which they are valid (their maturity or period until expiry) and the value of the underlying security.

There is a relatively simple method of looking at the price of one warrant relative to other warrants – using the conversion premium. This is the price of the warrant plus the **exercise price** required to buy the underlying share, less the prevailing share price.

Example

For example, calculating the conversion premium for the Cambridge Investment Trust warrants in the example above involves the:

Warrant price	=	4p
Plus exercise price	=	100p
Less share price	=	77p
Conversion premium	=	27p

Note that if the resultant figure were a negative, the warrant would be trading at a conversion discount.

7.3 Property

Learning Objective

2.7.3 Understand the risks and rewards involved in investment in property and the differences between the different investment routes: direct investment; real estate investment trusts; open-ended funds

Property as an asset class has certain distinguishing features:

- Each individual property is unique in terms of location, structure and design.
- Valuation is subjective, as property is not traded in a centralised marketplace, and continuous and reliable price data is not available.
- Property is subject to complex legal considerations and high transaction costs upon transfer.
- It is relatively illiquid as a result of not being instantly tradeable.
- It is also illiquid because it is often indivisible: the investor generally has to sell all of the property or nothing at all. It is not generally feasible for a commercial property investor to sell, for example, one factory unit out of an entire block (or at least, to do so would be commercially unattractive) – and a residential property owner cannot sell a spare bedroom to raise a little cash.
- Since property can only be purchased in discrete and sizeable units, **diversification** is made difficult.
- The supply of land is finite and its availability can be further restricted by legislation and local planning regulations. Therefore, price is predominantly determined by changes in demand.

Property or real estate can be subdivided into two types – residential and commercial. Residential property is where people live, whereas commercial property is used for business purposes; commercial property includes shops and offices, industrial premises and farmland.

Some key differences between commercial and residential property are shown in the following table.

	Residential Property	Commercial Property
Direct investment	Range of investment opportunities, including second homes, holiday homes and buy-to-let property	Size of investment required means direct investment in commercial property is limited to property companies and institutional investors
Tenancies	Typically short renewable leases	Long-term contracts with periods commonly in excess of ten years
Repairs	Landlord is responsible	Tenant is usually responsible
Returns	Largely linked to capital – increase in house prices	Significant component is income return from rental income

As an asset class, property has, at times, provided positive real long-term returns allied to low volatility and a reliable stream of income. An exposure to property can provide diversification benefits owing to its low **correlation** with both traditional and alternative asset classes.

Many private investors have chosen to become involved in the property market through buying-to-let or simply by purchasing a second home. Other investors wanting to include property within a diversified portfolio generally seek indirect exposure, either via a mutual fund or shares in publicly quoted property companies. It needs to be remembered, however, that investing via a mutual fund does not always mean that an investment can be readily realised. During the financial crisis of 2007–08, property prices fell and, as investors started to cash in their holdings, property funds brought in measures to stem outflows, in some cases imposing 12-month moratoria on encashments.

However, property can be subject to prolonged downturns and its lack of liquidity, significant maintenance costs, high transaction costs on transfer and the risk of having commercial property with no tenant (and, therefore, no rental income) really only makes commercial property suitable as an investment for long-term investing institutions, such as pension funds. The availability of indirect investment via shares in companies or stakes in collective funds, however, makes a diversified property portfolio more accessible to individual investors.

7.3.1 Real Estate Investment Trusts (REITs)

Real estate investment trusts (REITs) are well established in countries such as the UK, US, Australia, Canada and France. They are listed investment companies that pool investors' funds to invest in commercial and possibly residential property.

One of the main features of REITs is that they provide access to property returns without the previous disadvantage of double taxation. Until recently, when an investor held property company shares, not only would the company pay corporation tax, but the investor would be liable to tax on dividends and any growth. Under the rules for REITs, no corporation tax is payable, provided that certain conditions are met and distributions are instead taxable on the investor.

Broadly, tax-exempt business conditions are the following:

- The property rental business carried on by a UK REIT must contain at least three single rental properties. These can be commercial or residential, and a property includes each separately rented unit in a multi-let property but must not involve a property representing more than 40% of the total value of the property rental business
- For each accounting period, the REIT must distribute at least 90% of its property rental business profits by way of dividend.

REITs give investors access to professional property investment and may provide them with new opportunities, such as the ability to invest in commercial property. This allows them to diversify the risk of holding direct property investments.

REITs also remove a further risk from holding direct property, namely **liquidity risk**, or the risk that the investment will not be able to be readily realised. REITs are **closed-ended** funds quoted on stock exchanges, and shares in REITs are bought and sold in the same way as other listed company shares.

7.3.2 Open-Ended Funds

Open-ended funds are collective funds pooling the money of investors to buy portfolios of investments, such as stocks or bonds. In return for their money, the investors are given units in the fund. The funds are open-ended because they can grow by selling more units or shrink by buying back and cancelling units. This gives the fund the attraction of liquidity.

However, this process works less well for funds investing in physical property. Individual properties take time to sell, sales prices can suffer cyclical downturns and properties are usually indivisible – it is the case of selling the whole property or none at all. As such, open-ended funds investing in property may need to resort to redemption moratoria. This means that investors cannot sell back their units for a period, or an extended redemption period, meaning that they have to be more patient than usual and may need to wait months before receiving the proceed of the sale of units.

8. Foreign Exchange (FX)

8.1 Introduction

Learning Objective

2.8.1 Know the principal features and uses of spot, forward and cross rates: quotation as bid-offer spreads; forwards quoted as bid-offer margins against the spot; quotation of cross rates

The foreign exchange ('forex' or 'FX') market is the collective way of describing all the transactions in which one currency is exchanged for another, anywhere in the world. There is no physical exchange for the currency market in London; it is purely OTC and dominated by the banks.

There are two types of transaction conducted on the FX market:

1. Spot transactions are immediate currency deals that are settled within two working days.
2. Forward transactions involve currency deals that are agreed for a future date at a rate of exchange fixed now.

Both spot and forward rates are quoted by dealers in the form of a buying rate (the bid) and a selling rate (the offer). The spread between these two prices enables the FX dealer to make a profit.

The users of the FX market fall into two broad camps.

First, FX transactions are driven by international trade. If a Japanese company sells goods to a US customer, it might invoice the transaction in US dollars. These dollars will need to be exchanged for Japanese yen by the Japanese company and this is the FX transaction. The Japanese company may not be expecting to receive the dollars for a month after submission of the invoice. This gives it two choices:

1. It can wait until it receives the dollars and then execute a spot transaction.
2. It can enter into a forward transaction to sell the dollars for yen in a month's time. This will provide it with certainty as to the amount of yen it will receive and assist in its budgeting efforts.

The second reason for FX transactions is speculation. If an investor feels that the US dollar is likely to weaken against the euro, they can buy euros in either the spot or forward market to profit if they are right.

Trading of foreign currencies is always done in pairs. These are currency pairs when one currency is bought and the other is sold, and the prices at which these take place make up the exchange rate. When the exchange rate is being quoted, the name of the currency is abbreviated to a three-character reference.

The most commonly quoted currency pairs and their three-character references are:

- US dollar and Japanese yen (USD/JPY)
- Euro and US dollar (EUR/USD)
- US dollar and Swiss franc (USD/CHF)
- British pound and US dollar (GBP/USD).

When currencies are quoted, the first currency is the **base currency** and the second is the counter or quote currency. The base currency is always equal to one unit of that currency, in other words, one pound, one dollar or one euro. For example, at the time of writing, the EUR:USD exchange rate is 1:1.1229 which means that €1 is worth $1.1229.

When currency pairs are quoted, a market maker or foreign exchange trader will quote a bid and an ask price. Staying with the example of the EUR/USD, the quote might be 1.1228/30. So if you want to buy €100,000 then you will need to pay the higher of the two prices and deliver $112,300; if you want to sell €100,000 then you get the lower of the two prices and receive $112,280.

Generally, exchange rates around the world are quoted against the US dollar. A cross rate is any foreign currency rate that does not include the US dollar, eg, GBP/JPY is a cross rate, with the exception of GBP and EUR. Obviously a cross rate will be of particular interest to companies doing international business between the constituent countries, eg, a UK company selling goods or services to Japanese consumers, and receiving payment in yen.

8.2 Spot and Forward Transactions

Learning Objective

2.8.2 Be able to calculate spot and forward settlement prices using: adding or subtracting forward adjustments; interest rate parity

A typical sterling/dollar spot quote might look something like this:

GBP/USD spot rate 1.3055–1.3145

- Buyer's rate: £1 buys $1.3055.
- Seller's rate: $1.3145 buys £1.

The buyer's rate and seller's rate refer to buying and selling dollars respectively. The difference between the buyer's and seller's rates is generally referred to as the bid-offer spread. It enables the bank offering the deals to make money.

How much will an investor receive if the above spot rate is applied? If the investor wants to sell $50,000 for pounds sterling, they will receive £38,037. This is based on the seller's rate of $1.3145:£1.

The forward market is almost exactly the same as the spot market, except that currency deals are agreed for a future date, but at a rate of exchange fixed now. These rates of exchange are not directly quoted. Instead, quotes on the forward market state how much must be added to, or subtracted from, the present spot rate.

For example, the three month GBP/USD quote might be:

spot $1.3055–$1.3145

three-month forward 1.00–0.97c pm

pm stands for premium. It is used when the dollar is going to be more expensive relative to sterling in the future. It is deducted from the quoted spot rate in order to arrive at the forward rate. £1 will buy fewer dollars in three months' time and, if you have dollars in three months' time, the bank will sell you more sterling per dollar than it will now. The premium is quoted in cents, unlike the spot rate, which is quoted in dollars. So 1.00 pm is a premium of 1 cent or 0.01 dollars. And 0.97 pm is a premium of 0.97 cents or 0.0097 dollars.

The three-month forward quote is, therefore: $1.2955–$1.3048.

Alternatively the three-month forward rate might exhibit a discount, rather than a premium, for example:

spot   1.3055–1.3145

three-month forward   0.79–0.82c dis

dis stands for discount. The discount is used when the dollar is going to be cheaper relative to sterling in the future. It needs to be added to the quoted spot rate to arrive at the forward rate. £1 will buy more dollars in three months' time and, if you have dollars in three months' time, the bank will sell you less sterling per dollar than it will now. The three-month forward quote is therefore:

three-month forward $1.3134–$1.3227

The logic is that the forward rate will always exhibit a wider spread than the spot rate.

8.2.1   Interest Rate Parity

The concept of interest rate parity in determining the exchange rate between currencies arises from one of the cornerstone ideas in financial theory, which is that of rational pricing and the notion of arbitrage.

Rational pricing is the assumption in financial economics that asset prices will reflect the arbitrage-free price of the asset as any deviation from this price will be 'arbitraged away'.

Arbitrage is the practice of taking advantage of a pricing anomaly between securities that are trading in two (or possibly more) markets. One market can be the physical or underlying market; the other can often be a derivative market.

When a mismatch or anomaly can be exploited (ie, after transaction costs, storage costs, transport costs and dividends), the arbitrageur 'locks in' a risk-free profit. In general terms, arbitrage ensures that the law of one price will prevail.

Interest rate parity results from recognising a possible arbitrage condition and arbitraging it away.

Consider the returns from borrowing in one currency, exchanging that currency for another currency and investing in interest-bearing instruments of the second currency, while simultaneously purchasing futures contracts to convert the currency back at the end of the investment period. Under the assumption of arbitrage, the returns available should be equal to the returns from purchasing and holding similar interest-bearing instruments of the first currency.

If the returns are different, investors could theoretically arbitrage and make risk-free returns.

Interest rate parity says that the spot and future prices for currency trades incorporate any interest rate differentials between the two currencies.

A forward exchange contract is an agreement between two parties to either buy or sell foreign currency at a fixed exchange rate for settlement at a future date. The forward exchange rate is the exchange rate set today even though the transaction will not settle until some agreed point in the future, such as in three months' time.

The relationship between the spot exchange rate and forward exchange rate for two currencies is simply given by the differential between their respective nominal interest rates over the term being considered. The relationship is purely mathematical and has nothing to do with market expectations.

The idea behind this relationship is embodied in the principle of interest rate parity and is expressed as follows:

$$\text{Forward rate for GBP/USD} = \text{£ Spot rate} \times \left[\frac{(1 + \text{US \$ Short-term interest rate})}{(1 + \text{UK £ Short-term interest rate})} \right]$$

Example

The GBP/USD spot exchange rate = 1.5220. If the three-month interest rate for the UK is 4.88% and for the US, 3.20%, what will the three-month forward exchange rate be?

As the three-month interest rates are quoted on a per annum basis, they must be divided by four to obtain the rate of interest that will be payable (%) over three months:

Sterling: 4.88%/4 = 1.22%
Dollar: 3.20%/4 = 0.8%

Applying the interest rate parity formula:

$$\text{Forward rate for GBP/USD} = \$1.5220 \times \left[\frac{(1 + 0.008)}{(1 + 0.0122)} \right] = \$1.5157$$

The forward exchange rate in the example of $1.5157 is lower than the spot exchange rate of $1.5220. That is, in three months' time, £1 will buy $1.5157 or $0.0063 fewer dollars than is available at the spot rate (ie, the difference is 63 pips).

If this relationship did not exist, then an arbitrage opportunity would arise between the spot and forward rates.

It is important to realise that the forward rate calculated under the notion of arbitrage and interest rate parity is not a forecast of what the rate of exchange will actually be in three months. The actual rate will vary according to all of the factors which influence exchange rates in the **forex** market. The three-month forward rate in this example is simply a mathematically derived rate resulting from the interest rate differentials prevailing between the two currencies being exchanged.

8.3 Factors Affecting Foreign Exchange Rates

Learning Objective

2.8.3 Understand the factors that affect foreign exchange rates: freely floating exchange rates; purchasing power parity; currency demand and supply

Historically, exchange rates were fixed as part of the 1944 Bretton Woods agreement and not subject to market forces. Resetting or changing these exchange rates took place, as it did in the UK in the 1960s, by a formal devaluation whereby the rates which had been set in 1944 were modified. The UK Government undertook a devaluation of the pound against the dollar from £1= $2.80 to £1= $2.40 in 1968.

The era of fixed exchange rates came to an end during the 1970s, largely as a result of a currency crisis for the US dollar and the end of the official convertibility of currencies into gold, which was abandoned in August 1971. There have been attempts by governments to reintroduce managed exchange rates but these efforts have essentially failed, and the current regime of freely floating exchange rates is now accepted as the only feasible way for the FX market to function effectively.

There are exceptions to floating currencies; for example, some Middle Eastern countries, such as Saudi Arabia and the UAE, peg their currencies to the US dollar.

Questions regarding the determination of the FX rates by the markets comes down to several related issues concerning the demand and supply for individual currencies, monetary and interest rate policy, issues relating to purchasing power parity (PPP), and speculation.

8.3.1 Purchasing Power Parity (PPP)

In the short term, it appears that the primary factors affecting the manner in which market participants decide on the appropriate exchange rates are those of supply and demand and, to a greater or lesser extent, market sentiment.

Purchasing power parity (PPP) theory concerns the rate to which exchange rates should tend to move over the long term. PPP theory predicts that amounts of different currencies (at current exchange rates) should have equal purchasing power.

The concept of PPP can be appreciated by considering an example.

Example

If a basket of goods costs £100 in London and the same basket of goods costs $200 in New York, the PPP theory predicts that the exchange rate between the two countries will be £1 = $2.

If two economies experience differing rates of inflation then, over time, the exchange rate will tend to alter in the direction of restoring PPP.

If, after a number of years, the basket of goods now costs £150 in London due to the impact of inflation on UK prices and yet it only rises to $210 in New York, this suggests that the exchange rate between the two currencies should now be £1 = $1.40: there should have been a decline in the value of sterling.

PPP has some plausibility over the long term and gives an underlying theme to the FX markets. If one economy consistently has an inflation rate in excess of its competitors, then its currency will deteriorate against its trading partners.

Factors Affecting the Supply and Demand for a Currency

The following is a list of factors that affect the supply and demand for a particular currency, using the US dollar as an example:

Factors Affecting the Demand for US Dollars

- Overseas operators needing sterling to pay for exports of US goods to overseas markets.
- Overseas investors wanting to invest capital in the US.
- Speculation – if the US dollar is expected to increase relative to one or more other currencies, speculators will buy US dollars ahead of the increase.
- Currency rate management activities of central banks, including the Federal Reserve.
- Demand will be downward-sloping with respect to price – less demand for exports and less interest from overseas investors as the US dollar advances relative to other currencies.

Factors Affecting the Supply of US Dollars

- When US importers purchase overseas currencies to pay for imported goods arriving in the US, they are increasing the supply of US dollars into the markets.
- US residents wishing to invest in overseas assets will have to sell US dollars to buy overseas currency.
- Speculation – if the US dollar is expected to decrease relative to one or more other currencies, speculators will sell US dollars.
- The Federal Reserve may sell the domestic currency to purchase additional overseas currency reserves in order to influence the exchange rate as part of macroeconomic policy.
- Supply will be upward-sloping with respect to price.

8.3.2 Foreign Currency Trading and Speculation

Learning Objective

2.8.4   Understand the factors that affect foreign exchange trading and speculation

While the previous discussion has focused on the underlying economic and fundamental factors which influence exchange rates, there is no question that the FX market is also one where there is a huge amount of speculative trading activity. Much of this trading is conducted by the large banks, which are the dominant players in the OTC market for FX.

The volume of transactions has been estimated by the Bank for International Settlements (BIS) at approximately $5.3 trillion in nominal amounts traded daily. However, as with **derivatives**, the nominal amount traded is somewhat misleading since the speculative activity in FX is focused on the amount that is traded at the margin. In other words, if someone places an order to sell $1 million to purchase £600,000, but only holds the position for a few hours or minutes, there is a sense in which the nominal amounts are not really exchanged; it is the marginal difference which is really being traded or at risk.

According to the BIS, the most widely traded currency pair is the USD/EUR. Approximately 24% of overall turnover each year is between these two currencies. USD/YEN is the next most traded currency pair, generating 18% of turnover, followed by USD/GBP with 9%.

The FX market is extremely liquid and, in the case of major currency pairs such as the trade in EUR/USD, there is great depth to trading within the interbank market. Some other currency pairs, involving more exotic or less traded currencies such as the Hungarian forint, will obviously be far less liquid, with much wider spreads between the bid and the ask than for EUR/USD or GBP/USD.

FX markets can be extremely volatile at times, especially when the markets in other asset classes are acting in an erratic manner. There is a fascinating correlation between certain currency pairs and equity markets and some of this is explicable by reference to the carry trade. In essence, the carry trade in FX involves the borrowing of funds in a currency where the rate of interest is relatively low – examples are the Japanese yen and the Swiss franc – and then the purchase of securities, often government bonds, which have a relatively high yield, such as short-term instruments available from the Australian government.

The more volatile periods for FX trading are often seen when central bank officials (such as the Federal Reserve chairman) talk to the press or release minutes of meetings. Any hint of a change in central bank policy will tend to impact the FX rates. Another key mover of FX rates is when the US Labour Department issues its monthly employment data, more commonly known as the Non-Farms Payroll (NFP) report, on the first Friday of each month at 8:30 Eastern time.

Other economic events which can strongly impact the FX market are releases of inflation data, **gross domestic product (GDP)** data, and retail sales data from major government organisations, such as the Office for National Statistics (ONS) in the UK and Eurostat which provides economic data for the EU. Also important to the sudden movements of exchange rates are the results of auctions of government securities and any changes in short-term rates announced by central banks.

9.   Collective Investment Schemes (CISs)

A collective investment is a way of investing money with other people to participate in a wider range of investments than those feasible for most individual investors, and to share the costs of doing so.

Terminology varies with country, but collective investments are often referred to as investment funds, managed funds, mutual funds or simply funds. Across the world large markets have developed around collective investment, and these account for a substantial portion of all trading on major stock exchanges.

Collective investments are promoted with a wide range of investment aims either targeting specific geographic regions (eg, emerging Europe) or specified themes (eg, technology). Depending on the country, there is normally a bias towards the domestic market to reflect national self-interest as perceived by policymakers, familiarity, and the lack of currency risk. Funds are often selected on the basis of these specified investment aims, as well as their past investment performance and other factors, such as fees.

9.1 Regulated and Unregulated Collective Investment Schemes (UCISs)

Learning Objective

2.9.1 Understand the differences between regulated and unregulated collective investment schemes and their advantages and disadvantages to the issuer and investor

Financial services regulations in certain jurisdictions tend to include particular requirements that need to be met before a CIS can be marketed to retail investors. These requirements aim to make sure that retail investors do not become involved in inappropriate schemes, such as ones that are excessively complex or risky. In the UK, schemes meeting the requirements to enable them to be marketed to retail investors are referred to as regulated schemes, and those that do not meet the requirements and cannot be marketed to retail investors are referred to as unregulated schemes.

Definition of a CIS

The definition of a CIS as given by the International Organization of Securities Commissions (IOSCO), and which is used by many international organisations, is that a CIS is an instrument that:

- invests in transferable securities
- is publicly marketed, and
- is open-ended.

It is typical to distinguish two types of CIS:

- **Regulated CISs** that are either authorised by the local financial regulator or, if they are from outside the country, are recognised by the local financial regulator. Recognition generally enables overseas CISs to be marketed to the public in the country concerned and the financial regulator will only recognise an overseas scheme if certain specified criteria are met.
- **Unregulated collective investment schemes (UCISs)** are schemes that are not authorised or recognised by the local financial regulator.

UCISs are described as unregulated because they are not subject to the same restrictions as regulated CISs (eg, in terms of their investment powers and how they are run). Schemes that are not authorised or recognised are subject to marketing restrictions, particularly in relation to retail investors. UCISs are generally regarded as being characterised by a high degree of volatility, illiquidity or both and, therefore, are usually regarded as speculative investments. This means that, in practice, they are rarely regarded as suitable for more than a small proportion of an investor's portfolio. The schemes can offer exotic investments, such as golf courses in Mexico, forests in Brazil or off-plan property in Eastern European countries, and some not so exotic investments, such as wine in France.

9.1.1 The Risks of Unregulated Collective Investment Schemes (UCISs)

As with most other investments, a client investing in a UCIS could lose some or all of their principal investment. However, this risk is likely to be particularly relevant to UCISs. UCISs frequently invest in assets that are not available to regulated CISs (for example, because they are riskier or less liquid), or are structured in a way that is different from regulated CISs. Unlike regulated CISs, UCISs are often not subject to investment and borrowing restrictions aimed at ensuring a prudent spread of risk. As a result, UCISs are generally considered to be a high-risk investment and firms should always ensure that clients fully understand, and are financially able to assume, the associated risks before investing.

Typical risks encountered in an individual UCIS are likely to include the following:

- **Liquidity** – most unregulated investments will not offer daily liquidity. It is normal for investors wishing to redeem their investment to need to serve notice of their intention and for the redemption to take effect at the next available redemption date – typically at the end of the month in which notice is served. The investment will be sold at the price prevailing at the end of the following month and the realisation value returned to the investor approximately 14 days later. It can be seen, therefore, that the elapsed time from serving notice to receiving the proceeds can be up to two and a half months.
- **Fixed- or long-term commitment** – mainly due to the liquidity constraints set out above, investment must be regarded at the outset as long-term.
- **There is no guarantee of capital or income return** – while this represents a risk, it is not necessarily significantly different to the risk associated with a regulated investment.
- **High charges** – some unregulated investments may have higher administration charges associated with them. This can only be determined on an individual fund basis. Some unregulated investments include a performance fee for the manager if they hit a level of performance in excess of, say, 20% pa. It is usual, in these cases, for there also to be a high-water mark which means that if the price of the investment falls in a year only to rise again in the next, the manager will not become eligible to receive an additional fee, until the previous maximum fund price is surpassed.
- **Gearing** – this means that the fund can borrow money to enhance the total funds available to it for investment. If the fund goes up in value (and the capital value of the loan remains static) this can lead to a higher multiple of gains (net of interest charges) being available for distribution to the investors. The risk is that in the event of a loss in the value of the fund's assets, this can lead to a higher multiple of loss to the investor, because the loan will still require repayment in its entirety before the net asset value (NAV) can be attributed to the investors.
- **Currency/geopolitical** – an offshore investment may have a base currency other than the investor's home currency. For example, if the investor was from the US, this means that there is currency exposure in the translation of value back into US dollars from whatever the base currency is. If, during the period of investment, the base currency strengthens against sterling, this is advantageous to the investor; and vice-versa. Similarly, investing offshore may expose the investor to parts of the world which are less politically stable.
- **Single asset** – an unregulated investment may represent a single project, the success of which is dependent upon certain criteria. This may be deemed high-risk.

9.2 Open-Ended and Closed-Ended Collective Investment Schemes (CISs)

Learning Objective

2.9.2 Understand the differences between open-ended and closed-ended collective investment schemes and their advantages and disadvantages to the issuer and investor

2.9.3 Understand the circumstances under which a collective investment scheme may be exchange-traded or offered by a fund manager

2.9.4 Understand the circumstances where a collective investment scheme would be issued under a deed of trust and where it may be company- or private equity-based

As well as distinguishing between regulated and unregulated collective investment schemes, funds can also be subdivided based on their legal structure and the way the scheme operates. A major subdivision is between schemes that are open-ended and ones that are closed-ended.

An open-ended fund is an investment fund that can issue and redeem shares or units in the scheme at any time. Each investor has a pro rata proportion of the underlying portfolio and so will participate in any growth of the fund. The value of each share or unit is in proportion to the total value of the underlying investment portfolio.

If investors wish to invest in an open-ended fund, they approach the fund directly and provide the money they wish to invest. The fund can create new shares or units in response to this demand, issuing new shares or units to the investor at a price based on the value of the underlying portfolio. If investors decide to sell, they again approach the fund, which will redeem the shares or units and pay the investor the value, again based on the value of the underlying portfolio.

An open-ended fund can, therefore, expand and contract in size based on investor demand, which is why it is referred to as open-ended. Key examples of open-ended funds around the world include US mutual funds, the UK's open-ended investment companies (OEICs) and mainland Europe's Sociétés d'Investissement à Capital Variable (SICAVs).

A closed-ended investment company is another form of investment fund. When a closed-ended investment company is first established, a set number of shares are issued to the investing public, and these shares are then subsequently traded on a stock market. Investors wanting to then buy shares do so on the stock market from investors who are willing to sell. The capital of the fund is, therefore, fixed, and does not expand or contract in the way that an open-ended fund's capital does. For this reason, they are referred to as closed-ended funds. Traditionally, such funds have been referred to as **investment trusts** although, increasingly, they are also referred to as investment companies.

9.2.1 Open-Ended Vehicles

Before looking at the relative advantages and disadvantages of open-ended and closed-ended CISs, it is important to see the more detailed mechanics behind each of them. There are two major forms of open-ended schemes – unit trusts and OEICs.

Unit Trusts

A unit trust is a professionally managed collective investment fund.

- Investors can buy units, each of which represents a specified fraction of the trust.
- The trust holds a portfolio of securities.
- The assets of the trust are held by trustees and are invested by managers.
- The investor incurs annual management charges and possibly also an initial charge.

An authorised unit trust (AUT) is essentially a unit trust that is allowed to be marketed to the investing public, and must be constituted by a trust deed made between the manager and the trustee.

The Role of the Trustees

The primary duty of the trustees is to protect the interests of the unitholders. The investors in a unit trust own the underlying value of shares based on the proportion of the units held. They are effectively the beneficiaries of the trust.

The following requirements apply in the UK in relation to trustees and the trust deeds of AUTs:

1. Trustees of a unit trust must be authorised by the FCA and be fully independent of the trust manager.
2. Trustees are required to have capital in excess of £4 million and, for this reason, are normally large financial institutions, such as banks or insurance companies.
3. The trust deed of each unit trust must clearly state its investment strategy and objectives, so that investors can determine the suitability of each trust.
4. The limits and allowable investment areas for a unit trust fund are also laid out in the trust deed together with the investment objectives.

The Role of the Manager

In the UK, the manager of an AUT must also be authorised by the FCA. The role of the fund manager covers:

- marketing the unit trust
- managing the assets in accordance with the trust deed
- maintaining a record of units for inspection by the trustees
- supplying other information relating to the investments under the unit trust as requested
- informing the FCA of any breaches of regulations while the manager is running the trust.

Buying and Selling Units

Units in AUTs can be purchased in a number of ways; for example, via a newspaper advertisement, over the phone or over the internet. These methods will generally require payment with the order, or some form of guarantee of payment. A contract note will be produced and sent to the investor as evidence of the purchase.

Investors can sell their units via the same source that they purchased them, or can contact the fund managers direct, for example by telephone.

Unit Trust Pricing

The calculation of buying and selling prices will take place at the valuation point, which is at a particular time each day. The fund is valued on the basis of the net value of the constituent assets and a typical spread between buying and selling prices in the market will be in the range of 5%-7%.

Some fund managers use single pricing, in which case there is the same price quoted for buying and selling units, with any charges being separately disclosed.

Charges

The charges on a unit trust can be taken in three ways – an initial charge which is made upfront, an annual management charge made periodically and an exit charge levied when the investor sells. Whatever charges are made must be explicitly detailed in the trust deed and documentation. The documents should provide details of both the current charges and the extent to which the manager can change them.

The upfront initial charge is added to the buying price incurred by the investor. Initial charges tend to be higher on actively managed funds, often in the range of 3%–6.5%. Lower initial charges are typically levied on index trackers. Some managers will discount their initial charges for direct sales including sales made over the internet. It is not unusual for those managers that charge low or zero initial charges to make exit charges when the investor sells units.

When they apply, exit charges are generally only made when the investor sells within a set period of time, such as the first three or five years. Furthermore, these exit charges tend to be made on a sliding scale with a more substantial charge made for those exiting earlier than those exiting later. Both the set period and the sliding scale reflect the fact that, if the investor holds the unit for longer, the manager will benefit from the regular annual management charges that effectively reduces the need for the exit charge.

The annual management charge is generally levied at a rate of 0.5–1.5% of the underlying fund. Like the initial charge, the annual management charge will typically be lower for trusts that are cheaper to run, such as index trackers, and higher for more labour-intensive actively managed funds.

Open-Ended Investment Companies (OEICs)

Open-ended investment companies (OEICs) are a type of open-ended collective investment formed as a corporation under the Open-Ended Investment Companies Regulations of the United Kingdom. Pronounced oiks, they are also known as ICVCs, which is an acronym for investment companies with variable capital. The terms ICVC and OEIC are used interchangeably, with different investment managers favouring one over the other.

A share in an OEIC entitles the holder to a share of the profits of the OEIC, and the value of the share will be determined by the value of the underlying investments. For example, if the underlying investments are valued at £125,000,000 and there are 100,000,000 shares in issue, the net asset value (NAV) of each share is £1.25.

Holders of shares in an OEIC can sell them back to the company, resulting in the number of shares issued by the OEIC reducing. Similarly, new or existing investors can buy new shares from the OEIC, resulting in the number of shares issued by the OEIC increasing. In both cases the price at which the deal is done is based on the NAV of the shares.

An OEIC may take the form of an umbrella fund with a number of separately priced sub-funds, adopting different investment strategies or denominated in different currencies. Each sub-fund will have a separate client register and asset pool.

Classes of shares within an OEIC may include income shares, which pay a dividend; and accumulation shares, in which income is not paid out and all income received is added to net assets.

As the name suggests, OEICs are companies with corporate structures. They differ from other companies in that they have the flexibility to issue and redeem their shares on an ongoing basis.

9.2.2 Investment Trusts

Investment trusts began in the UK and the Foreign & Colonial Investment Trust was the first to be founded in 1868 with the aim of *giving the investor of moderate means the same advantage as the large capitalist'*. Today, the Foreign & Colonial Investment Trust invests in more than 600 different companies in 35 countries and investment trust vehicles are found in many developed markets.

In general, investment trusts provide a way for the small investor to have some exposure to investments in very large portfolios of assets, primarily equities, which are impractical for the investor to buy individually.

Investment trusts are a form of collective investment, pooling the funds of many investors and spreading their investments across a diversified range of securities.

Investment trusts are managed by professional fund managers who select and manage the stocks in the trust's portfolio. Investment trusts are generally accessible to the individual investor, although shares in investment trusts are also widely held by institutional investors, such as pension funds.

Despite their name, investment trusts are not trusts but are companies. However, whereas other companies may make their profit from providing goods and services, an investment trust makes its profit solely from investments. Like most investors, investors who buy shares in an investment trust hope for dividends and capital growth.

Buying and Selling Shares in Investment Trusts

Prices

The quotation of the price of investment trust shares is similar to that for equities generally, and a dealer will give two prices:

- The higher price is the **offer price**, at which an investor can buy the shares.
- The lower price is the bid price, at which a holder of the shares can sell.

In a price quote in the financial media, a single price may be given: this will typically be the mid-market price, between the offer and bid prices.

The difference between the offer price and the bid price is the spread.

Shares in investment trusts can be bought through a stockbroker, who is likely to charge the same level of commission as for other equities. If a broker is not providing any advice and is providing an execution-only service, then commission may be as low as 0.5%, or a minimum commission of around $7.50 per deal. If the broker is providing an advisory service, commission will be higher, for example, 1.5% or 2% of the purchase consideration.

Net Asset Value

The NAV is essentially the net worth of an investment trust company's equity capital and is calculated from adding together the following:

- the value of the trust's listed investments at mid-market prices
- the value of its unlisted investments at directors' valuation
- cash and other net current assets.

The company's liabilities are deducted from this figure, including any issued preference capital at nominal value. The resulting figure is the asset value for the ordinary shareholders of the company. Dividing by the number of shares gives the NAV per share. The valuation may be carried out monthly, weekly or daily.

By way of illustration, the NAV of an investment trust with assets worth $10 million, and with liabilities of $4 million, is $6 million ($10m – $4m). The NAV per share is the NAV divided by the number of shares outstanding. Assuming this investment trust has 12 million ordinary shares outstanding, the NAV per share is calculated as: $6 million ÷ 12 million shares = 50c per share.

Most investment trusts operate at a discount to NAV. The level of premium or discount relates to the demand for shares, and any factor that influences demand will affect it.

9.2.3   Comparison Between Open-Ended and Closed-Ended Funds

Generally, closed-ended investment trusts have wider investment freedom than authorised open-ended investment funds, such as unit trusts and OEICs. Unlike authorised OEICs, closed-ended investment trusts can:

- invest in unquoted private companies as well as quoted companies
- provide venture capital to new companies or companies requiring new funds for expansion.
- borrow money to help them achieve their objectives. Authorised open-ended collective schemes' powers to borrow are more limited. The ability to borrow allows an investment trust to leverage returns for the investor. Such gearing also increases the volatility of returns.

As seen, in an open-ended fund, new shares or units can be created when new investors subscribe and shares or units can be cancelled when investors cash in their holdings. In the case of closed-ended funds, such as closed-ended investment companies, new investors have to buy from existing holders of the shares who wish to sell.

As closed-ended vehicles, the number of shares in issue in an investment trust is not affected by the day-to-day purchases and sales by investors, which allow the managers to take a long-term view of the investments of the trust. With an open-ended scheme, such as an OEIC, if there are more sales of units or shares by investors than purchases, the number of units reduces and the fund must pay out cash. As a result, the managers may need to sell investments, even though it may not be the best time to do so from a strategic and long-term viewpoint.

Being closed-ended also means that the prices of shares of an investment trust rise and fall according to the demand for, and the supply of, the shares of the investment trust, and not necessarily directly in line with the values of the underlying investments. In this way, investment trust prices can have greater volatility than OEICs, where the share prices are directly related to the market values of the underlying investments.

It is also the case for investment trusts that as prices are dependent on supply and demand, the price of the shares can be lower than the NAV per share. This means investors can buy investment trust shares at a discount, while the income produced by the portfolio is based on the market value of the underlying investments. The income yield is, therefore, enhanced.

9.2.4   Exchange-Traded Funds (ETFs)

An exchange-traded fund (ETF) is a type of investment fund that trades on many global stock exchanges in the same manner as a typical company share. ETFs invest in assets, such as equities or bonds, and most ETFs track an index, such as the S&P 500 or MSCI EAFE (Europe, Australasia and Far East).

Only authorised participants (typically large institutional investors) actually buy or sell shares of an ETF directly from/to the fund manager, and then only in creation units – large blocks of tens of thousands of ETF shares – which are usually exchanged in kind with baskets of the underlying securities. Authorised participants may wish to invest in the ETF shares long-term, but usually act as market makers on the open market, using their ability to exchange creation units with their underlying securities to provide liquidity of the ETF shares and help ensure that their intra-day market price approximates to the NAV of the underlying assets. Other investors, such as individuals using a retail broker, trade ETF shares via a secondary market such as the NYSE/Arca exchange in the US, or the LSE in the UK.

Closed-ended funds (like investment trusts) are not considered to be ETFs, even though they are funds and are traded on an exchange. ETFs are relatively recent, having been available in the US since 1993 and in Europe since 1999. Although most ETFs are index-tracking funds, in 2008 the US Securities and Exchange Commission (SEC) began to authorise the creation of actively managed ETFs.

Trading Features of an Exchange-Traded Fund

The selection of ETFs available is now very diverse and provides investors with a real alternative to some of the more traditional funds. One of the key features of ETFs is that, since they are listed securities and trade in the same manner as shares, the pricing takes place in real time and the funds can be bought or sold during all times when markets are open. This is unlike the position with many types of collective investment vehicles, such as unit trusts and other investment funds, where the pricing of the fund based on the NAV of the constituents is computed at the end of each day and where the ability to transact is also limited to certain prescribed times. For investors and traders who want to be able to react quickly to market movements and have immediate pricing and settlement for their positions (subject only to the normal settlement period for any listed share), the variety of ETF products is often preferable to the more traditional structured investment products.

Available ETFs include those that have been designed and constructed to track a general stock index, such as the S&P 500 (SPY) or the Nasdaq 100 Index (QQQQ); or indices for market sectors (eg, industrials, financials), geographical regions, currencies, commodities such as gold, silver, copper and oil, and even certain managed funds with objectives and management criteria laid out in an offering **prospectus**.

ETFs are also available to track the performance of various fixed-income instruments such as US T-bonds or indices which track high-yield bonds and other corporate bonds. Again, these can be used to take a **long position** on higher yields, in effect to be short the bond on a price basis. One well-known ETF traded in the US under the symbol TBT tracks the yield on US T-bonds of 20 years plus maturity. The fund moves in line with the real-time yields of the long end of the US Treasury curve, and therefore the fund moves inversely to the price of such US T-bonds.

Charges and Taxation

Many ETF products are managed by large financial intermediaries, including BlackRock, Vanguard and JP Morgan Chase, and the fees and charges are very competitive and often considerably lower than those applied for more traditionally managed funds.

Tracking Impact

While the operation, marketing and construction of an ETF requires skills on the part of the ETF management company, many funds are in effect tracker funds and therefore have to reflect the composition of a reference index or commodity.

The large amounts of funds invested in tracker funds can have a distorting effect on the market, for example if many tracker funds buy a particular share at the point when it is included in the index. Undoubtedly, inclusion in an index can be beneficial to the price of a share, while exclusion may be a factor causing a share to receive less attention from investors and to fall out of favour.

Physical Versus Synthetic Exchange-Traded Funds (ETFs)

When tracking an index, the providers of ETFs can use either physical or synthetic replication to ensure their ETFs mimic their designated indices as accurately as possible.

Physical replication means the ETF will buy and own most or all of an index's constituents in order to replicate the index's performance. Despite being simple and transparent, since physical replication involves buying and selling index components, this strategy is inherently labour-intensive and costly. These additional costs are ultimately passed along to investors in the form of higher charges.

In contrast, synthetic replication involves the ETF provider entering into a contract with a counterparty (typically a bank) to deliver the return of the fund's benchmark index in exchange for a fee. This **swap** contract means that, for example, an equity ETF will not actually hold any stocks at all. Instead, it will have a contractual relationship with the counterparty bank. This may generally reduce costs and any possibility of tracking error, but it increases risk for investors. This is because there is a danger of the counterparty being unable to honour its obligation under the contract, known as counterparty risk.

9.2.5 Specialist Funds

Closed-ended funds can also be set up to invest in areas such as private equity, property or infrastructure. These vehicles essentially turn illiquid assets, or assets that investors would find difficult to invest in, into liquid investments that are available to institutional and retail investors. These are also classed as alternative assets.

Typically, these are long-term investment strategies and so the closed-end nature of the structure is more appropriate to their needs. This can have advantages for a fund in that it does not need to realise assets at possibly distressed prices to meet investor redemptions. It may require investors to commit their money for long periods of time so that the planned investments have time to deliver their expected returns.

Closed-ended companies may not be traded on a stock market and so periodic redemptions may be made available to offer investors a way to realise all or part of their investment.

Private Equity

Private equity investment is usually structured as a limited partnership arrangement and looks to target institutional investors and only the wealthiest private investors. Access to private equity is possible, however, for ordinary investors through listed, closed-ended funds.

Private equity firms invest in other businesses and then try to maximise their returns by exiting the company at a profit.

There are a number of further factors to consider with regard to private equity funds:

- Private equity funds are a specialist and widely varied sector. Some hold direct investments in companies and others do so indirectly through investment in other funds.
- Private equity funds make money by investing in businesses that need access to growth capital or that need overhauling. The types and spread of investments they hold need to be analysed along with any commitments they may have to provide further capital.
- They will often use high levels of debt and so are exposed to interest rate rises and credit squeezes. Funds will look to take their profit by a trade sale or flotation and so their planned exit route needs evaluation.
- Private equity is highly correlated with the economic cycle and realising a profit can be problematic. Given the timescales needed for such investments to work, the sale can occur at a time when there is little market interest in a sale or floatation.
- In stable economic environments, the drivers of outperformance and the ability to exit investments are in place. In such scenarios, discounts can be expected to narrow while, once the economic environment deteriorates, discounts will widen.
- The size of fund also varies widely and the market capitalisation of the fund needs to be judged in terms of the level of liquidity that is present and whether this would present any issues when buying or trying to realise the investment.

Exercise Answers

Exercise 1

a. Calculate the flat yield on a 4% gilt, redeeming in eight years and priced at £98.90.

$$(4/98.90) \times 100 = 4.04\%$$

b. Calculate the flat yield on a 7% gilt, redeeming in three years and priced at £108.60.

$$(7/108.60) \times 100 = 6.45\%$$

Exercise 2

The share value of the conversion choice is currently 15 x £6.40 = £96.

The bond is trading at £110, so the premium is £14 per £100 nominal value.

Expressed as a percentage: 14/96 x 100 = 14.6%.

Exercise 3

a.

Time	Cash flow	Discount factor	Present value
End of year one	$100	$1/1.06$	94.33
End of year two	$1,100	$1/1.06^2$	978.99
Sum of the individual present values = price of the bond			$1,073.33

b.

Time	Cash flow	Discount factor	Present value
End of year one	$100	$1/1.04$	96.15
End of year two	$1,100	$1/1.04^2$	1,017. 01
Sum of the individual present values = price of the bond			$1,113.16

End of Chapter Questions

1. What is the key difference between an ordinary share and a bearer instrument?
    Answer reference: Section 1.1

2. What are the four types of preference share?
    Answer reference: Section 1.2

3. What is the date on which a borrower agrees to pay back the nominal value of a bond known as?
    Answer reference: Section 2.1

4. What are three drawbacks in using flat yield as a robust measure in assessing bond returns?
    Answer reference: Section 2.3.3

5. What is an index ratio used for?
    Answer reference: Section 3.2.3

6. What are two of the serious drawbacks with investing in cash?
    Answer reference: Section 5.1

7. How do global depositary receipts differ from American depositary receipts?
    Answer reference: Section 7.1

8. What are the two types of transaction conducted on the FX market and how do they differ?
    Answer reference: Section 8.1

9. Name four typical risks encountered in an individual UCIS.
    Answer reference: Section 9.1.1

10. Which type of investment trust can invest in unquoted private companies as well as quoted companies?
    Answer reference: Section 9.2.3

Chapter Three
Primary Markets

1.	The Primary and Secondary Markets	83
2.	Types of Offer	85
3.	Participants in an Equity Offering Securities	94
4.	Stock Exchanges	98
5.	Bond Offerings	102

This syllabus area will provide approximately 16 of the 100 examination questions

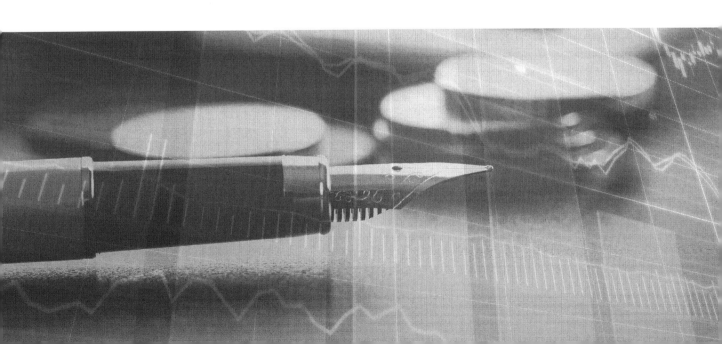

1.   The Primary and Secondary Markets

Learning Objective

3.1.1   Know the principal characteristics of, and the differences between, the primary and secondary markets. In particular: the role of the governing authority; users of the primary market; users of the secondary market; uses of primary and secondary markets

Stock exchanges are organised marketplaces for issuing securities and then trading those securities via their members. All stock exchanges provide both a primary and a secondary market.

1. The primary market, or the new issues market, is where securities are issued for the first time. The primary markets exist to enable issuers of securities, particularly companies, to raise capital, and to enable the surplus funds held by potential investors to be matched with investment opportunities the issuers offer. It is a crucial source of funding. The terminology often used when companies raise capital on a stock exchange is that they access the primary market and float. The process that the companies go through when they float is often called the **initial public offering (IPO)**. Companies can use a variety of ways to achieve this flotation, such as offers for investors to subscribe for their shares (offers for subscription).
2. The secondary market is where existing securities are traded between investors, and the stock exchanges provide a variety of systems to assist in this. These systems provide investors with liquidity, giving them the ability to sell their securities if they wish. Trading activity in the secondary market also results in the ongoing provision of buy and sell prices to investors via the exchange's member firms.

Each jurisdiction has its own governing rules and regulations for companies seeking a **listing**, and continuing obligations for those already listed. For example, the UK has the United Kingdom Listing Authority (UKLA) which is a division of the Financial Conduct Authority (FCA). The formal description of the UKLA is that it is the competent authority for listing – making the decisions as to which companies' shares and bonds (including UK government bonds or gilts) can be admitted to be traded on the London Stock Exchange (LSE). The rules are contained in a rule book called the Listing Rules.

The UKLA sets the rules relating to becoming listed on the LSE, including the implementation of any relevant European Union (EU) directives. The LSE is responsible for the operation of the exchange, including the trading of the securities on the secondary market, although the UKLA can suspend the listing of particular securities and therefore remove their secondary market trading activity on the exchange.

Developed markets generally have a similar structure to the UK. The US Securities and Exchange Commission (SEC) requires companies seeking a listing on the US exchanges, such as the New York Stock Exchange (NYSE) and Nasdaq, to register certain details with the SEC first. Once listed, companies are then required to file regular reports with the SEC, particularly in relation to their trading performance and financial situation.

1.1 Users of the Markets

1.1.1 Users of Primary Markets

Issuers of new securities, such as corporations engaging in IPOs or follow-on offerings as well as the issuers of certain kinds of debt instruments, are the main suppliers of new securities in the primary markets.

The main purchasers of newly issued securities are large institutional investors, such as pension funds, insurance companies and collective investment vehicles, such as exchange-traded funds (ETFs) and mutual funds, who buy the securities being offered on behalf of their clients, who are primarily members of the general public.

1.1.2 Users of Secondary Markets

In the secondary market, where existing securities are bought and sold throughout the daily trading sessions, there will be a variety of participants. In addition to the previously mentioned institutional investors engaged in the purchase of newly issued securities, these same institutions will, as a result of changes in their **asset allocation** decision-making, be engaged in selling previously owned securities within their portfolio and, in turn, adding other securities which have previously been available on the secondary market. The constant shifting of priorities in portfolio allocation constitutes a large part of the transactional volume which arises each day, for example, in the activities of the LSE and the NYSE.

Also the secondary markets will be used by short-term speculators and traders who may hold securities for very short periods – perhaps seconds, minutes or hours – when the motivation is to attempt to make profits from anticipating the direction of short-term price changes in the variety of securities which are available for trade in the secondary markets.

Members of the general public also have access to the secondary market through stockbrokers and therefore users also include individuals who choose to hold individual securities.

Increasingly, the principal users of secondary markets are various funds and trading vehicles which engage in automated trading strategies that are triggered by computer-programmed algorithms. These algorithmic trading strategies can be very short-term, perhaps involving buying one minute, and selling the next, and trigger automatically executed trades on multiple occasions each day. When the objective is to exploit transitory price discrepancies, such strategies are referred to as high-frequency trading (HFT).

1.2 Motivations for the Use of Primary and Secondary Markets

The principal reason behind the primary markets is for issuers, like companies, to raise capital by accessing the substantial market made up of potential investors. The issuers might want to raise capital for a variety of purposes, such as business expansion or acquisitions, and the buyers of the offerings may want to allocate their capital across what they perceive as attractive investment opportunities. In general terms, the holders of these newly issued securities are seeking longer-term investment objectives. However, some activity in the primary market – such as when there is a highly publicised

IPO – may be for short-term speculative purposes. The manner in which some buyers of newly issued securities buy a new offering, and then, in the midst of some rather exaggerated market excitement about the new issue, sell the new issue shortly afterwards, is known as **flipping**.

The principal use and benefit of secondary markets is that they provide a liquid environment within which owners of securities can sell a current holding and where willing buyers can purchase existing securities. The larger capitalisation issues are usually bought and sold in substantial amounts during each trading session and the spread, ie, the difference between the price that the securities are being offered at – or the ask price – and the price at which buyers are prepared to buy these securities – the bid price – is narrow. One characteristic of a liquid market is that spreads are narrow. Another feature which provides for more liquidity is the activity of speculators – including HFT activities – where the continuous buying and selling of securities with very short-term holding period horizons provides a depth to the secondary market, which would not be available if the secondary market only existed for institutions seeking longer-term investment reallocations.

2. Types of Offer

2.1 Initial Public Offerings (IPOs)

Learning Objective

3.2.1 Understand the use of an initial public offering: why would a company choose an IPO; structure of an IPO – base deal plus greenshoe; stages of an IPO; underwritten versus best efforts

An IPO is the initial offering of a company's shares which, until the IPO, are privately owned (and controlled) by a wider group of investors (the public). The current owners are likely to include the founders of the company and/or relatives or close acquaintances. By issuing company shares via an IPO, which is also known as 'going public', the original owners are giving up a substantial amount of control, as the new owners, shareholders, will not only own stock in the company, but will also have voting rights. These rights enable shareholders to be included in decision-making procedures and to elect the board of directors. It is possible that public shareholders may have different interests from the existing owners, as owners of listed shares are usually most interested in an increased share price. Furthermore, they can sell the shares on the market and the existing owners will lose control over who becomes a shareholder (and, therefore, a decision-maker) in the future.

The key advantages of IPOs over other capital-raising methods are that IPOs can raise substantial sums of capital and create a great deal of publicity for the issuing companies. The money raised in the form of an IPO is known as risk capital and the company assets are not encumbered or hypothecated in the same manner as they would be if the capital were raised from a debt offering.

An IPO is usually structured with a base number of shares that the company is planning to issue. However, the issuing company may also reserve the right to increase the number of shares it issues, if significant levels of demand would remain unsatisfied if only the base number of shares were issued. The option to increase the number of shares is referred to as a greenshoe.

As seen, there are three broad stages to an IPO:

1. **The decision** – the issuing company (in conjunction with its advisers, particularly an investment bank) makes a decision to raise capital via an IPO. This will involve careful consideration of the pros and cons of a public offer.
2. **The preparation of the prospectus** – this is the necessary document that must accompany an IPO, involving the whole team of advisers, including the investment bank, reporting accountants and legal advisers.
3. **The sale of securities** – the investment bank will lead-manage the sale and may well establish a syndicate of co-managers to assist in selling the securities to its clients.

Underwriting of the offer is generally the responsibility of the investment bank(s) and it typically arranges firm underwriting when there are guarantees in place to buy the securities. Investment banks may not provide a firm undertaking to place all of the securities on behalf of their clients. Instead, the lead underwriter, along with the co-managers of the offer, may provide a best efforts underwriting, in which they will do their best to sell the shares involved in the offering but when there is no formal guarantee that this will be achieved. In practice this means that the managers of the underwriting are not committing to purchase any unplaced securities for their own account in an unconditional manner. By an underwriter and the co-managers inserting the best efforts conditionality, should there be a failure to fully complete a sale of the offering, the underwriter will avoid the immediate monetary loss that purchasing the shares would entail. However, the result is likely to be that the underwriter will suffer reputational damage and not be invited to participate in future IPOs.

2.2   Follow-on Offerings

Learning Objective

3.2.2   Understand the use of follow-on offerings: why would a company choose a follow-on offering; structure of a follow-on – base deal plus greenshoe; stages of a follow-on offering; underwritten versus best efforts

An already listed company looking to raise more capital can choose to go through a follow-on offering. A follow-on offering is alternatively referred to as a secondary offer. Clearly, issuing more shares in a follow-on offering will only be considered if the equity markets are sufficiently robust. In a **bear market** there is unlikely to be sufficient demand for the shares at the price the issuing company wants.

Like an initial public offering, a follow-on offering will be structured with a base number of shares that the company is planning to issue. Again, the issuing company may also retain a **greenshoe option** to increase the number of shares that it issues, if significant levels of demand would otherwise remain unsatisfied.

A secondary offering will inevitably be quicker, easier and cheaper than an IPO, simply because the company has been through the stages before in its IPO. The broad stages of a follow-on offer are the same as an IPO:

1. **The decision**.
2. **The preparation of the prospectus** – this should be relatively easy, since the issuing company has prepared a prospectus before, when it first became a listed entity.
3. **The sale of securities** – as in an IPO, the appointed investment bank will lead-manage the sale and may well establish a syndicate of co-managers to assist in selling the securities to its clients.

As with an IPO, the follow-on offering may also be underwritten, with a potential combination of firm underwriting by the investment bank(s) and best efforts underwriting by clients such as stockbroking firms.

As with an IPO, a follow-on offering is said to be underwritten when there is a firm undertaking by the investment bank(s) that is conducting the offering that all of the offering will be fully subscribed. In other words, the underwriting bank(s) will guarantee that any shortfall by subscribers will be purchased by the bank(s) for its own account.

A best efforts agreement provides no such guarantee. In this case the underwriting bank(s) agrees to use its best efforts to sell as much of an issue as possible to the public. If the underwriter is unable to sell all of the offering because of adverse market conditions, they do not take responsibility for placing any of the unsold inventory. Arrangements that are made on a best efforts basis are often found with high-risk securities.

2.3 Open Offers and Offers for Subscription

Learning Objective

3.2.3 Understand the use of open offers and offers for subscription: why would a company choose an open offer; structure of an offer; stages of an offer; tenders, strike price, who is involved in the offer process

One way to achieve an IPO and to raise capital is by making an offer for subscription.

An offer for subscription involves the company sending a prospectus (including the share price) and an application form to potential investors. The company's sponsor, along with reporting accountants and legal advisers, will assist in the preparation of the prospectus. Those potential investors who want to invest in the company apply for shares. The company then issues allotment letters to successful applicants.

Only new (not previously issued) shares may be issued in this way.

Diagrammatically:

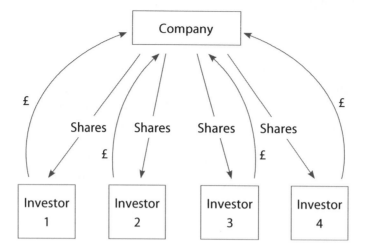

This method is rare in large IPOs, mainly because issuing companies like to use the expertise of the investment banks to facilitate their IPOs, in particular their ability to price and sell shares to their substantial client base. As a result, large IPOs tend to follow the offer for sale route outlined in the following section.

An open offer is similar in that it is an invitation to subscribe for new shares. However, open offers are follow-on offers that only offer new shares to the existing shareholders, in proportion to their existing shareholding. This meets the pre-emptive rights of the shareholders, but it differs from a rights issue in that the rights are not able to be sold nil-paid. The offer is simply open for the existing shareholders to take up, or not.

2.4   Offers for Sale

Learning Objective

3.2.4   Understand the use of offers for sale: why would a company choose an offer for sale; structure of an offer for sale; stages of an offer for sale; tenders, strike price, who may receive an allotment, who is involved in the offer process

Offers for sale are a much more common way of achieving a listing. The company seeking to sell the shares approaches an issuing house (usually an investment bank) that specialises in approaching potential shareholders and preparing the necessary documentation. The issuing company sells its shares to the issuing house (usually an investment bank), which then invites applications from the public at a slightly higher price than the issuing house has paid and on the basis of a detailed prospectus, known as the offer document. For a company applying for a full listing, this provides comprehensive information about the company and its directors and how the proceeds from the share issue will be applied. This document must be prepared by the company's directors and assessed by their sponsor to satisfy the regulatory authorities of the company's suitability to obtain a full listing.

Diagrammatically:

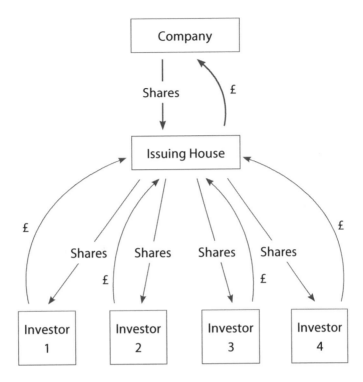

Offers for sale do not necessarily require the company to create new shares specifically for the share issue. Indeed, offers for sale are often used by a company's founders to release part, or all, of their equity stake in their company, and have also been the preferred route for government privatisation programmes, when former nationalised companies have been sold to the public. In both cases, existing shareholdings are disposed of, rather than new shares created, in order to obtain a listing.

An offer for sale, or an offer for subscription, can be made on either a fixed- or a tender-price basis:

Fixed-price offer – when a fixed-price offer is made, the price is usually fixed just below that at which it is believed the issue should be fully subscribed, so as to encourage an active secondary market in the shares. Subscribers to a fixed-price issue apply for the number of shares they wish to purchase at this fixed price. If the offer is oversubscribed, as it nearly always is, given the favourable pricing formula, then shares are allotted either by scaling down each application or by satisfying a randomly chosen proportion of the applications in full. The precise method used will be detailed in the offer document.

Tender offer – given the judgement required in setting the price at a level that does not lead to the issue being excessively oversubscribed but which leads to a successful new issue, and the fact that market sentiment can and often does change between the announcement of the IPO and the end of the offer period, offers for sale and offers for subscription can be made on a tender basis when the issuer does not stipulate a fixed price for the shares but invites tenders for the issue, usually by setting a minimum tender price. Investors state the number of shares they wish to purchase and state the price per share they are prepared to pay.

Once the offer is closed, a single strike price can then be determined by the issuing house or by the company, as appropriate, to satisfy all applications tendered at, or above, this price.

Although this auctioning process is the more efficient way of allocating shares and maximising the proceeds from a share issue, tender offers are also more complex to administer and, as such, tend to be outnumbered by fixed-price offers.

2.4.1   Over-allotment Options

An allotment provision used in the case of an IPO that has become almost standard in the case of new offerings undertaken by US investment banks is the greenshoe. It is known as the greenshoe option because the term comes from a company founded in 1919 as Green Shoe Manufacturing Company, now called Stride Rite Corporation, which was the first company to be permitted to use this practice in an offering.

More properly known by its legal title as an over-allotment option, the greenshoe provision gives the underwriters of an IPO the right to sell additional shares in a registered securities offering, if demand for the securities is in excess of the original amount offered. It is used as a tool in providing price stabilisation and a successful execution of the offering on behalf of the issuer. In essence, it is one strategy that underwriters have developed which enables them to smooth out price fluctuations if demand surges on the one hand, and to help support the IPO if there are adverse market conditions. The way a greenshoe operates is best illustrated by the following simplified example:

Example

ABC is a company planning an IPO and using the services of an investment bank. The number of shares to be sold is initially agreed to be 100,000. The investment bank is also granted an over-allotment option (the greenshoe) that enables it to buy a further 15,000 shares from ABC if demand is sufficient.

During book-building the investment bank finds buyers for 115,000 shares rather than just 100,000. On the day following listing, if the price of the shares holds at the listing price or higher, the investment bank simply exercises the over-allotment option to cover the additional 15,000 shares sold.

In contrast, if ABC shares struggle to stay at the listing price and fall in the immediate aftermarket, the investment bank can buy back 15,000 shares to help support the price. If it does this, the over-allotment option will not be exercised.

By using the over-allotment provision the issuer may ensure a more successful marketing and distribution of the offering. However, some issuers have refrained from providing their underwriters with a greenshoe option.

2.5 Selective Marketing and Placing

Learning Objective

3.2.5 Understand the basic process and uses of selective marketing and placing: advantages to the issuing company; what is a placing; what is selective marketing; how is a placing achieved; how is selective marketing achieved

In placing its shares, a company simply markets the issue directly to a broker, an issuing house or other financial institution, which in turn places the shares with selected clients. Although the least democratic of the three IPO methods, given that the general public does not initially have access to the issue, a placing is the least expensive, as the prospectus accompanying the issue is less detailed than that required for the other two methods and no underwriting is required.

A placing is often referred to as a selective marketing, because the intermediary is selecting the clients to whom the offer is directed.

Diagrammatically:

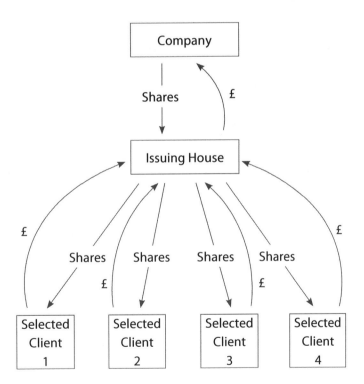

2.5.1   Private Placements

For most public offerings of securities a vital prerequisite is a prospectus or offering document which the issuer has to make available to all prospective investors and the exchanges upon which it intends to list its securities. The prospectus has to fully disclose all the pertinent details regarding the offering, including a detailed business plan, an explanation of how the proceeds from the offering will be used, details of all owners/directors of the entity, and most importantly a comprehensive disclosure of all of the risks associated with the investment.

A special provision exists for offerings marketed to a restricted class of investors, known as either sophisticated, qualified or accredited investors. These investors, and the investment banks who advise them, are able to purchase investments through which a formal prospectus is either not issued, or when the regular disclosure requirements associated with issuing shares are far less onerous than those which would be required for a public offering.

The specific requirements for this type of offering in the European Union (EU) are outlined in the Prospectus Directive (PD). In the US, the SEC also has special provisions for these so-called private placements.

2.6   Introductions

Learning Objective

3.2.6   Understand the use of introductions: why would a company undertake an introduction; structure of an introduction; stages of an introduction

An **introduction** is not actually an issue at all. It is used by a company that wishes to become listed in order to gain access to the secondary market that an exchange will provide.

An introduction is unusual because most companies use listing as an opportunity to raise extra funds and some companies are forced to issue more shares to comply with regulations that typically require a minimum percentage of shares to be held by people other than the founders and other significant shareholders.

An introduction is used by a company that does not need to raise extra capital through share issues, but wishes to gain the extra liquidity in its shares that a listing provides. This might be a company that is already listed on another, overseas stock exchange, a new company formed from two previously listed companies that have merged, or a demutualised organisation.

As an introduction does not raise funds, it is not a marketing operation in the same way as an offer for sale, offer for subscription or placing.

2.7 Exchangeable/Convertible Bond Offerings

Learning Objective

3.2.7 Understand the use of exchangeable/convertible bond offerings: the difference between exchangeable and convertible bonds; structure of an offering – base deal plus greenshoe; stages of an offering; underwritten versus best efforts

Exchangeable bonds and convertible bonds are similar instruments – they both can be described as hybrid instruments, with characteristics of both equities and bonds. A **convertible bond** is a bond, paying a coupon and with a nominal value to be repaid on maturity, that offers the holder of the bond the right to convert the bond into a set number of ordinary shares of the company that issued the bond.

Example

XYZ plc issues convertible bonds paying a 6% annual coupon and redeeming in five years' time. The holder of the convertible can choose to convert £100 nominal value of the bonds into 25 XYZ plc shares at redemption.

The holder of the bonds will convert as long as the shares are trading at more than £4 each (£100 divided by 25 shares) at the redemption date. Say the shares are trading at £4.60 each at redemption, by converting the bondholder will get 25 x £4.60 = £115 worth of securities. This is preferable to the £100 alternative.

An **exchangeable bond** is also a bond that pays a coupon and has a set redemption date. Like a convertible, it gives the holder the right to exchange the bond for a set number of shares, but these shares are not those of the bond issuer, but of another company's shares that are held by the issuer.

Example

A listed company holds ABC plc shares and issues exchangeable bonds paying a 6% annual coupon and redeeming in five years' time. The holder of the exchangeable bonds can choose to convert £100 nominal value of the bonds into 20 ABC shares at redemption.

Clearly the holder of the bonds will exchange as long as the ABC shares are trading at more than £5 each (£100 divided by 20) at the redemption date.

The holder of either a convertible or an exchangeable bond has the safety of coupons and repayment, combined with the potential upside of equity growth. Both types of bond will enable the issuer to raise borrowed funds more cheaply, because the bonds have the upside potential of the conversion/exchange into shares.

The structure of an offering of a convertible or exchangeable bond mirrors that of equities – the issuer will set a base amount of bonds it wishes to issue and perhaps retain a greenshoe, reserving the right to issue more if demand is strong.

The stages of the convertible/exchangeable offer are the same as an IPO:

1. The decision.
2. The preparation of the prospectus.
3. The sale of securities.

As with an IPO, the offer may also be underwritten, with a potential combination of firm underwriting by the investment bank(s) and best efforts underwriting by clients of the investment bank(s) such as stockbroking firms.

3. Participants in an Equity Offering Securities

Deciding to list (or float) securities on a stock exchange, such as the New York Stock Exchange (NYSE), the LSE or any of a host of other exchanges worldwide, is a significant decision for a company to take. Flotations have both pros and cons – the fact that the company can gain access to capital and enable its shares to be readily marketable are often-quoted positives. The most often-quoted negatives are the fact that the original owners may well lose control of the company and that the ongoing disclosure and attention paid to the company after listing is much greater than previously.

3.1 Listing Advisers and Continuing Obligations

Learning Objective

3.3.2   Know the role of advisers: listing agent; corporate broker

3.3.3   Know the issuer's obligations: corporate governance; reporting

In order to have its securities listed, the company concerned will have to find and appoint certain advisers. The precise requirements and roles are laid down in the local regulations that apply to the particular exchange. Generally, the advisers will include both a listing agent at the IPO stage and a corporate broker to act for the company both at the IPO and afterwards.

Once the decision has been made to list, the company will have to find and appoint a listing agent, alternatively referred to as a sponsor. The sponsor is likely to be an investment bank, a stockbroking firm or a professional services firm such as an accountancy practice. The role of the sponsor includes assessing the company's suitability for listing, the best method of bringing the company to the market, and coordinating the production of the prospectus. The prospectus is a detailed document about the company, including financial information that should enable prospective investors to decide on the merits of the company's shares.

The sponsor is only part of the origination team helping the company in the flotation. In addition to the sponsor, the issuing company will appoint a variety of other advisers, such as reporting accountants, legal advisers, public relations (PR) consultants and a corporate broker.

The reporting accountants will attest to the validity of the financial information provided in the prospectus. The legal advisers will make sure that all relevant matters are covered in the prospectus and that the statements made are justified. The combination of the reporting accountants and the legal advisers is said to be providing due diligence for the prospectus – making sure the document is accurate and complies with the regulations.

A PR consultant is generally appointed to optimise the positive public perception of the company and its products and services in the run-up to listing.

Finally, the origination team is likely to include a corporate broker, who may be the same firm as the listing agent. The responsibilities of the corporate broker are to act as an interface between the company on the one hand, and the stock market and investors in the company's securities on the other. In particular, the corporate broker advises the company on market conditions – the way existing and potential investors are viewing the company in relation to its peers, and the general direction of the market.

An issuer that is planning to have its securities listed will have to accept certain obligations. Like the requirements for advisers, the precise obligations can vary across jurisdictions, but they always include obligations in relation to good corporate governance and regular reporting.

Corporate governance is the way a company (the corporate) manages and controls its activities (governs itself). Corporate governance is often described as the set of laws, rules, customs and both external and internal policies that guide how a company is directed and managed. In particular, it is expected (and, in some jurisdictions, required) that the listed companies have put in place appropriate corporate and management structures. Examples include reducing the influence of a single individual by splitting the roles of chairman and chief executive of the company, appointing a reasonable proportion of non-executive directors (NEDs) to the board, and having a suitably qualified finance director.

Reporting requirements are designed to make sure that existing and potential investors are kept informed of progress and developments at the listed company. It is particularly important that financial information is provided regularly and that the information is reliable, and so listed companies are generally required to provide audited annual accounts; and less detailed half-yearly, or perhaps quarterly, reports.

3.2   The Syndicate Group

Learning Objective

3.3.1   Understand the role of the syndicate group: different roles within a syndicate: book runner, co-lead; co-manager; marketing and book-building

For large listings, when the issuing company is planning to issue substantial quantities of shares to interested investors, the sponsor will gather together a syndicate of investment banks and stockbrokers to market the share issue to their clients. These clients may be a mixture of both institutional clients (such as insurance companies and asset management firms) and retail clients. The sponsor will generally act as the lead manager of the syndicate, appointing a host of co-managers to assist. Sometimes the issue may be large enough to warrant the appointment of more than one lead manager, perhaps with each co-lead manager taking responsibility for particular geographical areas – for example, one lead manager for Europe, another for the US.

The process of finding buyers for the issuing company's shares is known as bookbuilding, and the lead managers coordinate the overall level of demand across the syndicate. This role is commonly referred to as that of the book runner.

During the book-building, the syndicate will gather the willingness of investors to purchase the shares, which will be sensitive to the price at which the shares are sold. Usually, the book-building begins with an indicative range of prices; the finalisation of the price will come just prior to listing. This is illustrated in the following example.

Example

Cauldron Stanley is a large investment bank. It is acting as lead manager and sponsor for a new issue of shares for a client, Wizard Enterprises plc, which is looking to raise several billion pounds. Because of the size of the issue, Cauldron Stanley sets up a syndicate of ten investment banks to assist in the marketing and act as co-managers.

The syndicate initially markets the shares at an indicative price range of £2 to £2.20 each. The strength of demand is strong so that, as listing approaches, the final price is set at the top of the range, at £2.20 per share.

3.3 Underwriting

Learning Objective

3.3.4   Understand the purpose and practice of underwriting, rights and responsibilities of the underwriter: benefits to the issuing company; risks and rewards to the underwriter

In circumstances where a company is attempting to sell shares to the investing public, there is a danger that the demand is not sufficient, perhaps because of a general fall in share prices near to the flotation date. This could lead to the flotation failing, so it is usual to underwrite new issues of shares. Underwriting is agreeing with financial institutions, such as banks, insurance companies and asset managers, that, if the demand is insufficient, the financial institutions will buy the shares. Effectively, underwriting creates an insurance policy that the issue will happen because, in the worst case, the underwriters (the financial institutions that have agreed to underwrite the offer) will buy the shares. The underwriters also work closely with the issuing company, prior to an offering period, to determine demand for the shares, to help determine an appropriate share price for the listing and in the distribution of the shares to their network of institutional or retail clients.

In such circumstances, the price at which the underwriters guarantee to buy is generally at a discount to the share price at which the shares are offered to the public, eg, shares offered to the public at £5 each might be underwritten at £4.75 each.

The benefits to the issuing company of an underwriting arrangement are obvious – the sale of the shares and minimum proceeds are guaranteed. For the underwriters, the risk is that they may end up buying shares for more than they are worth. However, in return for accepting this risk, the underwriters will be paid fees, regardless of whether or not there is a lack of demand for the shares from the public.

3.4 Stabilisation

Learning Objective

3.3.5 Understand stabilisation and its purpose: governing principles and regulation with regard to stabilisation activity; who is involved in stabilisation; what does stabilisation achieve; benefits to the issuing company and investors

Stabilisation is the process whereby, to prevent a substantial fall in the value of securities when a large number of new securities are issued, the lead manager of the issue agrees to support the price by buying back the newly issued securities in the market if the market price falls below a certain predefined level. This is done in an attempt to give the market a reasonable chance to adjust to the increased number of securities that have become available, by stabilising the price at which they are traded.

By increasing the demand for the securities in the market at the same time as more securities become available, the price should remain more stable. This will mean the issuing company's securities appear less volatile, and existing investors will be less likely to begin panic-selling, creating a downward spiral in the security's price. The securities that are bought back by the lead manager of the issue will then be sold back into the market over time.

An alternative way of stabilising the price of shares after an IPO is to use a greenshoe option.

There are strict rules laid down by regulators regarding stabilisation practices. For example, the UK's FCA requires disclosure to the market that stabilisation is happening, and that the market price may not be a representative one because of the stabilisation activities. Prices can also be stabilised by exchanges using **circuit breakers** to temporarily suspend trading in periods of volatility.

4. Stock Exchanges

Learning Objective

3.4.1 Know the role of stock exchanges and their regulatory frameworks

The basic role of a stock exchange is to facilitate secondary market trading of shares in quoted companies. The participants include investors, many of which are institutional investors, such as asset managers, trading the shares held in their clients' funds and insurance companies. The trades they undertake are arranged by stockbrokers (often simply referred to as brokers), and the arranged trade will often involve purchasing from, or selling to, a bank which is acting as a dealer or, in some cases, a market maker. The larger banks that provide their clients with the capacity to both arrange and deal are often termed broker/dealers.

There are major exchanges in each of the world's financial centres, and their regulatory frameworks are all broadly similar in that they must:

- determine which securities can be traded, most obviously laying down conditions that must be satisfied before an issuing company is 'quoted' on the exchange
- lay down rules and regulations for subsequent trading of those securities by the participants ('members') using the exchange.

Generally speaking, the regulatory framework that surrounds initial/primary and secondary markets in securities consists of three strands – the law, the requirements of the local regulator and the rules of the stock exchange itself. To illustrate the interaction of these three strands, it is instructive to look at the framework that has developed in the UK.

Illustration – The Regulatory Framework Surrounding the LSE

The regulatory framework that lies behind the way that the LSE operates includes three major constituents: the law (in particular the UK Companies Act), the requirements of the FCA and the rules laid down by the exchange itself (in its rule book).

The Companies Act details the requirements for companies generally, such as the requirement to prepare annual accounts, to have accounts audited and for annual general meetings (AGMs). Of particular significance to the LSE are the Companies Act requirements to enable a company to be a plc, since one of the requirements for a company to be listed and traded on the exchange is that the company is a plc.

The FCA has to give its recognition before an exchange is allowed to operate in the UK. It has granted recognition to the LSE and, by virtue of this recognition, the exchange is described as a recognised investment exchange (RIE). In granting recognition, the FCA assesses whether the exchange has sufficient systems and controls to run a market. Furthermore, the FCA (through its division the UK Listing Authority (UKLA)) lays down the detailed rules that have to be met before companies are admitted to the Official List that enables their shares to be traded on the exchange.

The LSE also has its own rules in relation to who can access its systems and become members of the exchange, as well as how those members must behave when trading on the exchange.

4.1 Admission Criteria for Listing

Learning Objective

3.4.2 Understand the purpose of admission criteria for main markets and how they can differ for other markets dealing with smaller companies: appointment of advisers and brokers; transferability of shares; trading record; amount raised; percentage in public hands; shareholder approval; market capitalisation

Listing securities, such as a company's shares, is typically a two-stage process that aims to make sure potential investors have relevant and reliable information about the securities and their issuer, and that there are likely to be sufficient securities available to make them relatively easy to buy and sell.

The first stage usually involves the filing of a prospectus with the regulator that contains information about the securities' issuer, its history, financial situation and its operations. This will be coordinated by a sponsor (generally an investment bank) and supported by reporting accountants vetting the numbers and legal advisers ensuring the sponsor has discharged its legal responsibilities. The prospectus is filed and made available to interested investors (the public).

The second stage is an application to the stock exchange to have the securities traded. The exchange will want to see that there is at least a minimum number of shares held by persons other than the issuing company's directors and other dominant investors (a sufficient 'free float') and that there are investment banks willing to buy and sell the securities once listed.

It is common in developed markets around the world to have more than one market for company securities: a major or main market for securities issued by the bigger, well-established companies, and a junior market for securities issued by smaller, less well-known companies. Examples include the UK and Hong Kong. In the UK, the LSE has established two markets for company securities: the Official List and **AIM**. The Official (or full) List is the senior market and is often referred to as the Main Market. Entry rules are stringent, ensuring that only companies of a high quality can be involved. AIM was created with less stringent admission requirements to provide a market for smaller, less well-established companies. In Hong Kong, the senior and junior markets are referred to as the Main Board and the Growth Enterprise Market. The latter captures the logic of providing a facility for trading smaller companies' shares, where entry requirements are less stringent. It is a fact that small companies can, if they are successful, grow very quickly and provide extremely attractive returns to their early-stage investors.

The following outlines how the Main Market admission requirements typically differ from those of the junior/growth market using the UK as an example.

The UK Main Market versus the Junior Market

The Main Market in the UK is typically referred to as the Official List and the criteria for admission to the Official List are set out in the Listing Rules – a rule book is maintained by the United Kingdom Listing Authority (UKLA), itself a division of the regulator, the FCA.

The UKLA actually has two sets of requirements that may be met by an applicant to be admitted to the Official List. The first is the so-called Standard Listing, with the requirements derived from the EU, and the second is the so-called Premium Listing, which has further requirements over and above the European minimum. Only equity shares are eligible for Premium Listing, so issuers of other securities, such as bonds, can only seek a Standard Listing.

The main requirements contained in the Listing Rules for admission to a Premium Listing are:

- Every company applying for a listing must be duly incorporated (UK companies need to be plcs), and must be represented by a sponsor (alternatively referred to as a listing agent), which will usually be an investment bank, stockbroker, law firm or accountancy practice. The sponsor provides a link between the company and the UKLA, guiding the company through the listing process.
- The expected market capitalisation of the company should be at least £700,000 for the company's shares to be listed.
- The company should have a trading record of at least three years.
- At least 25% of the company's shares should be in public hands, or be available for public purchase. The term 'public' excludes directors and their associates and anyone who holds 5% or more of the shares.
- The company and its advisers must publish a prospectus, a detailed document providing potential investors with the information required to make an informed decision on the company and its shares.
- The company must restrict its ability to issue warrants to no more than 20% of the issued share capital.
- Listing is not free, and a further requirement before a company's shares can be admitted is that the appropriate fee has been paid.

For issuers listing debt securities, where the Premium Listing is not available, the requirements for Standard Listing include that the aggregate market value of the debt securities should be at least £200,000.

Once listed, companies are expected to fulfil certain continuing obligations: they are obliged to issue a half-yearly report in addition to annual accounts, and they have to notify the market of any new, price-sensitive information.

The UK's Junior Market: AIM

In contrast to the Official List, to which access is via application to the UKLA and the UKLA's Listing Rules must be complied with, AIM companies' application and regulations are set by the LSE. AIM companies are usually smaller than their fully listed counterparts, and the rules governing their listing are much less stringent. For example, there is no restriction on market value, percentage of shares in public hands or trading history.

Among the more important rules for the AIM is the requirement that AIM companies need to have a nominated adviser. The nominated adviser is often referred to as the 'nomad' and is typically a firm of stockbrokers or accountants or an investment bank. Each nomad needs to be approved by the LSE for assessing the appropriateness of the applicant for AIM, and for guiding and advising AIM companies on their responsibilities under the rules of the market that have been laid down by the LSE.

The main requirements for a company's shares to be admitted to the AIM are twofold:

1. That there is no restriction on the transferability of the shares.
2. That the AIM company appoints two experts to assist it:
   a. the nominated adviser – as seen, the nomad can be thought of as an exchange expert, advising the company on all aspects of AIM Listing Rules and compliance
   b. the broker – AIM companies' shares are usually less liquid than those of fully listed companies; it is the broker's job to ensure that there is a market in the company's shares, to facilitate trading in those shares and to provide ongoing information about the company to interested parties.

As with the Official List, the LSE imposes similar continuing obligations on AIM companies. There are also certain other aspects in relation to AIM companies and their broker and nominated adviser:

- The broker and adviser can be the same firm; they are often firms of stockbrokers or accountants.
- If a company ceases, at any time, to have a broker or adviser, then the firm's shares are suspended from trading.
- If the company is without a broker or adviser for a period of one month it is removed from AIM.

Similar structures exist elsewhere in Europe, with two paths open to companies wishing to access the primary market for capital – through markets regulated by the EU and through markets that are regulated by the exchanges themselves. An important example is Frankfurt in Germany.

Example

On the Frankfurt Stock Exchange, a listing in the EU-regulated market can be in the General Standard segment or in the Prime Standard segment. The market that the Frankfurt exchange itself regulates includes the Scale segment.

General Standard

The General Standard segment is primarily intended for medium-sized and large corporations who seek to address national investors and want to use a cost-effective listing for that purpose. It has the following key conditions:

- Valid and audited securities prospectus, satisfying the requirements of the Federal Financial Supervisory Authority (BaFin).
- Reporting history dating back at least three years.
- Probable total price value of at least €1.25 million.
- Number of shares admitted to trading to be at least 10,000.
- Free-float to be at least 25%.

Prime Standard

The Prime Standard is considered to be the premium segment for raising equity with ongoing requirements that exceed those of the General Standard. The Prime Standard sets the very highest transparency requirements of all segments in the Frankfurt Stock Exchange and, indeed, in all of Europe. The additional admission follow-up duties for the Prime Standard stand out not only for the higher transparency yardstick but also because the requirements always have to be met in English. The Prime Standard is, therefore, an attractive choice for issuers who want to appeal to international investors.

Scale

Scale for equities is the segment for small and medium-sized enterprises (SMEs). It targets German and European SMEs seeking capital for growth.

5. Bond Offerings

5.1 Types of Issuer

Learning Objective

3.5.1 Know the different types of issuer: supranationals; governments; agency; municipal; corporate; financial institutions and special purpose vehicles

Bonds are essentially IOU (I owe you) instruments that specify a face value, coupon rate and redemption date. They are issued by a variety of organisations including:

- **Supranationals** – organisations like the World Bank raise money through issuing bonds.
- **Governments** – most governments have a requirement to borrow money at some stage, and the long-term borrowing is generally financed by bond issues, such as UK gilts and US Treasury bonds.
- **Agencies** – agencies (often backed by the government) issue bonds for particular purposes. These are common in the US, where examples include the Federal National Mortgage Association ('Fannie Mae'), created to provide mortgage finance for the disadvantaged, and the Student Loan Marketing Association ('Sallie Mae') created to finance student education.
- **Municipalities** – municipalities in the US issue municipal bonds to finance local borrowing. These municipal bonds are often tax-efficient, particularly for investors who reside in that municipality. Municipal bonds are usually guaranteed by a third party, known in the US market as a **monoline insurer**, and their credit quality may be enhanced by such a guarantee, which enables the municipality to secure funds on more advantageous terms.
- **Corporates** – large companies often use bonds to finance borrowing needs.
- **Financial institutions and special purpose vehicles (SPVs)** – like other corporates, financial institutions issue bonds to finance borrowing. These financial institutions also arrange borrowing for themselves and others by creating SPVs to enable money to be raised that does not appear within the accounts of that entity. This type of finance is often described as off-balance-sheet finance because it does not appear in the balance sheet that forms of part of the company's accounts.

The use of special purpose vehicles (SPVs) continues to be popular in the asset-backed securities markets.

5.2 Bond Issuance

Learning Objective

3.5.2 Know the methods of issuance: scheduled funding programmes and opportunistic issuance, eg, medium-term notes (MTNs); auction/tender; reverse inquiry (under MTN)

Traditionally, borrowing money via a bond issue was only sensible when large sums of money were being raised in a single capital-raising transaction. The sums had to be large enough to make the costs involved in issuance worthwhile. The details of the bond would be established, including its coupon and maturity, and the bonds would be marketed to potential investors. The investors would either be invited to bid for the bonds in an auction-type process, or a tender method was adopted. Both of these are illustrated in the example that follows in relation to UK government bonds.

Example

The Debt Management Office (DMO) is the part of the UK Treasury that oversees gilt issues. It uses a number of different issue methods, depending on the circumstances. Most commonly used is the **auction** method, when the DMO announces the auction, receives bids and allocates the gilts to those that bid highest, at the price they bid. Gilt-edged market makers (GEMMs) are expected to bid for gilts when the DMO makes a new issue, and the DMO reserves the right to take the gilts onto its own books if the auction is not fully taken up. Applicants bid for the gilt and successful bidders pay the price at which they bid.

Imagine an auction is for £1m nominal.

- A offers to buy £0.5m nominal, willing to pay £101.50 for every £100 nominal.
- B offers to buy £0.5m nominal, willing to pay £100.75 for every £100 nominal.
- C offers to buy £0.5m nominal, willing to pay £100.50 for every £100 nominal.

A and B are awarded the gilts for **the prices that they bid** and there is nothing left for C.

Up until 1987, instead of the auction method, the tender method was standard, when all bidders paid a common strike price. In a tender, a minimum price is set by the DMO and investors make bids. The gilts are awarded at the highest price at which they can all be sold.

Imagine the auction is for £1 million nominal and the minimum price is £100 for £100 nominal. The bids submitted are:

- A offers to buy £0.5 million nominal, paying £101.50 for every £100 nominal.
- B offers to buy £0.5 million nominal, paying £100.75 for every £100 nominal.
- C offers to buy £0.5 million nominal, paying £100.50 for every £100 nominal.

In this instance, A and B are awarded the gilts, but both pay the lower price: £100.75 (the highest price at which all the gilts could be sold).

As many issuers, particularly companies, needed to borrow money regularly in line with the developments of their business, they tended to prefer to set up scheduled programmes with their banks under which they would be able to borrow money, instead of issuing bonds.

However, a US innovation has been introduced that has been subsequently adopted in many other jurisdictions which enables bond financing to be much more flexible. Traditionally, it was awkward and expensive to regularly raise bond finance because each bond issue had to be separately registered with the financial regulator (the SEC in the US). A process known as 'shelf registration' was introduced that enabled a single registration to be used for a number of bond issues over a period of up to two years. This has been heavily used in the medium-term note (MTN) market for bonds with generally two to ten years between issue and maturity. Shelf registration introduced flexibility to the bond market, allowing companies to issue smaller batches of bonds, with the coupons and maturity varying according to market demand at the time.

The process involves the bond issuer finding two or more dealers that are willing to offer their services to market the bonds to their clients on a best efforts basis. The issuer will then issue bonds as and when the money is required, with coupon rates and maturity in accordance with market demand. Indeed, it is not unusual for some MTNs to be issued in response to an enquiry from clients of the dealers that want a particular maturity and coupon. These are termed reverse inquiries in the US, and the issuer can decide whether to accept the terms and issue the bonds or not.

5.3   The Role of the Origination Team

Learning Objective

3.5.3   Understand the role of the origination team including: pitching; indicative bid; mandate announcement; credit rating; roadshow; listing; syndication

Many of the activities in originating bond issues are similar to those in originating equity issues, particularly if the bonds are going to be listed and therefore need a prospectus. In such cases there will be a whole **origination team** involving the issuer, its investment bank, reporting accountants, legal and PR advisers.

A typical new issue of bonds could contain any, or all, of the following stages:

1. **Pitching** – the issuer of the bonds will need to decide that a bond issue is appropriate and which investment bank(s) it wants to assist in the issue. The final decision will be dependent upon an assessment of the qualities of the potential banks. A final decision is usually made on the basis of a presentation (pitch) made by the banks, to the issuer.
2. **Indicative bid** – during the pitching stage, the banks will detail their views of how much finance the issuer is likely to raise given the terms of the bond issue.
3. **Mandate announcement** – once the issuer has decided upon the bank(s) to raise the finance on its behalf, it will announce the names of the banks that have been given the mandate to arrange the issue on its behalf.

4. **Credit rating** – given by one of the credit rating agencies or an investment bank, this will be vital to the amount of finance that can be raised. The details of the proposed terms and conditions of the bond will have to be provided to get a credit rating, and there may be a need for credit enhancements, such as insurance, to enable a higher rating to be achieved.

5. **Roadshow** – once the bank running the issue has been appointed, it will arrange and run a series of visits to the potential buyers of the bonds. This is commonly described as the roadshow, because it involves travelling around a number of major financial centres to see the key investors.

6. **Listing** – if the bond is to be listed it will need a prospectus to submit to the relevant listing authority.

7. **Syndication** – for larger bond issues there will be a number of banks acting for the issuer, described as a lead manager (the primary contact with the issuer) and the other co-managers that will sell into their particular client base, perhaps based on geographical regions. The total of all the banks involved is the syndicate.

End of Chapter Questions

1. What is the definition of the primary market?
   Answer reference: Section 1

2. Who are the main investors in newly issued securities?
   Answer reference: Section 1.1.1

3. What is the main motivation for issuers in the primary market?
   Answer reference: Section 1.2

4. What are the main uses and benefits of secondary markets?
   Answer reference: Section 1.2

5. How does an offer for subscription differ from an offer for sale?
   Answer reference: Sections 2.3 and 2.4

6. What is a greenshoe?
   Answer reference: Section 2.4.1

7. What is the role of the listing agent or sponsor in an IPO?
   Answer reference: Section 3.1

8. What requires UK issuers to prepare annual audited accounts and hold AGMs?
   Answer reference: Section 4

9. For how long must a company applying for a Premium Listing in the UK have a trading record?
   Answer reference: Section 4.1

10. What is a reverse inquiry in relation to medium-term notes?
    Answer reference: Section 5.2

Chapter Four
Secondary Markets

1.	**Trading Venues**	**109**
2.	**Methods of Trading and Participants**	**112**
3.	**Stock Exchanges**	**116**
4.	**Indices**	**121**
5.	**Government Bonds**	**126**
6.	**Corporate Bond Markets**	**130**
7.	**Dealing Methods**	**132**

This syllabus area will provide approximately 14 of the 100 examination questions

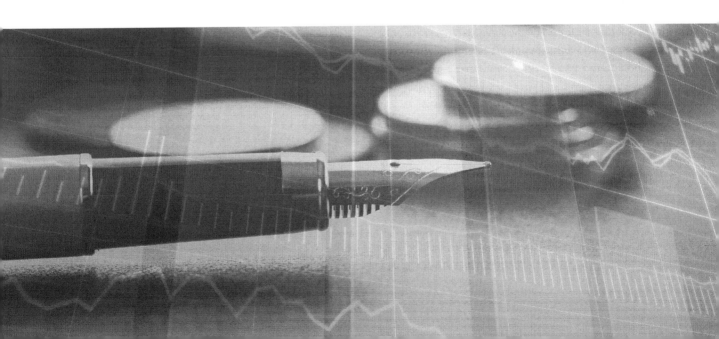

1. Trading Venues

Learning Objective

4.1.1 Understand the main characteristics and practices in the developed markets

4.1.2 Understand the main characteristics and practices in the undeveloped and emerging markets

4.1.3 Understand the purpose, role and main features of stock exchanges generally. In particular: scope; provision of liquidity; price formation; brokers versus dealers

4.1.4 Understand the purpose, role and main features of alternative trading venues: off-exchange trades; dark pools; OTC; private transactions; multilateral trading facilities

1.1 Developed Markets

Trading venues facilitate the purchase and sale of listed equities and have traditionally been dominated by national stock exchanges, including the US New York Stock Exchange (NYSE), the UK London Stock Exchange (LSE), Germany's Deutsche Börse and Japan's Tokyo Stock Exchange (TSE). Typically, these exchanges started out as meeting places, where buyers and sellers would gather to carry out deals, and which gradually developed to become regulated entities where one investor's wish to buy is matched with another investor's wish to sell via middlemen (the brokers). Unsurprisingly, these exchanges have taken advantage of huge strides in technology to introduce electronic systems that match orders efficiently and effectively.

Stock exchanges offer membership to investment banks and firms of stockbrokers. Becoming a member of an exchange enables these banks and stockbrokers to be involved in secondary market trades. As a consequence of the ongoing activities of the major participants in the secondary market – institutional investors, banks, and speculators – these exchanges provide liquidity to existing and potential investors, enabling existing investors to sell their securities and allowing potential investors to become actual investors by purchasing securities. Furthermore, because these exchanges aggregate and integrate the trading activity on their systems as well as some alternative venues, the prices at which trades are executed is the market price at any given time. This is described as the price formation process, and sometimes markets are characterised as price discovery mechanisms.

Brokers arrange deals for their clients, as well as potentially giving advice to their clients, as to which securities they should buy, sell or retain. In return for arranging (and potentially advising), the brokers will earn a commission that is typically calculated as a set percentage of the value of the deal. Acting as a broker is often described as dealing as agent. The broker never actually buys or sells securities – the broker is simply an agent that facilitates the transaction(s) between two parties. Firms of stockbrokers tend to act as brokers on the stock exchanges.

Dealers, in contrast to brokers, actually buy or sell securities. If a client wants to sell shares, a dealer may buy those shares; if another client wants to buy shares, a dealer may sell those shares. Acting as a dealer is often described as dealing as principal, because the dealer is taking a principal position by either buying, or selling the securities. It is the investment banks that tend to act as dealers on the stock exchanges.

Firms, such as investment banks, that are involved in both acting as agent (broking) and as principal (dealing), are often described as **broker-dealers.**

However, over recent decades, the equity markets in developed markets have seen a proliferation of venues beyond the single national exchange. A number of developed markets now have a multitude of regulated exchanges, plus a variety of so-called alternative trading systems (ATSs), including firms (such as investment banks) that internalise their customers' trades by executing them against other customers' trades or the firm's own inventory.

Example

The US is the largest developed market in the world and its equity trading venues include the following:

- 21 registered 'national securities exchanges' including the two dominant exchanges, Nasdaq and the NYSE
- more than 40 alternative trading systems, including those operated by investment banks, such as Goldman Sachs, Morgan Stanley, UBS and Bank of America Merrill Lynch.

The same type of venues for trading equities exist in developed markets elsewhere in the world although, sometimes, the terminology differs a little, such as that introduced in the European Union (EU).

Example

In Europe, the terminology used was originally introduced by the Markets in Financial Instruments Directive (MiFID). It distinguished three venues for trading equities:

1. Regulated markets – these are basically stock exchanges.
2. Multilateral trading facilities (MTFs) – these are systems other than regulated markets that are operated and/or managed by a market operator which bring together multiple third-party buying and selling interests in financial instruments (such as shares) in a way that results in a contract.
3. Systematic internalisers – these are investment firms (such as investment banks) which, on an organised, frequent, systematic and substantial basis, deal on their own account when executing client orders outside other markets.

A second Markets in Financial Instruments Directive (MiFID II) will subsequently be introduced in early 2018 that adds a fourth type of venue – the organised trading facility (OTF). This newly defined venue type is for instruments other than equities, such as bonds or derivatives, where multiple third-party buying and selling interests are able to interact in a way that results in a contract.

Over-the-counter (OTC) is the term given to trading which is conducted by networks of dealers and when the trading is not coordinated or subject to the formal procedures and standardised formats of an exchange.

Dark pool is the term that generally refers to an off-exchange trading venue where stocks are traded in large quantities without the prices being displayed until after the trade is done. The term 'dark' is used to describe the fact that pricing information cannot be seen. Trading undertaken in dark pools is commonly described as dark liquidity. The opposite of dark pools are known as 'lit pools'.

One investment manager has described the appeal of dark liquidity pools as follows:

A dark pool is a way you can hopefully capture lots of liquidity and achieve a large proportion of your order being executed without displaying anything to the market.

In the US, the dark pools are a form of what are referred to as alternative trading systems (ATSs) and, in Europe, they are a form of **multilateral trading facility (MTF)**.

Private transactions are those offerings of securities which are made, not to the general public, but to a subset of so-called sophisticated investors, when the same rigorous kinds of disclosures that have to be made in an initial public offering (IPO) prospectus (sometimes known in the US as a red herring) can be avoided.

In the US, the Securities and Exchange Commission (SEC) has special provisions for what are termed private placements. A private placement (or non-public offering) is a funding round of securities which are sold without an IPO, and without the formality of an approved prospectus, usually to a small number of chosen private investors.

Although these placements are subject to the Securities Act of 1933, the securities offered do not have to be registered with the SEC if the issuance of the securities conforms to an exemption from registrations as set forth in the Rules known as Regulation D. Private placements may typically consist of stocks, shares of common stock or preferred stock or other forms of membership interests, warrants or promissory notes (including convertible promissory notes), and purchasers are often institutional investors such as banks, insurance companies and pension funds.

1.2   Undeveloped and Emerging Markets

Less developed markets around the world, including those classified as emerging markets, tend not to have reached the same degree of sophistication as developed markets. Most of the equity trading in these markets takes place through stock exchanges.

Example

The Stock Exchange of Thailand

Originally incorporated in 1974, the Stock Exchange of Thailand's primary role is to serve as the centre for the trading of listed securities and to provide systems needed to facilitate securities trading.

The Stock Exchange of Thailand's core operations include listing securities, the supervision of information, disclosures by listed companies, oversight of securities trading, monitoring member companies involved in trading securities, as well as dissemination of information and educating investors.

China provides a good example of an equity market that is becoming more sophisticated all the time – partly as a result of China's rapid development and partly due to the size of the economy.

Example

China's equity market is relatively young and, on the Chinese mainland, is dominated by the Shanghai and Shenzhen Stock Exchanges which opened in December 1990. The Shanghai exchange has, historically, listed China's most prominent large-cap companies – state-owned enterprises (SOEs), banks and energy firms – sectors which are collectively known as 'Old China'. Shenzhen, however, plays host to mainly small- and mid-cap firms.

In addition to listing on mainland markets, the largest Chinese firms and SOEs also list on the Hong Kong Stock Exchange.

China's market structure is unusual in that there are multiple share classes. Historically, regulators restricted foreigners' access to mainland markets, depriving investors of the significant growth opportunities associated with China's emergence onto the global stage. The gradual loosening of these controls has resulted in the presence of different share classes, most notably A-shares and H-shares.

A-shares are traded on the mainland exchanges and are gradually being opened up to enable purchase by overseas investors. H-shares are mainland Chinese companies listed in Hong Kong and are available to, and popular with, global investors. Although the H-share universe consists of a more limited number of companies than on the mainland exchanges, international investors prefer the more familiar legal and market framework in Hong Kong.

2. Methods of Trading and Participants

2.1 Quote-Driven Versus Order-Driven Systems

Learning Objective

4.2.1 Understand the differences between quote-driven and order-driven markets and how they operate

Trading systems provided by exchanges around the world can be classified on the basis of the type of trading they offer. Broadly, systems are either quote-driven or order-driven:

- **Quote-driven systems** – market makers agree to buy and sell at least a set minimum number of shares at quoted prices. The buying price is the bid and the selling price is the offer. The prime example of a quote-driven equity trading system is Nasdaq in the US.
- **Order-driven systems** – the investors (or agents acting on their behalf) indicate how many securities they want to buy or sell, and at what price. The system then simply brings together the buyers and sellers. Order-driven systems are very common in the equity markets – the NYSE, the TSE and trading in the shares of the largest companies on the LSE are all examples of order-driven equity markets.

The presence of market makers on quote-driven systems provides liquidity that might be lacking on an order-driven system. Market makers are required to quote **two-way prices**, resulting in an ability for trades to be executed. In contrast, an order-driven system can lack liquidity, since transactions can only be matched against other orders – if there are insufficient orders, trades cannot be matched.

The orders that await matching are included in the so-called 'order book'. The buy side of the order book lists orders to buy, and the sell side of the order book lists orders to sell. New sell orders entered into the system potentially match existing orders on the buy side. New buy orders potentially match existing sell-side orders in the order book.

Generally, trading systems are run electronically, allowing participants to trade via computer screens. However, there are notable exceptions: the NYSE still retains a physical trading floor where buyers and sellers gather to trade in an open-outcry manner in addition to the electronic system.

Some trading systems combine features of both order-driven and quote-driven systems – these are referred to as hybrid systems and include the LSE's Stock Exchange Electronic Trading Service – quotes and crosses (SETSqx).

2.2 Participants

Learning Objective

4.2.2 Know the functions and obligations of: market makers; broker-dealers; inter-dealer brokers

Member firms of an exchange can act in two different capacities or roles – as a principal and as an agent. This does not preclude an individual firm from acting in both capacities; at times it may be acting as an agent and at others it may be acting as a principal.

When a firm is acting as a principal it is essentially buying shares for its own account, in the hope of the shares increasing in value before it sells them, or, in the case of a short transaction, selling borrowed shares at a higher price at the time of borrowing than the price it has to pay when it wishes to replace or cover. Firms acting in this way can also be described as performing their function as dealers and, in more specialised cases, as outlined below, as market makers.

When a firm is acting as an agent it is essentially arranging and making deals on behalf of other third parties, and it makes money, when acting in this capacity, by charging a commission on the deal. This agency role is commonly described as acting as a broker. For instance, when acting as an agent or broker a firm will receive orders to buy and sell equities on behalf of its clients, and find matches for the trades that its clients want to make. In return for these services, brokers charge commission.

If a firm decides to focus only on acting as a principal it is known simply as a dealer, and some exchange member firms may choose simply to buy and sell equities for their own account.

Most exchanges' members, however, are broker-dealers. This means they have the dual capacity to either arrange deals (acting as a broker), or to buy and sell shares for themselves (acting as a dealer).

Some of an exchange's member firms may choose to take on the special responsibilities of a market maker. When a firm acts as a market maker, it stands ready to provide a source of liquidity to certain sections of the market. By being prepared to provide a bid for shares that third parties want to sell and an ask for parties that want to buy shares at any time, the market maker smooths out the more erratic price movements that can occur without this additional source of market liquidity.

To become a market maker a member firm must apply to the stock exchange, giving details of the securities in which it has chosen to deal. It must provide prices at which it is willing to buy and sell a minimum number of its chosen shares throughout the course of the trading day. Because some of the exchange systems rely on market makers to honour their commitments, the exchange closely vets firms before allowing them to quote prices to investors. In return for agreeing to take on these extra responsibilities, market makers hope to enjoy the benefits of a steady stream of business, from broker-dealers and from other investors.

An inter-dealer broker (IDB) is an exchange member firm that has registered with the exchange to act as an agent between dealers (such as market makers). When one dealer trades with another, it often prefers its identity to remain a secret. This is the key benefit of using an IDB. The IDB is acting as agent for the dealer but settles any transactions as if it were principal in order to preserve the anonymity of the dealer. An IDB is not allowed to take principal positions, and it has to be a separate firm, not a division of another broker-dealer.

2.3   High-Frequency Trading (HFT)

Learning Objective

4.2.3   Understand high-frequency trading: reasons; consequences for the market (eg, flash crashes); types of company that pursue this strategy

High-frequency trading (HFT) has evolved recently, particularly over the past 15 years or so, since the advent of electronic trading systems. Indeed, estimates for exchanges such as the NYSE put the proportion of trading done by high-frequency traders at 50% or more.

HFT involves the use of powerful computers that are programmed to transmit orders based on algorithms. These algorithms will respond extremely rapidly to market movements and, because the computers are usually located physically closely to those of the exchange, the orders will arrive ahead of other conventional orders. The high-frequency traders will enter into hundreds, or even thousands, of small orders in this way and will then reverse the deals (so if the initial deals were to buy, they will sell or vice versa) to make a 'turn' on each. The amount of money made on each deal might be very small, but because of the quantity of deals being done, the high-frequency trader can make a lot of money very quickly.

Potential criticisms of HFT include seeing the traders as 'vultures' exploiting the genuine, longer-term investors and, given their dominance of market turnover, the impact they can have on pricing. The impact on pricing can be substantial, as was exhibited in the so-called 'flash crash' that hit the US markets on 6 May 2010. On that day, stock prices fell rapidly, with around 600 points being wiped off the **Dow Jones Industrial Average (DJIA)** in five minutes, only to recover again around 20 minutes later. An official report from the SEC and the Commodity Futures Trading Commission (CFTC) put most of the blame for the volatility on high-frequency traders' algorithms. The initial impact came from movements in the Standard & Poor's (S&P) futures market and spilled over into the wider stock market with the high-frequency traders aggressively selling. After the Chicago Mercantile Exchange (CME) paused trading in the S&P futures by triggering a circuit breaker, prices stabilised and then recovered almost as quickly as the losses had crystallised minutes earlier.

Another 'mini' flash crash occurred in the US market on 23 April 2013 in response to a hoax Twitter posting about an attack on the White House and an injury to President Obama. The DJIA fell about 130 points and then rapidly recovered. Again some commentators placed the blame for the excessive volatility on the algorithms of the high-frequency traders.

HFT has also been criticised for the systemic risks that it can create. In the event of extreme price movements on one exchange, the arbitrage trades automatically placed by the high-frequency traders can rapidly spread the price movements to other exchanges where the same, or related, instruments are traded.

The original operators of the HFT algorithms were small, specialist firms; their success has attracted others, including hedge funds and the large investment banks.

2.4 Prime Broker Services

Learning Objective

4.2.4 Know the main services provided by an equity and fixed-income prime broker, including: securities lending and borrowing; leverage trade execution; cash management; core settlement; custody; rehypothecation

Prime brokerage is the term given to a collection of services provided by investment banks to their hedge fund clients.

The typical services that are provided by a prime broker include the following:

1. **Securities lending and borrowing** – eg, to cover short positions in a hedge fund's long/short strategy.
2. **Leveraged trade execution** – undertaking trades on the fund's behalf that are partly financed by borrowed funds.
3. **Cash management** – maximising the return that is generated from cash held by the fund.
4. **Core settlement** – taking the necessary steps to make sure that any securities purchased become the property of the fund, and that the appropriate cash is received for any sales made of the fund's securities in a timely manner.
5. **Custody** – keeping safe the securities held by the fund and processing any corporate actions promptly and in accordance with its targets.
6. **Rehypothecation** – in addition to holding collateral and having a charge over the fund's portfolio, the prime broker might also require a right to re-charge, dispose of, or otherwise use the customer's assets which are subject to the security, including disposing of them to a third-party. This is commonly described as a 'right of rehypothecation'. When assets have been rehypothecated, they become the property of the prime broker as and when the prime broker uses them in this way, for instance, by depositing rehypothecated securities with a third-party financier to obtain cheaper funding or by lending the securities to another client.

3. Stock Exchanges

3.1 Rules and Procedures

Learning Objective

4.3.1 Understand the rules, procedures and requirements applying to dealing through stock exchanges' bespoke electronic systems and hybrid trading systems relating to: order book features; order management; limitations and benefits of trading through bespoke systems; right to call a halt in trading; liquidity; market makers

Most stock exchanges operate electronic order-driven systems that automatically match orders to buy and sell equities.

Such systems are centred on an electronic order book into which member firms submit their orders in order to to buy and sell equities and, when there are orders that can be matched, the system automatically brings them together.

3.1.1 The Order Book

In the order book, orders are given priority first by price and then by time.

The electronic screen reflecting the order book for the shares of the fictional company ABC plc might look something like this:

Company: ABC			
Orders to buy		**Orders to sell**	
Volume	**Price**	**Volume**	**Price**
10,000	315	4,000	316
2,000	315	12,000	317
4,000	314	14,000	318
8,000	313	3,000	318
5,000	312	5,000	319
5,000	311	5,000	319

The order priority adopted is by price first, and then time. The best buy and sell prices are always at the top of the two columns of orders and will be executed first. In the case of the buy orders, this is the highest-priced order (315 in the above example, where the order to buy 10,000 shares must have been entered into the system before the order to buy 2,000 shares).

In the case of the sell orders, this is the lowest-priced order (316 in the above example). Below the best-priced orders, all the other orders are displayed, giving an immediate picture of the depth of liquidity on the order book.

Essentially, the way that this system works is that exchange members have access to the order book and can enter orders electronically. If a firm of brokers enters a sell order on behalf of a client for up to 12,000 shares in ABC at the best available price, the order will be executed by the system by matching with the best buy orders (10,000 and 2,000 shares). The matched order will proceed to settlement at 315 per share and be immediately revealed to the market in terms of size (12,000 shares) and price (315).

3.1.2 Opening Auctions and Automatic Execution

At the start of each day's trading, an opening price is often established using an auction process. Typically, this sees member firms entering orders in the period leading up to the auction. In this period, no trading takes place.

The auction itself uses an uncrossing algorithm through which those orders that overlap on the order book are executed at the single price that maximises the number of shares traded. Simultaneously, the opening price for the security is calculated. Once the opening auction is complete, automatic execution commences. As orders are entered on to the system, the exchange's system tries to match them. If the exchange system finds a buyer and seller with agreeable prices and volumes, the trade is automatically executed.

During the trading day, there is typically a possibility of an interruption to this automatic execution of orders. If the price of a trade is more than the price tolerance level away from the previous trade price, an automatic execution is suspended for a period to allow investors time to react to large price changes. The price tolerance level is typically set at between 5% and 25%, depending upon the exchange and the share concerned.

3.1.3 Viewing the Order Book

Any market participant can view the exchange's order book for a particular security (by looking at a Bloomberg screen, for example). However, membership of the exchange is required to interact with the order book. It is for brokers and dealers only.

The exchange typically reserves the right to prohibit any transaction from being dealt on-exchange for any reason. This is referred to as a trading halt, and often arises from the suspension of a security's listing.

If a security is suspended, permission is required from the exchange before a member firm can effect a transaction in that security. The length of the trading halt is at the discretion of the exchange. Trades that have occurred but have not yet settled at the time of suspension are settled as normal.

3.2 Order Types

Learning Objective

4.3.2 Understand the following order types and their differences: market; limit; fill or kill; all or none; execute and eliminate; iceberg; multiple fills

There are a number of types of order that can be entered onto a stock exchange's bespoke order-driven system, and each will be treated slightly differently. The following outlines and explains the major order types.

1. **Limit orders** have a price limit and a time limit, eg, a limit order may state: *'sell 1,000 shares at 360 by next Tuesday'* and the system will attempt to sell these shares at a price no worse than 360 by next Tuesday. Limit orders can be partially filled, and it is only limit orders that are displayed on the order book.

2. **Iceberg orders** are a particular type of limit order. They enable a market participant with a particularly large order to partially hide the size of their order from the market and reduce the market impact that the large order might otherwise have. The term comes from the fact that just the top part of the order is on view (the peak of the iceberg); the rest is hidden (the bulk of the iceberg is below the water). Once the top part of the order is executed, the system automatically brings the next tranche of the iceberg order on to the order book. This process continues until the whole of the iceberg order has been executed, or the time limit for the order expires.

3. **Market orders** do not specify a price. They are submitted to the order book to deal in a specified number of shares.

4. **Execute and eliminate orders** will execute as much of the trade as possible and cancel the rest. However, unlike an at best order, this order type has a specified price and will not execute at a price worse than that specified.

5. **Fill or kill orders** or **all-or-none orders** normally have a specified price (although they can be entered without one) and either the entire order will be immediately filled at a price at least as good as that specified, or the entire order will be cancelled (ie, if there are not enough orders at the price specified or better).

If the order placed on the system does not perfectly match an equal and opposite order, then it may be subject to what are known as 'multiple fills'. For example, a market order to buy 5,000 shares may be satisfied against a number of sell orders, say, a limit order to sell 1,000 shares at $20.00 or better, another to sell 2,500 shares at $20.02 or better, and a third to sell 1,500 shares at $20.03 or better. The buy order has been filled by three individual deals (a multiple fill) and will pay a weighted average price of just less than $20.02.

Number of shares	Price per share ($)	Number x price ($)
1,000	20.00	20,000
2,500	20.02	50,050
1,500	20.03	30,045
5,000		100,095
Weighted average price paid	=100,095/5,000	= $20.019

3.3 The Central Counterparty (CCP)

Learning Objective

4.3.3   Understand the operation, purpose, benefits and limitations of using a central counterparty

Most stock exchanges utilise a central counterparty (CCP); the impact of a CCP is best illustrated by way of an example:

Example

A trade is executed on an exchange's order book that involves A agreeing to sell shares to B. The CCP steps in between the two parties and two new obligations replace the initial obligation of A to sell to B. The two obligations are for A to sell to the CCP and then for the CCP to sell to B. This transfer of obligation is known as 'novation'.

If either of the two parties to this transaction (A or B) were to default, it would no longer affect the other party, as they no longer have a contract with each other. It would only impact the CCP.

The use of a central counterparty provides certain benefits to market participants, particularly:

- **Reduced counterparty risk** – the risk that the other side of the transaction will default is reduced because it is replaced by the CCP, which is invariably well-capitalised and has an insurance policy in place lessening the risk of default. This reduces the risk of systemic collapse of the financial system.
- **Providing total anonymity** – both sides of the trade do not discover who the original counterparty was.
- **Reduced administration** – all trades are settled with the CCP, rather than a variety of counterparties, improving operational efficiency.
- **Facilitating netting of transactions** – because all the trades are with a single CCP, receipts and payments for transactions in the same share that settle on the same day can be netted against each other.
- **Improved prices** – because more participants are willing to transact anonymously, it is argued that a CCP results in improvements in price.

The CCP typically charges a flat fee to both parties for fulfilling its role and also requires margin payments (similar to derivatives margin) to reduce its potential loss, should one party default.

3.4   Costs of Trading

Learning Objective

4.3.4   Understand the concept of stamp duties and other transaction taxes and costs on securities trades and the potential for their variation between types of security

Whenever a trade is undertaken in a security, be it a share or a bond, there will be costs. There are what might be described as tacit fees in the difference between the bid and offer prices: if an investor buys shares and pays the offer price, that investor would only be able to sell the shares at the lower bid price. There is also the dealing cost in the form of commission that needs to be paid to the broker arranging the transaction, but in particular environments there may be additional costs as outlined below:

*   **Broker's commission** – commission is typically based on a set percentage of the value of the securities being purchased or sold. The precise percentage varies by broker and market, but it is generally at least 0.5% of the value of the securities traded. It will invariably be higher when the broker is providing the client with research and advice, with these so-called full service brokers likely to charge a higher percentage of perhaps 1.5%. If the broker is offering little or no investment advice, perhaps providing their services over the internet, the firm is described as a discount broker and the fees will be lower. Both types of broker are likely to have a minimum charge that will apply if the value of the securities traded is small. This might be $7.50 or equivalent for a discount broker and perhaps £19.95 for a full service broker.
*   **Account fees** – brokers also tend to charge account fees to their ongoing customers, although a number of brokers will waive these fees where the client undertakes less than a minimum number of trades during a particular period such as a quarter or year.
*   **Exchange fees, regulatory fees, clearing fees, taxes/duties** – there are typically minor charges that are either subsumed within the brokers' commissions, or added separately to cover the charges the stock exchange makes per transaction, charges to contribute to the clearing system, and, in many jurisdictions, some form of tax such as the UK's stamp duty or stamp duty reserve tax. Since the financial crisis of 2007–08, there has been an ongoing debate about taxing the financial services profession, generally through a financial transactions tax, to provide for the costs to the taxpayer of bailing out banks. Further charges are also commonly made to contribute to other regulatory matters, like overseeing the conduct of takeovers and mergers or providing an investors' compensation scheme if a broker were to go bust.

4. Indices

Learning Objective

4.4.1 Understand how different indices are created and their purpose: types of index; purpose of weighted indices; purpose of unweighted indices; sector versus national indices; price return, total return and net total return indices; the implications of free-float on market capitalisation

4.1 Stock Market Indices

A stock market index is a method of measuring the performance of a section of the stock market which is segmented to represent a particular group. The group might be the largest companies listed on the market, or perhaps a group of companies that all operate in a similar industry. Many indices are cited by news or financial services firms and are used as benchmarks to measure the performance of portfolios and to provide the general public with an easy overview of the state of equity investments. Their methods of construction may vary according to whether they are capitalisation-weighted or not. Capitalisation-weighted refers to market capitalisation which is the number of shares in issue multiplied by the price per share.

There are various organisations that have become specialists in constructing and maintaining equity indices. This includes managing their composition, making periodic adjustments and making index data public in real time and on a historical basis. For example, Standard & Poor's (S&P), a well-known credit ratings agency in the US, is the manager of the S&P 500 index. This index represents 500 large American companies that trade on the NYSE and Nasdaq, which are considered to be representative of the US markets as a whole. The index is weighted according to the market share capitalisation of each company in the index and is used as a benchmark for comparison against other markets or investments within the US markets. The Dow Jones Industrial Average (DJIA), also known as 'the Dow', is another example of a US index. The DJIA, however, is made up of only 30 companies that trade on US exchanges: either the NYSE or Nasdaq. The Dow is one of the oldest and most-referenced stock market indices in the world. In addition, the Russell organisation in the US is well known for maintaining several indices of US stocks, including the Russell 2000, which represents the smallest capitalisation issues trading in US markets.

The Nikkei 225 is the premier index of Japanese stocks. It has been calculated for more than 60 years and consists of 225 stocks in the first section of the Tokyo Stock Exchange. The constituents are reviewed at the beginning of October each year, based on two factors: liquidity and sector balance.

In the UK, the best-known index is the FTSE (Footsie) 100 index, which consists of the 100 largest companies traded on the LSE as measured by market capitalisation. **FTSE 100** companies represent about 81% of the market capitalisation of the whole of the LSE. The index, maintained by the FTSE Group, is calculated in real time while the LSE is open for trading and published every 15 seconds.

The FTSE 100 started at a base level of 1000 points in January 1984, meaning that the value of the 100 constituent companies at that time equated to 1000 index points. As the value of the constituent companies increases (or decreases), the FTSE 100 increases (or decreases). So, if the value of the constituents grew by 10% in the first nine months following the index publication date, the index would have risen to 1100 index points.

All countries with active stock exchanges have indices that provide a quick and simple way of assessing whether the stock prices are moving up or down. The following table provides information on the composition and geographical scope of many of the largest and best-known global equity indices:

Index name	Composition	Geographical scope
FTSE 100	Largest 100 UK companies listed on the LSE as measured by market capitalisation	UK and multinationals
DJIA	30 large US companies selected by a committee that includes the managing editor of the Wall Street Journal	US-domiciled multinationals
Nikkei Stock 225	225 large and regularly traded Japanese companies traded on the Tokyo Stock Exchange (TSE)	Japanese corporations
Hang Seng	50 companies listed on the Hong Kong Stock Exchange selected on the basis of market value, turnover and financial performance	Hong Kong/China
STOXX	A family of indices, based around the STOXX Global 1800 index that consists of 600 of the largest capitalisation companies from each of three regions – Europe, the Americas and Asia/Pacific	Global developed markets
MSCI World	A market capitalisation-based index including companies from 23 countries, totalling approximately 1,700 companies	Global developed markets
FTSE Eurofirst 300	The 300 largest listed companies by market capitalisation from across Europe	European-domiciled corporations
Cotation Assistée en Continu (CAC) 40 (CAC quarante)	A capitalisation-weighted measure of the 40 most significant values among the 100 highest market caps on Euronext Paris	French-domiciled companies; approximately 45% of its listed shares are owned by foreign investors, more than any other main European index
Deutscher Aktien IndeX (DAX)	The DAX includes the 30 major German companies trading on the Frankfurt Stock Exchange	The base date for the DAX is 30 December 1987 and it was started from a base value of 1,000. The Xetra system calculates the index
S&P 500	Standard & Poor's manages the composition of the index. The 500 constituents are selected by S&P from the largest cap stocks traded in the US	US-traded stocks which are multinational companies operating in global markets

FTSE All-Share	The FTSE All-Share index, originally known as the FTSE Actuaries All-Share index, is a capitalisation-weighted index, comprising around 600 of more than 2,000 companies traded on the LSE	To qualify, companies must have a full listing on the LSE with a sterling- or euro-dominated price on the Stock Exchange Electronic Trading Service (SETS)
Nasdaq Composite	Covers issues listed on the Nasdaq stock market, with over 3,200 components, of which around 300 are non-US stocks. It is an indicator of the performance of stocks of technology companies and growth companies	Since both US and non-US companies are listed on the Nasdaq stock market, the index is not exclusively a US index
Nasdaq 100	Consists of the largest non-financial companies listed on the Nasdaq. It is a modified market value-weighted index	Does not contain financial companies, and includes companies incorporated outside the US
Wilshire 5000	Named after the close to 5,000 shares it contained on launch in 1974, the Wilshire 5000 contains all US equity securities with readily available price data. It is capitalisation-weighted and measures total return	Contains all US-headquartered equities with readily available prices

4.2 National and Sector Indices

A national index represents the performance of the stock market of a given nation and reflects investor sentiment on the state of its economy.

The most regularly quoted market indices are national indices, composed of the stocks of large companies listed on a nation's largest stock exchanges. The concept may be extended well beyond an exchange.

For example, the Wilshire 5000 Index, the original total market index, represents the stocks of nearly every publicly traded company in the US, including all US stocks traded on the NYSE (but not American depositary receipts or limited partnerships) and Nasdaq.

More specialised indices exist which track the performance of specific sectors of the market. Examples include the FTSE EPRA/NAREIT for real estate and the Nasdaq Biotechnology Index for the biotechnology industry.

4.3 Construction of Indices and Weighting

The construction of an index usually involves the total market capitalisation of the companies weighted by their effect on the index, so the larger stocks make a greater difference to the index than the smaller market cap companies.

However, the one major exception to this method of construction and calculation is the DJIA which is price-weighted rather than market capitalisation-weighted. Since it is such a widely quoted index, it is worth considering the method of calculation.

The sum of the prices of all 30 DJIA stocks is divided by the Dow Divisor. The divisor is adjusted in case of **stock splits**, spin-offs or similar structural changes, to ensure that such events do not alter the numerical value of the DJIA. Early on, the initial divisor was composed of the original number of component companies, which made the DJIA at first a simple arithmetic average. The present divisor, after many adjustments, is less than one, meaning the index is larger than the sum of the prices of the components.

That is:

$$DJIA = \frac{\Sigma p}{d}$$

where:

p = the prices of the component stocks.
d = the Dow divisor.

Events, such as stock splits or changes in the list of companies composing the index, will alter the sum of the component prices. In these cases, in order to avoid discontinuity in the index, the Dow Divisor is updated to instantly capture the effect of any events as soon as they occur. The value of the Dow Divisor is altered so that the quotations right before and after the event coincide:

$$DJIA = \frac{\Sigma p_{old}}{d_{old}} = \frac{\Sigma p_{new}}{d_{new}}$$

The DJIA is often criticised for being a price-weighted average, which gives higher-priced stocks more influence over the average than their lower-priced counterparts, but takes no account of the relative industry size or market capitalisation of the components. For example, a $1 increase in a lower-priced stock can be negated by a $1 decrease in a much higher-priced stock, even though the lower-priced stock experienced a larger percentage change. In addition, a $1 move in the smallest component of the DJIA has the same effect as a $1 move in the largest component of the average. Goldman Sachs and Visa are among the highest-priced stocks in the average and therefore have the greatest influence on it. Alternatively, General Electric and Cisco are among the lowest-priced stocks in the average and have the least amount of sway in the price movement. Many critics of the DJIA therefore recommend the float-adjusted market value-weighted S&P 500 or the Wilshire 5000 as better indicators of the US stock market.

All FTSE Equity Index constituents are fully free-float-adjusted, in accordance with the FTSE's Index rules, to reflect the actual availability of stock in the market for public investment. Each FTSE constituent weighting is adjusted to reflect restricted shareholdings and foreign ownership, so as to ensure an accurate representation of investable market capitalisation.

4.4   Total Return Index

A total return index is one that calculates the performance of a group of stocks, assuming that dividends are reinvested into the index constituents. For the purposes of index calculation, the value of the dividends is reinvested in the index on the ex-dividend date. Total return index data is not available at the stock level.

Some indices, such as the S&P 500, have multiple versions. These versions can differ, based on how the index components are weighted and on how dividends are accounted for. For example, there are three versions of the S&P 500 Index:

- **price return**, which measures the price performance and, therefore, disregards income from dividends
- **total return**, which measures the performance of both price return and dividend reinvestment, and
- **net total return**, which accounts for dividend reinvestment after the deduction of a withholding tax.

4.5   Free-Float and Market Capitalisation

The free-float of a public company is an estimate of the proportion of shares that are not held by large owners and that are not stock with sales restrictions (restricted stock that cannot be sold until it becomes unrestricted stock).

The free-float or a public float is usually defined as being all shares held by investors other than:

- shares held by owners owning 5% or more of all shares (those could be government holdings, institutional investors, strategic shareholders, founders, executives, and other insiders' holdings)
- restricted stocks (granted to executives who can be, but don't have to be, registered insiders)
- insider holdings (it is assumed that insiders hold stock for the very long term).

4.5.1   Free-Float Factor

For most market capitalisation-weighted indices, the total market capitalisation of a company is included, irrespective of who is actually holding the shares and whether they are freely available for trading.

The free-float factor represents the proportion of shares that is free-floated as a percentage of issued shares and is then rounded to the nearest multiple of 5% for calculation purposes. To find the free-float capitalisation of a company, first find its market cap (number of outstanding shares x share price) then multiply by its free-float factor.

A free-float adjustment factor is introduced into the calculations of most of the major global equity indices.

For example, the following press release from STOXX ltd, which maintains the various Euro Stoxx indices, reflects the adjustment to the free-float factor for Volkswagen in 2008, and the changes that this had on various indices.

Example

ZURICH (October 28, 2008) – STOXX ltd, the leading provider of European equity indices, today announced it was to change Volkswagen's free-float factor to 0.3732 from 0.4963. This decision reflects the changes in the shareholder structure of Volkswagen and results in a lower weighting of Volkswagen in the respective indices.

Indices affected are the Dow Jones EURO STOXX 50, Dow Jones STOXX 600 Large, Dow Jones STOXX Total Market Large, Dow Jones STOXX Sustainability and its respective sub- and sector-indices. The adjustment will be effective as of the opening of trading on Friday, 31 October, 2008.

In essence, free-float market cap equates to the total value of buying all the shares of a particular company which are traded in the open market.

The free-float method is seen as a better way of calculating market capitalisation, because it provides a more accurate reflection of market movements and is more representative of the investable universe. When using a free-float methodology, the resulting market capitalisation is smaller than what would result from a full market capitalisation method. This is useful for performance measurement, as it provides a benchmark more closely related to what money managers can actually buy.

5. Government Bonds

Learning Objective

4.5.1 Know the functions, obligations and benefits of the following in relation to government bonds: primary dealers; broker-dealers; inter-dealer brokers; government issuing authorities

5.1 Participants in Government Bond Markets

In addition to the government itself, there are four major groups of participants that facilitate deals in the government bond markets:

1. The government's issuing agency.
2. Primary dealers – such as gilt-edged market makers (or GEMMs) in the UK.
3. Broker-dealers.
4. Inter-dealer brokers.

The roles of these participants will be illustrated in a series of examples covering UK, US, Japanese and eurozone government bond markets.

Government Issues in the UK

Issuing Agency

The Debt Management Office (DMO) is the issuing agency for the UK government in respect of its government bonds. It is an executive agency of the UK Treasury, making new issues of UK government securities, which are known as 'gilt-edged securities' or just 'gilts'. Once issued, the secondary market for dealing in gilts is overseen by two bodies, the DMO and the LSE.

It is the DMO that enables certain LSE member firms to act as primary dealers, known as gilt-edged market makers or simply GEMMs. The DMO then leaves it to the LSE to prescribe rules that apply when dealing takes place.

Gilt-Edged Market Makers (GEMMs)

The GEMM, once vetted by the DMO and registered as a GEMM with the LSE, becomes a primary dealer and is required to provide two-way quotes to customers (clients known directly to it) and other member firms of the LSE throughout the normal trading day. There is no requirement to use a particular system for making those quotes available to clients, and GEMMs are free to choose how to disseminate their prices.

The obligations of a GEMM can be summarised as follows:

- To make effective two-way prices to customers on demand, up to a size agreed with the DMO, thereby providing liquidity for customers wishing to trade.
- To participate actively in the DMO's gilt issuance programme, broadly by bidding competitively in all auctions and achieving allocations commensurate with their secondary market share – effectively informally agreeing to underwrite gilt auctions.
- To provide information to the DMO on closing prices, market conditions and the GEMM's positions and turnover.

The privileges of GEMM status include:

- exclusive rights to competitively bid directly with the DMO at gilt auctions and other DMO operations, either for the GEMM's own account or on behalf of clients
- an exclusive facility to trade as a counterparty of the DMO in any of its secondary market operations
- exclusive access to the services of gilt inter-dealer brokers (IDBs).

A firm can register as a GEMM to provide quotes in either:

- all gilt-edged securities, or
- gilt-edged securities excluding index-linked gilts, or
- index-linked gilts only.

There are exceptions to the requirement to provide two-way quotes to customers. In particular the obligation does not include quoting to other GEMMs or gilt IDBs.

Broker-Dealers

These are non-GEMM LSE member firms that are able to buy or sell gilts as principal (dealer) or as agent (broker). When acting as a broker, the broker-dealer will be bound by the LSE's best execution rule, ie, to get the best available price at the time.

When seeking a quote from a GEMM, the broker-dealer must identify at the outset if the deal is a small one, defined as less than £1 million nominal.

Gilt Inter-Dealer Brokers (IDBs)

Gilt IDBs arrange deals between gilt-edged market makers anonymously. They are not allowed to take principal positions, and the identity of the market makers using the service remains anonymous at all times. The IDB will act as agent, but settle the transaction as if it were the principal. The IDB is only allowed to act as a broker between GEMMs, and has to be a separate company and not a division of a broker-dealer.

Government Issues in the US

The Federal Reserve is the coordinator of the issuance of US Government securities. As with the DMO in the UK, it conducts auctions on a regular basis and appoints primary dealers, which include the major investment banks as conduits in the auction process to place bids and to buy the issue on behalf of their clients or for their own account.

The US government securities are typically issued in one of three forms – bills, notes and bonds – that differ in the length of time between issue and maturity:

*   Treasury bills (T-bills) are issued for terms less than a year.
*   Treasury notes (T-notes) are issued for terms of two, three, five, seven and ten years.
*   Treasury bonds (T-bonds) are issued for terms of 30 years.

T-bills are issued in regular auctions with maturity dates of 28 days (or four weeks, about a month), 91 days (or 13 weeks, about three months), 182 days (or 26 weeks, about six months), and 364 days (or 52 weeks, about one year). T-bills are sold by single price auctions held weekly.

During periods when Treasury cash balances are particularly low, the Treasury may sell cash management bills (or CMBs). These are sold at a discount and by auction just like weekly T-bills. They differ in that they are irregular in amount; term (often less than 21 days); and day of the week for auction, issuance, and maturity. When CMBs mature on the same day as a regular weekly bill, usually Thursday, they are said to be on-cycle.

T-notes and T-bonds pay interest every six months until they mature. T-bonds have the longest maturity of 30 years. Both T-notes and T-bonds are issued by auction.

For T-notes, two-year notes, three-year notes, five-year notes, and seven-year notes are auctioned every month. Ten-year notes are auctioned at original issue in February, May, August, and November, and in reopenings in January, March, April, June, July, September, October and December. In a reopening, additional amounts of a previously issued security are auctioned. Reopened securities have the same maturity date and interest rate as the original securities.

For T-bonds, original issue auctions take place in February, May, August, and November, and reopening auctions in the other eight months.

Government Issues in Japan

Japanese Government Bonds (JGBs) are issued by the Bank of Japan (BoJ) and, as the name implies, they are the bonds issued by the government, which is responsible for interest and principal payments. Interest is paid every six months, and principal is repaid at maturity.

JGBs are available with various maturity periods. Coupon-bearing bonds, which feature semi-annual interest payment and principal payment at maturity, have maturities of two, five, five (for retail investors), ten, ten (inflation-indexed), ten (for retail investors), 15 (floating rate), 20, 30 and 40 years.

The Japanese Government also offers a separate strips programme.

Government Issues in the Eurozone

The eurozone consists of the 19 states which have adopted the euro as their currency and for whom their monetary policy is determined by monthly meetings of the European Central Bank (ECB). Each of the member states issues government bonds which have the credit rating associated with the country of issue rather than the eurozone as a whole. In the syllabus, the focus is on Germany and France.

German Government securities offer original maturities ranging from three months to 30 years. In the money market segment, the Federal Government issues Treasury discount paper (Bubills) with maturities of six and 12 months. The offering of capital market products begins with Federal Treasury notes (Schatz) with a maturity of two years, followed by five-year Federal notes (Bobls) (Bundesobligationen) and Federal bonds (Bunds) with maturities of ten and 30 years.

The German Federal Government usually places single issues by auction. Only credit institutions domiciled in an EU member state can be members of the auction group and participate directly in these auctions. The Bund uses a multiple price auction procedure. In other words, bids for Bunds, Bobls and Schatz accepted by the government are allocated at the price quoted in the respective bid and are not settled at a uniform price. Bids priced above the lowest accepted price are allotted in full, while bids priced below the lowest accepted price receive no allotment. Non-competitive bids are allotted at the weighted average price of the accepted price bids. The government reserves the right to reallot the bids at the lowest accepted price as well as the non-competitive bids, eg, to allot them only at a certain percentage rate. The same procedure is applied on a yield basis for Bubills.

To remain a member of the auction group, a credit institution must subscribe to at least 0.05% of the total issuance allotted at the auctions in a calendar year, weighted according to maturity. Members who do not reach the required minimum allotment drop out of the auction group Bund issues. There are no other requirements placed on the members of the auction group.

French Government securities consist of Obligations Assimilable du Trésor (OATs), Bons du Trésor à Taux Fixe et à Intérêts Annuels (BTANs) and Bons du Trésor à Taux Fixe et à Intérêts Précomptés (BTFs).

OATs, or fungible T-bonds, are the government's long-term debt instruments with maturities from seven to 50 years. Most OATs are fixed-rate bonds redeemable on maturity. OATs are auctioned on the first Thursday of each month.

BTANs, or negotiable fixed-rate medium-term T-notes with annual interest, represent medium-term government debt. On issue, their maturity is either two or five years. They are auctioned on the third Thursday of each month.

BTFs, or negotiable fixed-rate discount T-bills, are the government's cash management instrument. They are used to cover short-term fluctuations in the government's cash position (less than one year), mainly due to differences in the pace with which revenues are collected and expenses are paid and in the debt amortisation schedule. On issue, BTFs have a maturity of less than one year. They are auctioned every Monday.

The principal method of issuing French Government securities is the bid price system where participants compete in the auction, on an equal footing, through a transparent system of open bidding according to a planned issuance programme.

In the bid price system the highest bids are first served, followed by lower bids and so on, up to Agency France Trésor's target amount. Participants pay different prices, precisely reflecting their bids. Only institutions affiliated to Euroclear France and holding accounts with the Banque de France are eligible to bid.

6. Corporate Bond Markets

6.1 Characteristics

Learning Objective

4.6.1 Understand the characteristics of corporate bond markets: decentralised dealer markets and dealer provision of liquidity; the impact of default risk on prices; the differences between bond and equity markets; dealers rather than market makers; bond pools of liquidity versus centralised equity exchange; relevance of the retail bond market

The price of a corporate bond is based on the equivalent government bond, less a discount to represent the risk that the corporate may default, compared with the default-risk-free nature of the government bond. Unlike the market for equities, the method of dealing in corporate bonds tends to be away from the major exchanges in what is commonly described as a decentralised dealer market. The dealers provide liquidity by being willing to buy or sell the bonds. The systems that the dealers use to display their willingness to deal are numerous, with each being described as a separate pool of liquidity.

6.1.1 Default

In the corporate bond market, unlike the government bond markets where it is often assumed that no sovereign borrower will default, the determination of the likelihood that a corporate borrower may default is a vital part of the pricing mechanism.

6.1.2   Differences between Equity and Bond Markets

The primary difference between the corporate bond market and the equity market relates to the nature of the security being traded. A corporate bond usually has a specified income stream in the form of coupon payments which will be paid to the holder of the bond, and a bondholder has a more senior claim against the assets of the issuer in the case of a bankruptcy or restructuring.

Investors in equities may receive a dividend payment from the corporation, but this is less certain and can fluctuate. Indeed, less mature companies may not even pay a dividend. The equity-holder also has a greater risk that, if the corporation, which has issued the shares, becomes insolvent or undergoes a restructuring, there may be insufficient assets to be liquidated or reorganised and then distributed to shareholders. In such instances shareholders may find that their equity stakes in a corporation have little or no residual value.

6.1.3   Markets and Dealers of Corporate Bonds

The primary function and role of market makers in corporate bonds is to provide liquidity to the marketplace and to act as a facilitator or agent in trades between the principals. Dealers are those that have been appointed by the corporate issuer to act as distributors on their behalf in the issuance and underwriting of bond issues. There is often a combination of such roles by large financial institutions.

A decentralised dealer market structure is one that enables investors to buy and sell without a centralised location. In a decentralised market, the technical infrastructure provides traders and investors with access to various bid/ask prices and allows them to deal directly with other traders/dealers rather than through a central exchange.

The foreign exchange market is an example of a decentralised market, because there is no single exchange or physical location where traders/investors have to conduct their buying and selling activities; trades can be conducted via an interbank/dealer network that is geographically distributed. Much of the trading in corporate bonds is also conducted through a decentralised dealer network that can provide pools of liquidity for the conduct of trade between buyers and sellers, without the requirement for all trades to be cleared through an exchange.

6.1.4 Retail Bond Market

Although most trading of bonds is done by institutional investors through a decentralised network of dealers, there is also an active retail market provided by stock exchanges. An example of this is the LSE's Order Book for Retail Bonds (ORB).

Example

The ORB is an order-driven trading service offering access to a selected number of gilts, supranational and UK corporate bonds. Trading is available in more than 60 gilts and over 100 corporate bonds on an electronic order-driven system with continuous two-way pricing provided by market makers.

An example of a retail corporate bond and its trading statistics is as follows:

Bond issuer: Tesco Personal Finance – the banking subsidiary of the retailer Tesco

Maturity date: 21 November 2020

Coupon: 5% fixed

Average value traded per month: £7.7 million

Average number of trades per month: 72

Issuers are able to issue bonds via the ORB, which can provide an attractive alternative source of finance for the issuers wanting to raise relatively modest amounts of capital. Issue sizes tend to vary from as little as £20 million up to £300 million, and the minimum denominations that investors can trade are all less than £1,000, typically £100, although the minimum upfront investment is £2,000. The Tesco Personal Finance bond outlined above was a £200 million issue and can be traded in minimum denominations of £100.

7. Dealing Methods

Learning Objective

4.7.1 Know the different trading methods for bonds: OTC inter-dealer voice trading; inter-dealer electronic market; OTC customer-to-dealer voice trading; customer-to-dealer electronic market; on-exchange trading

7.1 Trading Methods for Bonds

Bond trading, including both corporate and government bonds, is either conducted between dealers, some of which is arranged by IDBs, or between dealers and their customers, like asset managers.

Dealer-to-dealer trading can occur in three ways:

- Direct telephone contact.
- Indirect via an IDB voice-broking the deal.
- Via an electronic market, known as an electronic trading platform, such as MTS Cash or BrokerTec. MTS Cash is actually a number of individual trading venues for the inter-dealer market regulated in a number of different jurisdictions.

Dealer-to-customer trading is done either by voice trading between the two parties, or via an electronic platform, such as TradeWeb, BondVision or proprietary single dealer systems developed by some of the larger banks.

A relatively small proportion of corporate bond dealing takes place via stock exchanges.

7.2   Trends in Trading Methods

Learning Objective

4.7.2   Understand the different trends between trading methods: characteristics of electronic trading; OTC; exchange-traded; price-driven via inter-dealer brokers (IDBs) – dealer-to-dealer; request for quote (RFQ) – customer-to-dealer

Traditionally, most trading in fixed-income instruments had been undertaken over-the-counter (OTC) by dealers at large banks buying from, or selling to, clients that they had managed to establish relationships with. The deals were mostly arranged over the telephone, with clients often ringing more than one dealer in an attempt to find the most advantageous price. When dealers wanted to trade with other dealers, the typical method was to speak to a 'voice broker' at an inter-dealer broking firm, who would arrange deals with other dealers.

As technology has improved, electronic trading has become much more important, particularly for the more liquid government bonds like US Treasuries, European sovereign bonds and Japanese Government Bonds (JGBs). It is in these markets where inter-dealer platforms like MTS Cash, BrokerTec and eSpeed have removed the need for voice brokers and replaced them with electronic trading.

Similarly, much of the dealer-to-customer trading in the more liquid bonds migrated to either single-dealer platforms run by individual banks, or multi-dealer platforms, such as Tradeweb Markets and MTS BondVision. However, electronic trading volumes of bonds through single-dealer platforms struggled to recover after the 2008 financial crisis, with banks much less willing to use valuable capital-taking positions in the bond market. In response, the multi-dealer platforms have expanded and some have tried to create competitive advantage by introducing or enhancing value-added services such as straight-through processing (STP), and expanding into OTC derivatives.

The dealer-to-customer systems typically operate on a request for quote (RFQ) basis. Investors will request quotes from a number of dealers' platforms simultaneously. Dealers respond to such requests very quickly and trades can be executed electronically.

These RFQ systems are a significant improvement over voice communication in terms of ease and speed of trading. RFQ systems also bring dealers into direct competition with each other which should deliver price improvement for investors.

7.3 Factors that Influence Bond Pricing

Learning Objective

4.7.3 Know the factors that influence bond pricing: issuer factors: yield to maturity, seniority, structure, technical factors, credit rating; market factors; benchmark bonds; liquidity premiums for highly traded bond issues; indicative pricing versus firm two-way quotes; availability of a liquid repo market and the difficulty in offering illiquid bonds; inability to borrow or cover shorts

Broadly, the factors that influence the prices of bonds can be subdivided into two: issuer factors and market factors.

Issuer Factors

The characteristics of a particular issue and the quality of the issuer encompass the following:

- **Issuer's current credit rating** (which itself will reflect the issuer's specific prospects and highlight the issuer's default risk).
- The **structure and seniority** of the particular issue, for example, the bonds may be high- or low-priority in the event of default by the issuer and may be structured in a way that gives the bonds particular priority in relation to particular assets (such as mortgage-backed bonds).
- The above aspects, combined with prevailing yields available on other benchmark bonds (such as government issues in the same currency, with similar redemption dates), will determine the required yield to maturity (YTM) and, therefore, the appropriate price.

Market Factors

Additionally, market factors that influence bond pricing will include the following:

- **Liquidity** – the more liquid bonds tend to be more expensive, encompassing a liquidity premium and having lower bid/offer spreads.
- **Method of trading** – some bonds attract firm quotes while others are traded with indicative quotes only; the precise price will only be arrived at by negotiation.
- **Ability to borrow** – bonds with active repo markets, and the ability to cover short positions relatively easily, will inevitably react more quickly to underlying interest rate changes and therefore yield changes.

The difficulties that can arise in the trading and pricing of bonds were especially acute during the 1998 crisis which began with the default by Russia on its bonds and led to the collapse of Long-Term Capital Management – a major fund that specialised in the trading of fixed-income instruments and various arbitrage strategies. One of the difficulties that arose during this crisis was the mispricing in the US Treasury market, where the most recently issued long-term bond, known as the on-the-run bond, trades at a premium to those bonds which had been issued previously and which are known as off-the-run. If investors have a preference, during a crisis, for the most liquid instruments, they may hoard the on-the-run bonds and force their price to be out of normal alignment with similar bonds which have slightly different maturity dates. This can result in a breakdown in complex strategies designed to exploit the spreads or price differences across the yield spectrum.

End of Chapter Questions

1. What is a dark pool?
   Answer reference: Section 1.1

2. How does order-driven trading differ from quote-driven trading?
   Answer reference: Section 2.1

3. What is a broker-dealer?
   Answer reference: Section 2.2

4. What is a prime broker?
   Answer reference: Section 2.4

5. What priority is normally given to orders on an exchange's order book?
   Answer reference: Section 3.1.1

6. What is an iceberg order?
   Answer reference: Section 3.2

7. What benefits do central counterparties bring to market participants?
   Answer reference: Section 3.3

8. How many companies are included in the Dow Jones Industrial Average and what markets does it represent?
   Answer reference: Section 4.1

9. What are the four types of participants that facilitate deals in the government bond markets?
   Answer reference: Section 5.1

10. What is the typical method of trading corporate bonds?
    Answer reference: Sections 6.1 and 7

Chapter Five
Corporate Actions

1.	Income Events	139
2.	Capital Events	142
3.	Capital Raising Events	149
4.	Share Capital and Changes to Share Ownership	159

This syllabus area will provide approximately 9 of the 100 examination questions

5

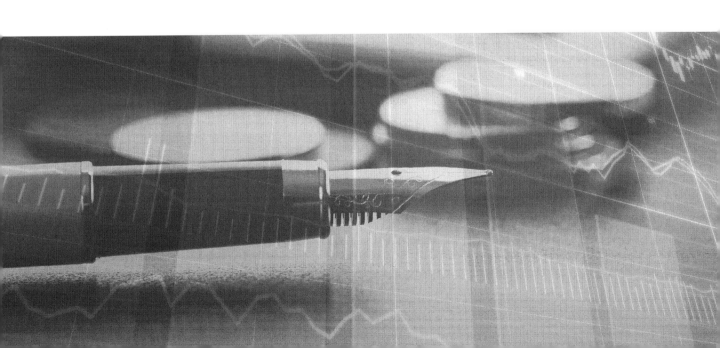

Corporate actions are events that are instituted by an issuer of securities, such as a company with shares in issue or an organisation with bonds in issue, that directly impact those securities. Perhaps the most obvious examples are when a company pays a dividend to its shareholders or a coupon to its bondholders. These are referred to as income events. Other corporate actions include those that bring about changes to the **share capital** of a company (capital events and capital raising events), such as when the company gives away new shares to existing shareholders for nothing (**scrip issues**), or offers new shares to existing shareholders at a discounted price (rights issues).

1. Income Events

Learning Objective

5.1.1 Understand the main types of dividends and bond coupon payments: characteristics; benefits to the investor; benefits to the issuing company

The two major classes of securities are equities and bonds; both typically incur regular costs for the issuer and regular benefits to the investor in the form of income events. If the investor holds equities, the income events will come in the form of dividend payments from the issuer to the shareholding investor. If the investor holds bonds, the income events are a series of coupon payments.

1.1 Bonds

The income from bonds is generally more predictable than income from equities. The contractual nature of a bond's coupon means that the investor knows in advance how much income is expected, based on the coupon rate per period and the nominal value of the bonds held. Most bonds pay coupons either semi-annually or annually, and the coupon is a fixed percentage that is set when the bond is issued.

Fixed-coupon bonds clearly give the investor the benefit of predictability of both the amount and the timing of the income. The investor knows how much income to expect and when it will be paid. An additional benefit for the investor could be that the bond is currently paying an attractive coupon relative to the prevailing level of interest because interest rates have fallen since the bond was issued.

The issuer of fixed-coupon bonds has the benefit of predictability too – knowing exactly how much is needed to pay for the capital provided by the bond and when it needs to be paid. An additional benefit for the issuer may arise when interest rates have generally risen and it managed to lock in an attractively low coupon when the bond was issued.

Awkwardness in the usually straightforward income events for bonds can arise in two situations – when the bonds are floating-rate notes (FRNs) and when the issuer is having difficulty in meeting the contractual payment of the coupons due to profitability and cash flow constraints.

FRNs specify a coupon based on a published rate of interest, usually based on a margin above one of the London Interbank Offered Rates, LIBORs, or Eurozone equivalents, EURIBOR. This clearly removes some of the predictability in the amount for both the investor in the bond and the issuer, as it will vary with changes in the level of the reference interest rate. It is also common for FRNs to have income events more regularly than most other bonds by paying quarterly coupons. By way of an example, below are some extracts from an FRN issued by the Dutch consumer goods giant, Unilever NV:

Example

Unilever NV

Issue of €750,000,000 floating rate notes: due June 2018; issued June 2015.

Extracts from the contractual terms:

- Issuer: Unilever NV, having its corporate seat in Rotterdam, the Netherlands.
- Title of notes: €750,000,000 floating-rate notes due June 2018.
- Specified currency: euro (€).
- Aggregate principal amount: €750,000,000.
- Issue date: 3 June 2015.
- Type of note: floating-rate note.
- Interest: the reference rate is three-month EURIBOR.
- The relevant margin is +0.18% per annum.
- The interest payment dates are 3 March, 3 June, 3 September and 3 December in each year, commencing on 3 September 2015 up to, and including, the maturity date.

The second potential issue that impacts the usual predictability of a bond's income events is where the issuer gets into difficulty and cannot meet the contractual coupon payment. This is clearly more likely if the bonds are lower on the credit rating scale – perhaps classified as junk.

1.2 Equities

The income from equities in the form of dividends is typically much less predictable than the income from bonds. Company dividends are generally variable in amount and will be dependent upon the profitability and cash flow generation of the issuer. That said, many larger, established and listed companies offer predictability in terms of both the frequency with which dividends are paid (for example, US companies tend to pay dividends quarterly), and the amount. This is because most companies do all they can to at least maintain the dividends paid per share from one year to the next. A pattern of growing dividends from year to year would be even better. This is clearly illustrated in the following example for the US-listed oil company, ExxonMobil.

Example

ExxonMobil Dividend Information

Latest announced dividend payment:

Rate	Ex-dividend date	Record date	Payment date
$0.77/share	10 May 2017	12 May 2017	9 June 2017

ExxonMobil dividends per common share:

	2017	2016	2015	2014	2013	2012	2011	2010	2009	2008
1st Quarter	0.75	0.73	0.69	0.63	0.57	0.47	0.44	0.42	0.40	0.35
2nd Quarter	0.77	0.75	0.7	0.69	0.63	0.57	0.47	0.44	0.42	0.40
3rd Quarter		0.75	0.73	0.69	0.63	0.57	0.47	0.44	0.42	0.40
4th Quarter		0.75	0.73	0.69	0.63	0.57	0.47	0.44	0.42	0.40
Total	$1.52	$2.98	$2.88	$2.70	$2.46	$2.18	$1.85	$1.74	$1.66	$1.55

ExxonMobil's dividend payments to shareholders have grown at an average annual rate of 6.4% over the last 34 years.

The benefits to the investors in equity from dividend income events are that the dividends tend to be predictable in terms of frequency and the amount can show some upside potential when the issuer does well.

The benefits to the issuer of equity financing include that the company can reduce, or even stop, the payment of dividends in times of lower profitability and/or the need to conserve cash.

Preference shares are often described as a hybrid instrument because they are essentially a halfway house between equities and bonds. The income events for preference shares are dividend payments, but the rate of dividend will be specified in advance in a similar way to the coupons on a bond. This will increase the predictability of income events for the investor compared with conventional equity. As preference shares are a form of equity, the issuer will retain the flexibility to stop paying dividends in times of stress. This option is not available for the contractual coupons on a bond.

2. Capital Events

2.1 Bond Repayments

Learning Objective

5.2.1 Know the main types of bond repayment events: bullet maturities; callable and puttable bonds; sinking funds

Capital events for bonds are the repayment of the principal. This usually involves a single repayment at the end of the single maturity date specified in the bond's contractual term. This is often described as a bullet issue.

There are variations on the single bullet maturity. This might be because the bond uses a sinking fund. A sinking fund involves the issuer setting aside a certain amount each year. The money is often paid to a separate trustee, who will either hold the money until the scheduled maturity date, or buy back bonds in the open market if they are trading at below par.

Example

The Zambian government has established a sinking fund for repayment of two sovereign eurobonds that it acquired.

Zambia issued its debut bond of US$750 million in 2012 and this was followed by another US$1 billion bond in 2014. The two bonds are expected to mature in 2022 and 2024 respectively, with concerns that the country may not be able to repay the funds due to economic challenges.

Chief Government Spokesperson, Chishimba Kambwili, said in a statement released after a Cabinet meeting that '*cabinet approved the establishment of the sinking fund which was expected to run over nine years and will help to ensure accumulation of resources for the repayment of the bonds at maturity*'.

A sinking fund approach may be combined with a bond issue that is callable. A callable bond is one where the issuer has the right, at specified points during the bond's life, to redeem some, or all, of the bonds at a pre-agreed amount, often at par value. Obviously, a call provision will give the issuer the ability to redeem a bond early if it is relatively expensive.

In contrast, some bonds are issued with put provisions. These puttable bonds give the bond investors the flexibility to require the bonds to be redeemed early, after giving the issuer due notice.

2.2 Equity Capital Events

Learning Objective

5.2.2 Understand the characteristics and rationale for capital restructuring events and the effect on the company's accounts: bonus issues; stock splits; reverse stock splits

In this section, three types of capital events for equities will be considered that do not involve any money flowing between the equity investor and the company. All three – bonus issues, stock splits and reverse stock splits – are undertaken to restructure the equity section of the company's accounts and, more importantly, change the amount for which the shares in the company trade.

2.2.1 Bonus Issues

A bonus issue is where a company issues new shares to its shareholders for no consideration or *pro bono*, raising no further capital. This corporate action is referred to in one of three ways – as a bonus issue, a scrip issue or a capitalisation issue. The reasons for doing this vary; sometimes it is as a public relations exercise to accompany news of a recent success or, more likely, it is simply as a means of reducing the current market price to make its shares more marketable.

It will have an impact on the way shareholders' funds are shown in the company's accounts by converting undistributable capital reserves into share capital. A company simply converts its reserves, which may have arisen from issuing new shares in the past at a premium to their nominal value and/or from the accumulation of undistributed past profits, into new shares. These new shares rank equally with those already in issue and are distributed to the company's shareholders in proportion to their existing shareholdings, free of charge.

Although as a result of the bonus issue the nominal value of the company's share capital will increase proportionately to the number of new shares issued, the net worth or intrinsic value of the business should remain the same. However, given that the company's earnings, or profits, and dividends will now be spread over a wider share capital base, the company's earnings per share (EPS) and dividends per share (DPS) should fall proportionately with the number of new shares in issue. This should result in the market price of the shares reducing by the same proportion, thereby leaving the company's overall market capitalisation unchanged.

Traditionally, once a UK company's share price starts trading well into double figures in pounds sterling, or, in the US, once the market price exceeds $200, it is felt that marketability starts to suffer as investors shy away from the shares they consider excessively expensive. Therefore, a reduction in a company's share price as a result of a bonus issue usually has the effect of increasing the marketability of its shares. It can also raise expectations of higher future dividends. This in turn might result in the share price settling above its new theoretical level and the company's market capitalisation increasing slightly.

2.2.2 Stock Splits and Reverse Stock Splits

An alternative to a bonus issue as a way of reducing a share price is to have a subdivision or stock split, whereby each share is split into a number of shares. For example, a company with shares having a nominal value of US$5 each and a market price of US$10 may have a split whereby each share is divided into five shares, each with a nominal value of US$1. In theory, the market price of each new share should be US$2 (US$10 ÷ 5).

There is little difference between a bonus issue and a stock split in terms of the impact on the share price, but the way the two impact the accounts of the company is different. A bonus issue will increase the share capital line reflected in the accounts, with a corresponding movement from reserves. A stock split will not alter the share capital line – it will be the same total amount but will be subdivided into a larger number of shares, each with a smaller nominal value.

By way of an example, the following is an extract from a CNN article that followed a stock split by technology giant Apple in 2014.

Example ⎯⎯⎯⎯⎯⎯⎯⎯⎯⎯⎯⎯⎯⎯⎯⎯⎯⎯⎯⎯⎯⎯⎯⎯⎯⎯⎯⎯⎯⎯⎯⎯

Apple Just Got 'Cheaper'. Will You Buy?

Apple is about to split its stock. A share of Apple worth about $647.50 will become seven shares at around $92.50.

Apple is the most valuable company in the world. Many consumers use (and love) its products. Yet for average investors, the stock has often been too expensive to touch.

You could buy a 16GB iPad Air with Wi-Fi and standard cellular connections for $629 – and that costs less than one share of Apple. But that just changed.

A share of Apple went from costing $645.57 (as of Friday's closing price) to about $92.44 – give or take a few cents. That is because the company did what is known as a stock split. It issued more shares to existing investors in order to bring down the price of the stock.

Current shareholders received seven shares of Apple for each one they owned. As a result, the stock price is one-seventh of where it used to be.

It is important to note that if you already owned Apple, nothing really changed. You just have more stock at a lower price. The value of your investment – and the market value of Apple – stays the same.

So why is Apple doing this? Companies with stock prices above $100 often decide to split their stock to try and lure more individual investors.

⎯⎯

A reverse split, or consolidation, is the opposite of a split: shares are combined or consolidated. For example, a company with a share price of US$0.10 may consolidate ten shares into one. The market price of each new share should then be US$1 (US$0.10 x 10). A company may do this if the share price has fallen to a low level and it wishes to make its shares more marketable. The impact on the share capital in the company's accounts will be similar to a stock split in that the total will remain the same, but the subdivision will be into a smaller number of shares each with a larger nominal value.

2.3 Impact of Capital Restructuring Events on the Share Price

Learning Objective

5.2.3 Be able to calculate the impact of bonus issues, stock splits and reverse stock splits on the share price

The following table shows the impact of a 1 for 3 scrip issue on a company. The company started with 750,000 $1 shares in issue trading at $3 each, so the market capitalisation of the company is 750,000 x $3 = $2.25 million. The $3 price is generally referred to as the cum bonus price (also known as cum scrip or cum capitalisation). It is the price including the forthcoming bonus before the issue has happened. Assuming the financial statement of the company reflects this market capitalisation, the company will have net assets of $2.25 million. A transfer of $0.25 million from retained profits to the share capital account is required to cover the 250,000 shares given away in the scrip issue. When the market capitalisation of $2.25 million is divided by this enlarged number of 1 million shares, the resulting share price is $2.25. So, the impact of the scrip issue has been to reduce the share price from $3.00 to $2.25. The $2.25 is the theoretical ex-bonus price that is expected after the issue. It is theoretical because it assumes nothing else has altered in the market for the shares. In reality, market movements may not mean that this is the actual resulting share price after the bonus issue.

Bonus, Scrip or Capitalisation			
Impact on the accounts (all amounts in $000)			
	Before	**Issue**	**After**
Net assets	2,250		2,250
Issued share capital			
1m $1 shares	750	250	1,000
Retained profit	1,500	(250)	1,250
Totals	2,250	0	2,250
Impact on the share price			
	Shares (000)	**Price $**	**Value ($000)**
Before	750	3.00	2,250
Scrip issue	250		
After	1,000		2,250
Market price for shares	$2.25		

An alternative way of calculating the theoretical ex-bonus price of the shares is to consider a shareholder that holds the minimum number of shares to qualify for the bonus issue – in this case three shares. As the table below shows, the shareholder started with three shares each worth $3, so the portfolio was worth $9. Since no cash has flowed into the company, after the free share has been received the portfolio should still be worth $9. Now the shareholder has four shares, so the theoretical ex-bonus price is $9 divided by 4 = $2.25.

	Number of shares	Price per share	Total value of holding
Before	3	$3	$9
Bonus	1	Nil	Nil impact
After	4	$9/4 = $2.25	$9

Example

XYZ makes a bonus issue to its shareholders on a 1 for 4 basis to coincide with the launch of a new product. Prior to the announcement of the issue, the company's shares traded at $2.00 per share. If the company had 1 million shares in issue, each with a nominal value of $0.25 in issue prior to the announcement, calculate:

- the number of shares and the nominal value of the company's share capital immediately before and immediately after the announcement
- the new theoretical market price for the shares
- the market capitalisation of the company immediately before and immediately after the announcement based on the pre-existing share price and the new theoretical market price.

Solution

Number of shares

- Immediately before = 1m.
- Afterwards, with one new share given away for every four = 1m + 0.25m = 1.25m

Nominal value of the company's share capital

- Immediately before = 1m x $0.25 = $250,000.
- Immediately after = 1.25m x $0.25 = $312,500.

Theoretical market price after the bonus issue

The theoretical market price will be $2.00 x (4/5) = $1.60.

Using the alternative approach considering the minimum number of shares to qualify for the bonus – here, four shares:

	Number of shares	Price per share	Total value of holding
Before	4	$2	$8
Bonus	1	Nil	Nil impact
After	5	$8/5 = $1.60	$8

Market capitalisation

- Immediately before = 1m x $2.00 = $2m.
- Immediately after = 1.25m x $1.60 = $2m.

The alternative way of lowering the price per share, but avoiding this problem, is to undertake a split. A stock split is achieved by dividing the existing share capital into a larger number of shares with a lower nominal value per share. The lower price should make the shares more accessible for investors and so therefore increase trading activity and liquidity for existing and prospective shareholders.

Example – Stock Split

A company has issued 1 million shares at $1 nominal or par value but now wishes to reduce the price of its shares by replacing that issue with a new issue of 5 million shares at a nominal value of $0.20. The results can be seen on the simplified section of the financial statement as follows. In effect, the company is engaging in a 5:1 stock split. Before the split, assume the shares are trading at $3 each.

Stock split			
Impact on the accounts (all amounts in $000)			
	Before	Issue	After
Net assets	2,000		2,000
Share capital			
1m $1 shares	1,000	(1,000)	
5m $0.20 shares		1,000	1,000
Reserves – retained profits	1,000		1,000
Totals	2,000	0	2,000
Impact on the share price			
	Shares (000)	Price $	Value ($000)
Before	1,000	3.00	3,000
Split issue	4,000		
After	5,000		3,000
Market price for shares	$0.60		

It can be seen that the price per share will drop to $0.60. In essence, each individual $1 nominal share has been split into five shares, each with a nominal value of $0.20. Therefore, the share price will theoretically fall to one fifth of the $3, that is $0.60.

The prior market capitalisation was $3 million based on 1 million shares but there are now 5 million shares issued and the market price for the shares is, therefore, $3 million divided by 5 million shares. The new market price for the shares of $0.60 is above the new nominal value of $0.20 per share, so the company would not encounter any problem in issuing these new shares with this nominal value.

In contrast, a reverse stock split entails consolidating the existing share capital into a smaller number of shares with a higher nominal value per share. The result should be a higher price per share.

Example – Reverse Stock Split

A company has issued 4 million shares at a nominal value of $1 but now wishes to increase the price of its shares by replacing that issue with a new issue of 2 million shares at a nominal value of $2. The results can be seen on the simplified section of the financial statement as follows. In effect, the company is engaging in a 4:1 reverse stock split. Before the reverse split, assume the shares are trading at $1.20 each.

Reverse stock split			
Impact on the accounts (all amounts in $000)			
	Before	**Issue**	**After**
Net assets	5,000		5,000
Share capital			
4 million $1 shares	4,000	(4,000)	
2 million $2 shares		4,000	4,000
Reserves – retained profits	1,000		1,000
Totals	5,000	0	5,000
Impact on the share price			
	Shares (000)	**Price $**	**Value ($000)**
Before	4,000	1.20	4,800
Reverse split issue	2,000		
After	2,000		4,800
Market price for shares	$2.40		

It can be seen that the price per share will rise to $2.40. In essence, each individual $1 nominal value share has been amalgamated into a single $2 nominal value share. Therefore, the share price will theoretically increase to twice the original share price of $1.20, that is $2.40.

The prior market capitalisation was $4.8 million based on 4 million shares, but there are now only 2 million shares in issue and the market price for the shares is, therefore, $4.8 million divided by 2 million shares. The new market price of the shares is $2.40.

Exercise 1

a. A company has a 1 for 1 bonus issue. What is the ex-bonus price (the price after the issue) if the cum-bonus price (the price before the issue) is $10? Here is a blank table to help:

	Number of shares	Price per share	Total value of holding
Before			
Bonus			
After			

b. What difference would it make if the shares were split with two shares replacing each previous share?

c. What difference would it make if a reverse stock split was carried out, with every five original shares becoming a single new share?

The answers to this exercise can be found at the end of this chapter.

3. Capital Raising Events

3.1 Rights Issues

Learning Objective

5.3.2 Understand the characteristics of rights issues: reasons for a rights issue; structure of rights issue; stages of rights issue; pre-emptive rights; trading nil-paid

Before considering rights issues, it is important to consider the concept of pre-emptive rights. Pre-emptive rights are legally required in many jurisdictions around the world and give existing shareholders the right to subscribe for new shares. What this means is that, unless the shareholders agree to permit the company to issue shares to others, they will be given the option to subscribe for any new share offering before it is offered to the wider public. The purpose of this is to ensure that the level of influence or control that a shareholder has is not diluted by any issue without that shareholder's prior knowledge and agreement.

Example of Dilution

Suppose an investor holds 400 shares out of a total of 10,000 shares in XYZ plc, a 4% stake in the company. XYZ then decides to issue 10,000 further shares. That means that there are now 20,000 shares in issue. The investor's original 400 shares now represents a 2% stake rather than a 4% stake. This is dilution.

The existence of **pre-emption rights** means that listed companies cannot issue equity shares, convertibles or warrants for cash, other than to the current equity shareholders of the company, except with the prior approval of the current shareholders in a shareholders' meeting. Jurisdictions typically require a **special resolution** from shareholders before allowing new shares to be allotted in cash to anyone other than the existing shareholders in proportion to their existing holding.

However, it is quite common to see the waiving of pre-emption rights as a proposed special resolution at the annual general meetings (AGMs) of listed companies, although best practice is to limit such issuance to 5% in any single year unless there is an identified purpose for the issue detailed in the resolution.

Example – Pre-emptive Rights

Investor X holds 400 ordinary shares of the 10,000 issued ordinary shares in ABC plc. Investor X therefore owns 4% of ABC plc.

If ABC plc planned to increase the number of issued ordinary shares by allowing investors to subscribe for 10,000 new ordinary shares, Investor X has the pre-emptive right to be offered 4% of the new shares, ie, another 400 shares. This would enable Investor X to retain their 4% ownership of the enlarged company.

In summary:

	Before the issue	Further issue	After the issue
Investor X	400 (4%)	400	800 (4%)
Other shareholders	9,600 (96%)	9,600	19,200 (96%)
Total	10,000 (100%)	10,000	20,000 (100%)

A rights issue is one method by which a company can raise additional capital, complying with pre-emptive rights, with existing shareholders having the right to subscribe for new shares.

A rights issue is an offer by a company of new shares for cash to the existing shareholders in proportion to their existing holding. The shares are usually priced at a discount to the current market price. The holder of the right, as the name suggests, has the right, but not the obligation, to purchase additional shares directly from the company at the discounted price. The right will have an expiry date, after which it will no longer be valid. Rights are short-term privileges and can be traded, usually on the exchange on which the company is listed, until they expire.

A rights issue is an attractive way for a company to raise new finance for the following reasons:

- There is no dilution of shareholders' interest, ie, someone who held 20% of the shares before the issue will hold 20% after (assuming they take up their rights).
- The issue is at a discount to the current market price to make it attractive.
- Existing ordinary shareholders of a company will receive a provisional allotment of new shares. After being granted such an allotment, each may decide to exercise the rights to add to their holding, but there is no obligation to take up the offer.
- A shareholder who does not want to subscribe more cash and take up their rights can sell them, receiving cash as payment for the dilution of interest that they will suffer.
- Such issues are generally underwritten to cater for those individuals who do not want to exercise their rights, thus the company can be sure of raising all the finance it requires.
- In essence, a rights issue is a way of avoiding the negative effects of dilution on shareholders.

The rationale for a rights issue is usually to fund expansion, perhaps to take over a rival or to diversify into a new business area. Existing shareholders receive a provisional allotment letter, which tells them how many shares they are entitled to and what the price will be.

Existing shareholders do not have to participate in the rights issue but can sell the rights nil-paid, either in part or in full. A fuller discussion of the method of calculating the nil-paid value is discussed below, but the essential feature is that the issuer provides the current shareholders with a transferable security (known as a provisional allotment letter) which can be sold to other investors.

By way of an example, the following are some extracts from a recent rights issue announcement by Singaporean-listed company, Tat Hong Holdings:

Example – Proposed Rights Issue Announcement

- The board of directors ('directors') (the 'board') of Tat Hong Holdings ltd (the 'company', and together with its subsidiaries, the 'group') wishes to announce that the company is proposing a renounceable underwritten rights issue of up to 125,776,884 new ordinary shares in the issued and paid-up capital of the company (the 'rights shares') at an issue price of S$0.33 for each rights share (the 'issue price'), on the basis of one (1) rights share for every five (5) existing ordinary shares in the issued share capital of the company (the 'shares'), held by shareholders of the company (the 'shareholders').
- Issue price – the issue price for each rights share is S$0.33, payable in full upon acceptance and application. The issue price represents a discount of approximately 27.5% to the closing market price of S$0.455 for trades done on the main board of the SGX-ST on the last market day on which the shares were transacted on the SGX-ST prior to the release of this announcement.
- Rationale of the rights issue – the rights issue has been proposed by the company as part of its ongoing and prudent balance sheet management to strengthen its financial position, enlarge its capital base and further enhance the financial flexibility of the group. In particular, the net proceeds of the rights issue will be used for (a) debt repayment; and (b) working capital and general corporate purposes including but not limited to (i) compliance and operating costs; and (ii) payment of trade and other payables, if necessary so as to provide the group with more flexibility and enhance its ability to formulate, strategise and execute its business plans.

3.1.1 Mechanics of a Rights Issue

New shares are offered in proportion to each shareholder's existing shareholding, usually at a price deeply discounted to that prevailing in the market, to ensure that the issue will be fully subscribed and sometimes to reduce, or even avoid, the cost of underwriting the shares. The number of new shares issued and the price of these shares will be determined by the amount of capital to be raised.

The right to participate in such an issue is only conferred upon those shareholders who hold the issuing company's shares cum-rights – that is, those who hold the company's shares before trading in the shares is conducted on an ex-rights, or without-rights, basis. The ex-rights period begins on, or shortly after, the day on which the rights issue announcement is made and runs for a further period, tending to be a minimum of ten business days, through to the acceptance date, the date by which the shareholder should have decided whether or not to take up these new shares.

Those entitled to participate in the rights issues are advised of their entitlement by means of a provisional allotment letter. The provisional allotment letter is renounceable and transferable and it sets out the shareholder's existing shareholding, the rights allotted over the new shares and the acceptance date. The ex-rights period begins on the day after the allotment letter is posted.

As these new shares rank equally, or *pari passu*, with the existing shares in issue, once the existing shares are declared ex-rights, the market price should fall to reflect the dilution effect that the new shares will have on the prevailing share price. The price to which the shares should fall is termed the theoretical ex-rights price, and its method of calculation is as follows:

$$\frac{\left[\left(\begin{array}{c}\text{No. shares held cum-rights}\\ \times\\ \text{cum-rights share price}\end{array}\right) + \left(\begin{array}{c}\text{No. rights allocated}\\ \times\\ \text{rights issue price}\end{array}\right)\right]}{\text{Total no. shares held assuming rights exercised}}$$

The difference between the theoretical ex-rights price and the rights issue price is known as the **nil-paid value**, and the calculation and significance of this will be illustrated in the following sections.

As noted above, shareholders typically have a minimum of ten business days to decide how to react to the announcement following receipt of the provisional allotment letter and must choose between one of the four following courses of action:

- **Option One – Take up the rights in full**
  Take up the rights in full by purchasing all of the shares offered. To take up the rights in full, the shareholder simply sends the company the provisional allotment letter, with a cheque, by the due date.
- **Option Two – Sell the rights nil-paid in full**
  If a shareholder entitled to take up the rights issue decides not to, they can sell the rights to these new shares nil-paid. The purchaser of the nil-paid rights will be able to take up the shares at the discounted price. Essentially they have a short-dated option on these new shares that can only be exercised, or traded, during the three-week ex-rights period. To sell the rights nil-paid in full the shareholder must sign the form of renunciation on the reverse of the provisional allotment letter and send it to their broker by the due date.

- **Option Three – Sell part of rights nil-paid to preserve current stake without dilution**
  The shareholder can sell sufficient of the rights nil-paid to finance the take-up of the remaining rights. This course of action would be taken by a shareholder wishing to retain their shareholding in the company but without any desire to invest any further capital at this stage. When selling the rights nil-paid in part, the shareholder does exactly the same as when selling them in full but requests that their broker split the allotment letter in accordance with the number of rights sold and those to be taken up. One of the split allotment letters will go to the purchaser of the rights, and the other to the original shareholder.

- **Option Four – Take no action**
  Any shareholder not taking any action by the acceptance date stipulated in the provisional allotment letter will automatically have their rights sold nil-paid. The proceeds, less any expenses incurred by the company, are then distributed to all such shareholders on a pro rata basis. For the smaller shareholder not wishing to increase their shareholding in the company, this is often the most economical way to proceed.

3.1.2 Impact of a Rights Issue on the Share Price

Learning Objective

5.3.3 Be able to calculate the impact of a rights issue on the share price

To illustrate the impact on the share price for a company which undertakes a rights issue, the following are the key variables in the example discussed below:

- Prior to the rights issue the company has 1 million shares in issue with a nominal value of £1.00 each. The nominal value is also referred to as the par value – it is the minimum price that the issuing company must receive when issuing shares.
- The share premium account (sometimes termed additional paid-in capital) shows a balance of £0.5 million. The share premium account is the capital that a company raises upon issuing shares that is in excess of the nominal value of the shares.
- The company wishes to raise new capital for expansion and undertakes a 1 for 4 rights issue at a price of £1.50 in order to raise £375,000.
- The company's accounts before the rights issue show that net assets are £2 million and retained profits are £0.5 million.
- The market price of the shares prior to the rights offering is £3.00 per share.

What is the impact on the accounts and the theoretical market price per share of this issue?

A 1 for 4 rights issue means that for every four shares previously in existence, one new share will be issued. In our example, 1 million shares were previously in issue, so 250,000 new shares will be issued at a price of £1.50 in order to raise the £375,000 cash required.

In terms of the accounts, the 250,000 new share issue will increase the share capital to 1.25 million shares, the retained profit (retained earnings) will remain unchanged but the share premium account will need to be adjusted. The reason for this adjustment is that for the £375,000 raised, each of the 250,000 new shares can be issued at the nominal value of £1 but the additional £125,000 raised in excess of the nominal value of the shares is allocated to the share premium account as indicated in the simple balance sheet perspective in the table below.

The total capitalisation of the company will have increased to £2.375 million and can be broken down according to the upper part of the table which reflects the rights issue from an accounting perspective.

The impact on the share price can be seen from the calculation of the theoretical market price in the lower part of the table. The price for the shares should have fallen from £3.00 per share before the rights issue to £2.70 after the issue to reflect the new capitalisation divided by the greater number of shares now outstanding.

Rights issue			
Impact on the accounts (all amounts in £'000)			
	Before	**Issue**	**After**
Net assets	2,000	375	2,375
Share capital			
1m £1 ordinary shares	1,000	250	1,250
Share premium	500	125	625
Retained profit	500		500
Totals	2,000	375	2,375
Impact on the share price			
	Shares ('000)	**Price £**	**Value (£'000)**
Before	1,000	3.00	3,000
Rights issue	250	1.50	375
After	1,250		3,375
Market price for shares	**£2.70**		

Another perspective on this can be seen simply by looking at the following formula, which only requires knowledge of the share price before the rights issue and the actual terms of the rights issue.

The formula for the theoretical ex-rights price is as follows:

$$\frac{\left[\left(\begin{array}{c} \text{No. shares held cum-rights} \\ x \\ \text{cum-rights share price} \end{array}\right) + \left(\begin{array}{c} \text{No. rights allocated} \\ x \\ \text{rights issue price} \end{array}\right)\right]}{\text{Total no. shares held assuming rights exercised}}$$

Description	Number of shares	Price per share (pence)	Total value of holdings (pence)
Shares held cum-rights	4	300	1,200
Rights allocated – new share entitlement	1	150	150
Post rights issue assuming rights taken up	5		1,350
Theoretical ex-rights price =1,350/5		270	

Exercise 2

A company's shares are currently trading at $5.00 each. The company announces a 1 for 3 rights issue at $3.00 per share. What is the theoretical ex-rights price? Here is a blank table to help:

	Number of shares	Price per share	Total value of holding
Before			
Bonus			
After			

The answer to this exercise can be found at the end of this chapter.

3.1.3 Nil-Paid Value

Learning Objective

5.3.5   Be able to calculate the value of nil-paid rights

The nil-paid rights is the theoretical value of the right to buy a share in a rights issue. This is calculated by comparing the theoretical ex-rights price to the price of exercising the right.

As can be seen, it is straightforward to substitute the following values using the minimum number of shares required to qualify for the rights issue (in this case four shares) from the company provided above:

Number of shares held cum-rights	=	4
Cum rights share price	=	£3.00
Number of rights allocated	=	1
Rights issue price	=	£1.50
Total shares assuming rights exercised	=	5
Solving	=	{[4 x £3.00] + [1 x £1.50]}/5 = £13.50/5 = £2.70

Given this example, the price of each nil-paid right should be calculated from the ex-rights share price – price of the new shares = 270p – 150p = 120p.

Obviously, it would not be rational to pay more than 120p for the right to purchase a new share for 150p when the ex-rights price of the existing shares in issue is 270p.

Exercise 3

A company's shares are currently trading at $8.00 each. The company announces a 1 for 6 rights issue at $4.50 per share. What is the nil-paid value? Here is a blank table to help:

	Number of shares	Price per share	Total value of holding
Before			
Bonus			
After			

The answer to this exercise can be found at the end of this chapter.

3.1.4   Selling Some Rights to Take Up Others (Swallowing the Tail)

Learning Objective

5.3.4   Be able to calculate the maximum nil-paid rights to be sold to take up the balance at nil cost

As discussed in the preceding section, the third possibility for a shareholder in a rights issue (instead of exercising their rights, or selling all of their rights [nil-paid]) is the situation when investors can choose to sell some of their entitlement and use the cash raised to take up the rest of the offer. In effect, they can buy a sufficient number of shares in the offering to preserve their position without dilution, but without having to invest additional funds into the business.

The number of nil-paid rights to be sold to take up the balance at nil cost is given by the equation:

$$\frac{\text{Issue price of new shares} \times \text{number of shares allocated}}{\text{Theoretical ex-rights price}}$$

As nil-paid rights cannot be sold in fractions, the number must be rounded up to the nearest integer or whole number value.

The actual process of preserving one's position without suffering any dilution but without having to invest new proceeds is sometimes known as swallowing the tail and can be demonstrated in the following table which is expanded from the one shown earlier. The table assumes the investor's current holdings, cum-rights, is 2,000 shares, and all of the information is the same as contained in the rights issue case study discussed, that is a 1 for 4 rights issue at an exercise price of 150p and a cum-rights share price of 300p.

Description	Number of shares	Price per share (pence)	Total value of holdings (£)
Shares held cum-rights	2,000	300	6,000.00
Rights allocated – new share entitlement	500	150	750.00
Post rights issue assuming rights taken up	2,500		6,750.00
Theoretical ex-rights price = 675,000/2,500		270	
Nil-paid rights value = 270 – 150		120	
Number of nil-paid rights to be sold*	278		
Amount raised from selling nil rights = 278 x 120			333.60
Number of nil-paid rights taken up to avoid dilution = 500 – 278	222		
Cost of purchasing rights to avoid dilution = 222 x 150			333.00
Gain/(loss) from financing to preserve current stake			0.60
Total value of shares post rights = (2,000 + 222) x £2.70			5,999.40
Total value of position post rights			6,000.00
Net change in position			0.00

* Number of shares to be sold is calculated by taking the issue price of the new shares (here £1.50) multiplied by the number of shares allocated (here 500) and dividing the result by the theoretical ex-rights price (here £2.70). The result is 277.7778, rounded to the nearest whole number = 278.

As can be seen from the bottom row, the net change in the investor's position is zero, ignoring transaction costs. By selling 278 nil-paid rights and using the proceeds to purchase 222 new shares, accompanied by the tiny cash gain of 60p on the proceeds, the investor is in exactly the same position as before the rights issue but now holds an additional 222 shares at no additional cost.

Exercise 4

A company's shares are currently trading at $5.00 each. The company announces a 1 for 3 rights issue at $3.00 per share. For a shareholder with 3,000 shares, how many shares should be sold nil-paid to prevent dilution?

The answer to this exercise can be found at the end of this chapter.

3.2 Placings and Open Offers

Learning Objective

5.3.1 Understand the main features and purpose of open offers and placings

As covered in chapter 3, when an already listed company wants to raise further capital by issuing equity, it can choose to do so with a placing of its shares. This involves a company marketing the issue directly to a broker, an issuing house or other financial institution which, in turn, places the shares with selected clients. Placings can be used for initial public offerings (IPOs), but also for secondary (or follow-on) issues. If the company is based in a jurisdiction that gives shareholders pre-emptive rights, a resolution at a shareholders' meeting will be required to enable the placing to happen.

In many European, Middle Eastern and Far Eastern markets, a variation on the rights issue theme can also be used when a company wants to raise finance: an open offer. An open offer is made to existing shareholders and gives the holders the opportunity to subscribe for additional shares in the company or for other securities, normally in proportion to their holdings. In this way, it is similar to a rights issue, but the difference is that the right to buy the offered securities is not transferable and so cannot be sold.

For normal open offers, holders of the shares cannot apply for more than their entitlement. However, an open offer can be structured so that holders may be allowed to apply for more than their pro rata entitlement, with the possibility of being scaled back in the event of the offer being oversubscribed.

4. Share Capital and Changes to Share Ownership

4.1 Share Buybacks

Learning Objective

5.4.1 Understand why share buybacks are undertaken: governing regulation: resolution at AGM; limits on percentage of shares and price; use of company's own money; key aspects of share buybacks – criteria to comply with: different structures regarding block trades; accelerated book build – best efforts basis; accelerated book build – back stop price; bought deal

A **share buyback** occurs when a company decides to use cash to repurchase shares from existing shareholders. There are two common scenarios where share buybacks may be considered worthwhile:

1. When the company has reduced its activities (perhaps having sold a major part of its business) and has surplus cash to return to shareholders.
2. When the company wants to reorganise its capital structure to include more debt and less equity. In these circumstances the company can borrow money (by issuing bonds or from banks), and use it to buy back and therefore reduce the number of shares it has in issue.

There will inevitably be restrictions on a company's ability to buy back its own shares, partly to prevent shareholders from being unfairly preferred to creditors, and partly to make sure that the company has gained approval to buy back from its own shareholders. To prevent unfair prejudice against the creditors, regulation limits the amount that can be used to repurchase shares. For example, in the UK, there are various accounting tests that need to be satisfied to prevent erosion of what is referred to as the creditors' buffer. In simple terms, the creditors' buffer is the money originally paid into the company as capital.

Approval from shareholders generally requires a resolution at the AGM to grant permission to buy shares back. Such permissions inevitably place limits on the percentage of shares to be purchased and the price paid to those shareholders that sell.

The actual mechanics of undertaking a share buyback, once regulatory and shareholder approval has been gained, can follow a variety of forms, such as:

*   **Block trades** – when an investment bank acting for the company will seek to do a small number of large trades with investors, perhaps through an exchange.

- **Accelerated book build** – the investment bank will contact a number of institutions, investors in the company, seeking their willingness to sell at particular price points. If the buyback is sufficiently large to require a syndicate (a group of dealers buying back shares, rather than just one), some of the more junior members may only be willing to be involved on a best efforts basis, and the whole syndicate will have a price which it cannot go above (the back stop price). A best efforts basis means that the dealer(s) will attempt to buy back shares, but do not guarantee any financial compensation, and cannot be held liable if they fail to meet the targeted number of shares they are seeking to buy. This is the opposite of a bought deal, in which the underwriter(s) actually purchase the shares themselves and then attempt to resell them to clients. If all of the inventory bought in a bought deal is not sold, the investment bank(s) guarantee the numbers of shares they will buy at an agreed price.

4.2 Stake Building

Learning Objective

5.4.2 Understand how and why stakebuilding is used: strategic versus acquisition; direct versus indirect: direct – outright purchase, ie, dawn raid; indirect – CFDs; disclosure thresholds, including mandatory takeover threshold

A stake is simply a shareholding, and many investors buy stakes in companies simply for the investment potential. Sometimes, however, stakes are built in companies for reasons over and above the simple investment potential.

Strategic stakes may be accumulated in order to prevent a company being taken over by a competitor and to influence the company concerned. This may be in order to protect supplies. The company may be a key supplier of raw materials to the strategic stakeholder, without which the strategic stakeholder may have difficulty obtaining the quantity and quality of raw materials it seeks.

Another example would be where a stake is accumulated in the hope of bringing about an acquisition. An acquisition of another company is achieved by purchasing more than 50% of the shares, and thereby gaining control of the votes and the company. It is usual to talk in terms of the acquiring company being the predator or offeror and the company being acquired as the target or offeree.

For a potential predator building a stake in order to eventually acquire a target company, there are generally certain regulatory restrictions.

Example – Stakebuilding Restrictions in the UK

First, as a stake becomes more significant, there are disclosure requirements. In the UK these disclosure requirements are contained within the FCA's Disclosure and Transparency Rules. An investor is judged to have a notifiable interest in a public company if they hold 3% or more of its shares. At this point they are obliged to inform the company of their holding. Once the investor's holding is above 3%, they must also inform the company if it rises or falls through a whole percentage point.

Indirect exposure to shares acquired under other financial instruments that have a similar economic effect, such as contracts for differences (CFDs) are included in these disclosure requirements.

The second regulatory restriction, and in addition to the rules relating to notification and disclosure of significant shareholdings, is the rules laid down by the Panel on Takeovers and Mergers (POTAM or PTM) in the UK that apply to stakebuilding during the course of a takeover bid. Under PTM rules, a mandatory offer is required if any person either:

- acquires shares that take their holding to 30% or more of the voting rights of the target company, or
- increases their holding from a starting point of 30% or more, but less than 50%.

If a mandatory bid is required, the consideration offered must be in the form of cash, or there must be a cash alternative. The cash offer must not be less than the highest price paid by the offeror in the previous 12 months.

There are some exceptions to this rule, the main one being for additions to the offeror's stake during the course of a formal offer. In any other instances the PTM's permission is required to acquire shares that breach the rule.

During the course of an offer, dealings in relevant securities by the offeror or the offeree company, or any associates, for their own account must be publicly disclosed. The requirement is that disclosure must be made to the Panel and a Regulatory Information Service (RIS) (such as the LSE's Regulatory News Service (RNS)) by noon on the business day following the transaction.

Relevant securities are the shares of the offeror and offeree, and any derivatives such as options on these shares.

Additionally, PTM rules require that anyone holding more than 1% (before or after the transaction) of the offeree or offeror company shares must disclose any further transactions (excluding acceptance of the offer itself) to the PTM and an RIS by noon on the next business day.

4.3   Takeovers and Mergers

Learning Objective

5.4.3   Know the characteristics of takeovers and mergers

Companies seeking to expand can grow organically or by purchasing or partnering with other existing companies. In the UK, purchases are often referred to as takeovers or mergers. In the US, the term 'takeover' is often referred to as an acquisition, and the initials 'M&A' are often used to describe a merger and/or acquisition or any blending of two existing companies. In both countries, the terms 'takeover/acquisition' and 'merger' are often used interchangeably in the press, however there is a difference between the two.

A takeover or acquisition occurs if one company buys a majority of the shares of another company; it gains control over the other company and is, therefore, termed the parent company, while the other company is its subsidiary. This takeover could be 'friendly' because the directors of the target company are positive about the merits of the takeover and recommend their shareholders accept it. Alternatively, it could be 'hostile' because the directors of the target company recommend rejecting the offer, perhaps because the amounts being offered are considered too low. Clearly, the shareholders of the target company could choose to accept or reject the takeover bid regardless of what their directors are recommending. Hostile takeover bids can be successful and friendly takeover bids can sometimes be unsuccessful.

In a successful takeover, the predator company will buy more than 50% of the shares of the target company. When the predator holds more than half of the shares of the target company, the predator is described as having gained control of the target company. Usually, the predator company will look to buy all, or almost all, of the shares in the target company, perhaps for cash, perhaps using its own shares, or even using a mixture of cash and shares.

Merger is the term reserved for the situation where two companies of a similar size come together to form a larger, merged entity. In a merger it is usual for one company to exchange new shares for the shares of the other. As a result, the two companies effectively come together to form a bigger entity under the joint ownership of the two original groups of shareholders.

Exercise Answers

Exercise 1

a. Bonus issue

	Number of shares	Price per share	Total value of holding
Before	1	$10.00	$10.00
Bonus	1	$0.00	$0.00
After	2	$10/2 = $5	$10.00

The theoretical ex-bonus price would be $5.

b. Share Split

If the shares were split into two, the impact would be the same. The price after the split would be half of the price before = $10/2 = $5.

c. Reverse Share Split

If there was a reverse share split, and five original shares become one new share, the per share price would rise. The new shares will theoretically be worth five times the previous value: 5 x $10 = $50.

Exercise 2

	Number of shares	Price per share	Total value of holding
Before	3	$5.00	$15.00
Bonus	1	$3.00	$3.00
After	4	$18.00/4 = $4.50	$18.00

The theoretical ex-rights price is $18.00 divided by 4 = $4.50.

Exercise 3

	Number of shares	Price per share	Total value of holding
Before	6	$8.00	$48.00
Bonus	1	$4.50	$4.50
After	7	$52.50/7 = $7.50	$52.50

The nil-paid value is the theoretical ex-rights price of $7.50 less the rights price of $4.50 = $3.00.

Exercise 4

	Number of shares	Price per share	Total value of holding
Before	3	$5.00	$15.00
Bonus	1	$3.00	$3.00
After	4	$18.00/4 = $4.50	$18.00

The theoretical ex-rights price is $18.00 divided by 4 = $4.50.

The number of shares to be sold is given by:

(Issue price of new shares x number of shares allocated)/theoretical ex-rights price = 3 x 1000/4.50 = 666.66.

Rounded up to 667 shares sold at the nil-paid value of (4.50-3.00) = 1.50 generates $1,000.50.

That would leave 333 shares to be taken up that will cost 333 x $3 = $999.

The shareholder will be left with an additional $1.50 ($1,000.50 – $999.00).

End of Chapter Questions

1. What is a bonus issue?
   Answer reference: Section 2.2.1

2. What is a stock split and how does it differ from a scrip issue?
   Answer reference: Section 2.2.2

3. Why would a company want to split its shares, or undertake a scrip issue that will result in the share price going down?
   Answer reference: Section 2.3

4. What is dilution in the context of a shareholding?
   Answer reference: Section 3.1

5. What is a rights issue?
   Answer reference: Section 3.1

6. What options exist for a shareholder when a company has a rights issue?
   Answer reference: Section 3.1.1

7. Explain nil-paid value in the context of rights issues.
   Answer reference: Section 3.1.3

8. Why might a company buy back its own shares?
   Answer reference: Section 4.1

9. What are the two main restrictions that companies face when they are considering buying back some of their own shares?
   Answer reference: Section 4.1

10. What is the difference between a takeover and a merger?
    Answer reference: Section 4.3

Chapter Six
Clearing and Settlement

1.	Introduction to Settlement Systems	169
2.	Settlement Models	171
3.	Custodianship	175
4.	Registered Title	179
5.	Designated and Pooled Nominees	180
6.	Cum- and Ex-Dividend	183
7.	Continuous Linked Settlement (CLS)	185
8.	Stock Borrowing and Lending	186

This syllabus area will provide approximately 9 of the 100 examination questions

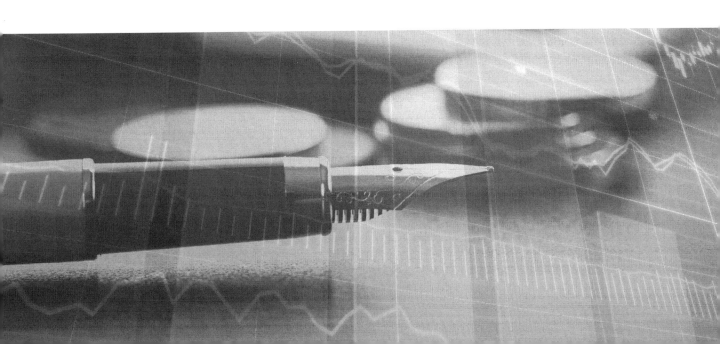

1. Introduction to Settlement Systems

Learning Objective

6.1.1 Understand the main stages of clearing and settlement

Settlement occurs after a deal has been executed. It is simply the transfer of ownership from the seller of the investment to the buyer, combined with the transfer of the cash consideration from the buyer to the seller. However, the process actually consists of several key stages, collectively described as clearing and settlement:

- **Pre-settlement and clearing** – as soon as a trade has been executed, a number of procedures and checks must be conducted before settlement can be completed. These include matching the trade instructions supplied by each counterparty to ensure that the details they have supplied for the trade correspond. It also involves conducting checks to ensure that the seller has sufficient securities to deliver and that the buyer has sufficient funds to cover the purchase cost.
- **Settlement** – the process through which legal title (ie, ownership) of a security is transferred from seller to buyer in exchange for the equivalent value in cash. Usually, these two transfers should occur simultaneously.
- **Post-settlement** – this entails the management of failed transactions and the subsequent accounting of trades.

When a trade has been executed, a key step in the management of risk in the post-execution, pre-settlement stage is for the two sides to the trade to compare trade details, and to eliminate any mismatches, prior to the exchange of cash and securities.

The matching of the buyer's and seller's trade data is typically conducted at two levels:

1. Trading counterparties compare trade details – this may take place bilaterally, via matching facilities extended by the securities settlement system (at the central securities depository (CSD) for example), or via a third-party central matching facility that will compare trade details electronically and issue a report on matching status (ie, whether matched or unmatched). Trades conducted via an electronic order book will effectively be auto-matched – matching engine software is integrated into the electronic order management technology that will provide automated matching of buyers' and sellers' orders in the order book. For centrally cleared transactions, matched instructions may be forwarded to the central counterparty (CCP) for clearing (see below).
2. Custodians acting on behalf of the buyer and seller will compare settlement instructions in order to identify potential mismatches prior to the settlement date.

Clearing (or clearance) is the process through which the obligations held by the buyer and seller to a trade are defined and legally formalised. In simple terms, this procedure establishes what each of the counterparties expects to receive when the trade is settled. It also defines the obligations each must fulfil, in terms of delivering securities or funds, for the trade to settle successfully.

Specifically, the clearing process includes:

- recording key trade information so that counterparties can agree on its terms
- formalising the legal obligation between counterparties
- matching and confirming trade details
- agreeing procedures for settling the transaction
- calculating settlement obligations and sending out settlement instructions to the brokers, custodians and CSD
- managing margin and making margin calls; this relates to collateral paid to the clearing agent by counterparties to guarantee their positions against default up to settlement.

Trades may be cleared bilaterally between the trading counterparties or via a CCP that interposes itself between buyer and seller. When trades are cleared bilaterally, each trading party bears a direct credit risk against each counterparty that it trades with.

CCP services are available in a range of markets in order to mitigate this risk. For example, LCH.Clearnet provides CCP services in the UK and NYSE Euronext European markets for trading in equity, derivatives and energy products, for platforms trading the majority of euro-denominated and sterling bond and repo products, along with commodity and energy derivatives and the bilaterally traded interbank interest rate swaps market.

In the US, clearing of broker-to-broker trades in equities, corporate bonds, municipal bonds, unit investment trusts (UITs) and exchange-traded funds (ETFs) takes place through the National Securities Clearing Corporation (NSCC), a subsidiary of the Depository Trust and Clearing Corporation (DTCC). Eurex Clearing AG, which is part of Deutsche Börse Group, provides a CCP service for exchange-traded equities executed on Xetra that are denominated in euros and listed on Xetra. Also, ISE Xetra is the electronic trading system for the Irish Stock Exchange, and Eurex Clearing provides clearing services for trades conducted via this system. In its role as clearing house, Eurex Clearing additionally assures the fulfilment and clearing of trades on the Eurex derivatives exchange, Eurex Bonds and Eurex Repo.

Since the implementation of the Markets in Financial Instruments Directive (MiFID), a number of new CCP facilities have been established in Europe, predominantly to clear trade flow from multilateral trading facility (MTF) platforms. These CCPs include the European Multilateral Clearing Facility and EuroCCP, which merged in December 2013 to form EuroCCP N.V.

There are two further basic elements to the settlement of trades that can differ across different instruments and/or markets:

- **Timing of settlement** – this is normally based on a set number of business days after the trade is executed and is often described as the processing cycle.
- **Structure of the settlement system** – the Bank for International Settlements (BIS) has identified three common structural approaches/models for linking delivery and payment in a securities settlement system that are all typically described as achieving delivery versus payment (DvP). These are described in detail in the following section.

2.   Settlement Models

Learning Objective

6.1.2   Understand the concept of DvP and the main differences between DvP models 1 to 3 as defined by the BIS

As mentioned, DvP is delivery versus payment and the concept is that, after agreeing a deal, the two parties to the deal, for example the buyer of shares and the seller of those shares, both face risks. The seller faces the risk that the buyer may not pay for the shares and the buyer faces the risk that the seller may not pass over ownership of the shares. A system that guarantees DvP will remove those risks by only transferring ownership of the shares when the payment is certain, and only making the payment when the transfer of ownership is certain. The BIS identifies the following three models for DvP settlement systems:

- **Model 1** – systems that settle transfer instructions for both securities and funds on a trade-by-trade (gross) basis, with final (unconditional) transfer of securities from the seller to the buyer (delivery) occurring at the same time as final transfer of funds from the buyer to the seller (payment).
- **Model 2** – systems that settle securities transfer instructions on a gross basis, with final transfer of securities from the seller to the buyer (delivery) occurring throughout the processing cycle, but settle funds transfer instructions on a net basis, with final transfer of funds from the buyer to the seller (payment) occurring at the end of the processing cycle.
- **Model 3** – systems that settle transfer instructions for both securities and funds on a net basis, with final transfers of both securities and funds occurring at the end of the processing cycle.

2.1   BIS Model 1: Gross, Simultaneous Settlements of Securities and Funds Transfers

The essential characteristic of model 1 systems is the simultaneous settlement of individual securities transfer instructions and associated funds transfer instructions. The system typically maintains both securities and funds accounts for participants and makes all transfers by book entry.

An against-payment transfer instruction is settled by simultaneously debiting the seller's securities account, crediting the buyer's securities account, debiting the buyer's funds account and crediting the seller's funds account. All transfers are final (irrevocable and unconditional) transfers at the time the debits and credits are posted to the securities and funds accounts. Overdrafts (negative balances) on securities accounts are prohibited. Funds account overdrafts are allowed in most model 1 systems, and an instruction to transfer securities against payment would not be executed either if the seller had an insufficient securities balance or if the buyer had an insufficient funds balance or overdraft facility.

Model 1 systems may require participants to maintain substantial money balances to ensure the completion of settlements, especially if participants are unable to adjust their money (or securities) balances during the processing cycle, or if the volume and value of transfers are relatively large. If balances cannot be adjusted during the processing cycle, participants must maintain balances sufficient not only to cover the net value of all funds debits and credits on the settlement date, but also to cover the largest debit balance during processing. The magnitude of the largest debit balance during processing can be very difficult to predict with any precision. Even if the debit balance after processing was known with certainty, the largest debit balance during processing could be considerably larger because the order in which transfers occur is determined by the availability of securities balances and cannot be predicted in advance. If participants do not maintain substantial money balances, and are unable to adjust their money balances during the processing cycle, high rates of failed transactions are likely to result in a model 1 system. In an extreme case, a high fail rate could escalate to a gridlock situation in which very few, if any, transactions could be completed on the settlement date.

Furthermore, if funds accounts are held by another entity, a communications link must be established between the operator of the securities transfer system and the other entity to provide the securities transfer system with real-time information on the completion of funds transfers.

The system may also allow participants to make free transfers, that is, transfers of securities without a corresponding transfer of funds, or free payments, that is, transfers of funds without a corresponding transfer of securities.

To avoid high fail rates, model 1 systems frequently employ some type of queue management technique and may also offer securities lending facilities. The system must also make decisions about the treatment of transfer orders that cannot be executed because of insufficient securities or money balances. The options available depend critically on whether participants are able to interact with the system during the processing cycle. If so, responsibility for queue management might be left to the participants.

Counterparties to a failed transaction could be promptly notified and given the opportunity to borrow the securities or funds necessary to allow execution of the instruction. The system could repeatedly recycle instructions on a simple first-in, first-out basis until participants had taken the steps necessary to allow execution.

In some model 1 systems, however, transfers are executed during one or more batch processing cycles in which participants have no opportunity to adjust their securities or money balances to make completion possible. Such systems typically employ complex chaining procedures that manipulate the order in which transfer instructions are executed so as to maximise the number or value of securities transferred and correspondingly minimise the number and value of failed transactions.

These systems may also offer automatic securities lending programmes, that is, programmes in which participants may pre-authorise the lending of available securities to other participants that have insufficient securities balances to allow execution of their transfer instructions.

Model 1 is primarily used in Europe and Eurasia, eg, the UK's **CREST** system.

Example

The majority of transactions in UK equities are settled via an electronic settlement facility called CREST.

CREST is a computer system that settles transactions in shares, gilts and corporate bonds, primarily on behalf of the London Stock Exchange (LSE). It is owned and operated by a company that is part of the Euroclear group of companies, called Euroclear UK & Ireland ltd.

The financial instruments settled by CREST are dematerialised: instead of using paper share certificates, the underlying company uses an electronic entry in its register of shareholders. This allows transactions in shares to be settled electronically.

CREST clears the trade by matching the settlement details provided by the buyer and the seller. The transaction is then settled when CREST updates the register of the relevant company, to transfer the shares to the buyer, and at the same time instructs the buyer's bank to transfer the appropriate amount of money to the seller's bank account.

In summary, to complete the settlement of a trade, CREST simultaneously:

- **updates the register of shareholders** – CREST maintains the so-called **operator register** for UK companies' dematerialised shareholdings
- **issues a payment obligation** – CREST sends an instruction to the buyer's payment bank to pay for the shares
- **issues a receipt notification** – CREST notifies the seller's payment bank to expect payment.

If a trading system provides a CCP to the trades (such as LCH.Clearnet), it is the CCP that assumes responsibility for settling the transaction with each counterparty. The buyer and seller remain anonymous to each other.

For frequently traded, listed company share trades, CREST gives the option to LSE member firms to settle with LCH.Clearnet on a gross basis or on a net basis. To illustrate this, if a firm has 20 orders executed in the same security through the Stock Exchange Electronic Trading Service (SETS), it could choose to either settle 20 trades with LCH.Clearnet (settling on a gross basis), or choose to have all 20 trades netted so that the firm just settles a single transaction with LCH.Clearnet (settling on a net basis).

The settlement period (the time between the trade and the transfer of money and registration) for UK equities is on a T+2 basis, where 'T' is the trade date and '2' is the number of business days after the trade date that the cash changes hands and the shares' registered title changes. In other words, if a trade is executed on a Tuesday, the cash and registered title will change two business days later, on the Thursday. So, if the trade is executed on a Thursday, settlement will occur on the following Monday.

2.2 BIS Model 2: Gross Settlements of Securities Transfers Followed by Net Settlement of Funds Transfers

The essential characteristic of the model 2 system is that securities transfers are settled on a trade-for-trade (gross) basis throughout the processing cycle, while funds transfers are settled on a net basis at the end of the processing cycle. The system maintains securities accounts for participants, but funds accounts are generally held by another entity, either a commercial bank or the central bank.

Securities are transferred by book entry, that is, by debiting the seller's securities account and crediting the buyer's securities account. These transfers are final at the instant the entries are made on the system's books. The corresponding funds transfers are irrevocable but not final. During the processing cycle the system calculates running balances of funds debits and credits. The running balances are settled at the end of the processing cycle when the net debit positions and net credit positions are posted on the books of the commercial bank or central bank that maintains the funds accounts.

Settlement of funds transfers may occur once a day or several times a day. Thus, final transfer of securities (delivery) precedes final transfer of funds (payment). Like model 1 systems, model 2 systems typically prohibit participants from overdrawing securities accounts but funds overdrafts are tacitly allowed since the running balances are permitted to be net debit balances. A securities transfer instruction is rejected if, and only if, sufficient securities are not available in the seller's account.

Without additional safeguards, model 2 systems would expose sellers of securities to the risk that they do not get the funds to which they are entitled. However, by allowing participants to settle funds transfer instructions on a net basis, the frequency of failed transactions is reduced, limiting the potential for fails to exacerbate such risks to participants.

Nonetheless, failed transactions would occur in the case of insufficient securities balances. Thus, queuing arrangements need to be developed, although they generally do not need to be as complex as in a model 1 system. Still, the system must decide whether to depart from first-in, first-out processing of securities transfer instructions and adopt more complex procedures that maximise the number or value of transfers completed.

Operators of model 2 systems have recognised the dangers inherent in allowing delivery prior to payment, and these systems are designed to provide strong assurances that sellers will receive payment for securities delivered. In most cases, an assured payment system is utilised, that is, a system in which the seller delivers securities in exchange for an irrevocable commitment from the buyer's bank to make payment to the seller's bank at the end of the processing cycle.

Model 2 is the settlement system that predominates globally, particularly in the US. Furthermore, since it is probably the easiest model in which to realise liquidity efficiencies, it is particularly popular in the emerging markets of Latin America, Africa and the Middle East.

2.3 BIS Model 3: Simultaneous Net Settlement of Securities and Funds Transfers

The essential characteristic of model 3 systems is the simultaneous net settlement of both securities and funds transfer instructions. Settlement may occur once a day or at several times during the day. The system maintains securities accounts for participants. Funds accounts may be maintained by a separate entity, either a commercial bank or a central bank. Securities are transferred by book entry, that is, by debiting the seller's securities account and crediting the buyer's securities account.

During a processing cycle, running balances of debits and credits to funds and securities accounts are calculated, and in some systems this information may be made available to participants.

However, book-entry transfers of securities do not occur until the end of the processing cycle.

The obligation of the seller's bank in the event of failure of the buyer's bank is a matter of negotiation between the seller's bank and the seller. In some cases, the seller's bank may guarantee that the seller will receive payment even if the buyer's bank fails.

If a participant has insufficient balances, it may be notified and given an opportunity to obtain the necessary funds or securities. If, and only if, all participants in net debit positions have sufficient balances of funds and securities, final transfers of the net securities balances and net funds balances are executed.

Model 3 systems can achieve, and most do achieve, DvP and, therefore, eliminate the risk of the seller not receiving their money. The exceptions involve systems that in certain circumstances allow provisional securities transfers to become final prior to the settlement of funds transfers.

DvP model 3 has the advantage of reducing both the funds and securities liquidity requirements within the settlement systems, but can potentially create large liquidity exposures if a participant fails to settle its net funds debit position, in which case some or all of the defaulting participant's transfers may have to be unwound.

3. Custodianship

Learning Objective

6.1.3   Know the concept of custody and the roles of the different types of custodian: global; regional; local; sub-custodian

3.1   Services Provided by Custodians

When an institutional investor invests in securities, it will commonly employ the services of a custodian to administer these securities by:

*   providing safekeeping of the investor's assets in the local market
*   making appropriate arrangements for delivery and receipt of cash and securities to support settlement of the investor's trading activities in that market
*   providing market information to the investor on developments and reforms within that market
*   collecting dividend income, interest paid on debt securities and other income payments in the local market
*   managing the client's cash flows
*   monitoring and managing entitlements through corporate actions and voting rights held by the investor in the local market
*   managing tax reclaims and other tax services in the local market
*   ensuring that securities are registered and that transfer of legal title on securities transactions proceeds effectively
*   ensuring that reporting obligations to the regulatory authorities, and to other relevant bodies, are discharged effectively.

3.2   The Role and Responsibility of a Custodian

The primary responsibility of the custodian is to ensure that the client's assets are fully protected at all times. Hence, it must provide robust safekeeping facilities for all valuables and documentation, ensuring that investments are only released from its care in accordance with authorised instructions from the client.

Importantly, the client's assets must be properly segregated from those of the custodian and appropriate legal arrangements must be in place to ensure that financial or external shock to the custodian does not expose the client's assets to claims from creditors or any other party.

3.3   Types of Custodian

An investor faces choices in selecting custody arrangements with regard to a portfolio of global assets. The possible paths can be summarised as follows:

- Appointing a local custodian in each market in which they invest (often referred to as direct custody arrangements).
- Appointing a global custodian to manage custody arrangements across the full range of foreign markets in which they have invested assets.
- Making arrangements to settle trades and hold securities and cash with a CSD within each market, or to go via an international central securities depository (ICSD).

3.3.1   Global Custody

A global custodian provides investment administration for investor clients, including processing cross-border securities trades and keeping financial assets secure (ie, providing safe custody) outside the country where the investor is located.

The term global custody came into common usage in the financial services world in the mid-1970s, when the Employee Retirement Income Security Act (ERISA) was passed in the US. This legislation was designed to increase the protection given to US pension fund investors. The Act specified that US pension funds could not act as custodians of the assets held in their own funds. Instead, these assets had to be held in the safekeeping of another bank. ERISA went further, to specify that only a US bank could provide custody services for a US pension fund.

Subsequently, use of the term global custody has evolved to refer to a broader set of responsibilities, encompassing settlement, safekeeping, cash management, record-keeping and asset servicing (eg, collecting dividend payments on shares and interest on bonds, reclaiming withheld taxes and advising investor clients on their electing on corporate actions entitlements), and providing market information. Some investors may also use their global custodians to provide a wider suite of services, including investment accounting, treasury and foreign exchange, securities lending and borrowing, collateral management, and performance and risk analysis on the investor's portfolio.

Some global custodians maintain an extensive network of branches globally and can meet the local custody needs of their investor clients by employing their own branches as local custody providers. Citigroup's custody business, for example, maintains a proprietary branch network covering 50 markets. Consequently, when Citigroup is acting as global custodian for an investor client, it may opt to use its own branch to provide local custody in many locations where the investor holds assets.

3.3.2   Sub-Custody

A sub-custodian is employed by a global custodian as its local agent to provide settlement and custody services for assets that it holds on behalf of investor clients in a foreign market. A sub-custodian effectively serves as the eyes and ears of the global custodian in the local market, providing a range of clearing, settlement and asset servicing duties. It will also typically provide market information relating to developments in the local market, and will lobby the market authorities for reforms that will make the market more appealing and an efficient target for foreign investment.

In selecting a sub-custodian, a global custodian may:

- appoint one of its own branches, in cases when this option is available
- appoint a local agent bank that specialises in providing sub-custody in the market concerned
- appoint a regional provider that can offer sub-custody to the global custodian across a range of markets in a region or globally.

A good example of a custodian that offers global services by selecting local specialists is the US bank Brown Brothers Harriman. Its adopts a *'non-captive sub-custodian bank strategy…independently selecting banks that are determined to be the best and most trusted service providers in each market'*.

Local Custodian

Agent banks that specialise in providing sub-custody in their home market are sometimes known as single market providers. Stiff competition from larger regional or global competitors has meant that these are becoming a dying breed. However, some continue to win business in their local markets, often combining this service with offering global custody or master custody for institutional investors in their home markets. Examples include Bank of Tokyo-Mitsubishi UFJ, Mizuho Bank and Sumitomo Mitsui Banking Corporation in Japan, Maybank in Malaysia and United Overseas Bank in Singapore.

A principal selling point is that they are local market specialists. Hence they can remain focused on their local business, without spreading their attentions broadly across a wide range of markets. A local specialist bank may be attractive in a market in which local practices tend to differ markedly from global standards, or where a provider's long-standing relationship with the local regulatory authorities and/or political elite leaves it particularly well placed to lobby for reforms on behalf of its cross-border clients.

Reciprocal arrangements may be influential in shaping the appointment of a local provider in some instances. Under such an arrangement, a global custodian (A) may appoint the local provider (B) to deliver sub-custody in its local market (market B). In return, the custodian (A) may offer sub-custody in its own home market (market A) for pension and insurance funds in market B that use provider B as their global custodian.

In summary, the strengths of a local custodian may include the following:

- They are country specialists.
- They can be the eyes and ears of the global custodian or broker-dealer in the local market.
- They will have regular dealings with financial authorities and local politicians – they may be well placed to lobby for reforms that will improve the efficiency of the local market.
- They have expert knowledge of local market practice, language and culture.
- They may offer opportunities for reciprocal business.

A local custody bank may be perceived to have the following disadvantages when compared with a regional custodian:

- Their credit rating may not meet requirements laid down by some global custodians or global broker-dealers.
- They cannot leverage developments in technology and client service across multiple markets (unlike a regional custodian) – hence product and technology development may lag behind the regional custodians that they compete with.
- They may not be able to offer the price discounts that can be extended by regional custodians offering custody services across multiple markets.

Regional Custodian

A regional custodian is able to provide agent bank services across multiple markets in a region.

For example, Standard Chartered Bank and HSBC have both been offering regional custody and clearing in the Asia-Pacific and South Asian region for many years, competing with Citigroup and some strong single market providers for business in this region. In Central and Eastern Europe, Bank Austria (subsidiary of the Unicredit Group), Deutsche Bank, Raiffeisen Bank International and Citigroup each offer a regional clearing and custody service. In Central and South America, Citigroup and Brazil's Bank Itau offer regional custody, in competition in selected markets with HSBC, Bank Santander and Deutsche Bank.

Employing a regional custodian may offer a range of advantages to global custodian or global broker-dealer clients:

- Its credit rating may be higher than that of a single market custodian.
- It can cross-fertilise good practice across multiple markets – lessons learned in one market may be applied, when appropriate, across other markets in its regional offering.
- It can leverage innovation in technology, product development and client service across multiple markets – delivering economies of scale.
- It can offer standardised reporting, management information systems and market information across multiple markets in its regional offering.
- Economies of scale may support delivery of some or all product lines from a regional processing centre – offering potential cost savings and efficiency benefits.
- Its size and regional importance, plus the strength of its global client base, may allow a regional custodian to exert considerable leverage on local regulators, political authorities and infrastructure providers. This may be important in lobbying for reforms that support greater efficiency and security for foreign investors in that market.

- A global client may be able to secure price discounts by using a regional custodian across multiple markets.

In some situations, a regional provider may be perceived to have certain disadvantages when compared with a local custody bank:

- A regional custodian's product offering may be less well attuned to local market practice, service culture and investor needs than that of a well-established local provider.
- A regional custodian may spread its focus across a wider range of clients and a wider range of markets than a single market provider. Hence, a cross-border client may not receive the same level of attention, and the same degree of individualised service, as may be extended by a local custodian.
- Some regional custodians may lack the long track record, customer base and goodwill held by some local custodians in their own market.

4. Registered Title

Learning Objective

6.1.4 Understand the implications of registered title: registered title versus unregistered (bearer); legal title; beneficial interest; voting rights; right to participate in corporate actions

Generally, when settling a trade involving shares, settlement must involve communicating the change in ownership to the company **registrar**. This is because the issuing company maintains a register listing all of its shareholders. Whenever shares are bought or sold, a mechanism is required to make the company registrar aware of the change required to the register.

Shares that are not registered are described as bearer shares, which means that the person holding the shares is the owner and there are no records to confirm or contradict this. With unregistered bearer shares, physically handing over the shares would be a valid transfer of their ownership, including their value and any associated voting rights.

So, registered title simply means ownership that is backed by registration. In terms of share ownership, registered title makes it straightforward for the company to give shareholders the right to vote on important company matters, to pay dividends to their shareholders and to enable participation in other corporate actions, such as rights issues. Most shares issued today are issued in registered form.

When shares are bought and sold, it is the company registrar who is responsible for updating the register of members and giving the new owner registered title.

Busy shareholders often want to avoid the administrative tasks connected with registered title, so they choose to appoint their stockbroker, or another professional, to act as a **nominee**. The nominee takes the registered title to the shares and all the responsibilities that go with it, but the nominee's client retains beneficial ownership – it is the client that ultimately receives all of the cash flows generated by the shares. The nominee is referred to as the legal owner of the shares, and the client retaining the benefits of ownership, mainly the dividends and capital growth, is known as the beneficial owner.

5. Designated and Pooled Nominees

Learning Objective

6.1.5 Understand the basics of designated and pooled nominee accounts and their uses, and the concept of corporate nominees: designated nominee accounts; pooled nominee accounts; details in share register; function of corporate nominees; legal ownership; beneficial ownership; effect on shareholder rights of using a nominee

5.1 The Share Register

When shares are held in registered form, any share certificate is simply evidence of ownership. The proof that counts is the name and address held on the company's share register.

5.2 Nominees

Upon the incorporation of a company (be it a new or ready-made shelf company or a tailor-made company), the investor can either act as a shareholder in their own name, or a financial services firm equipped to handle incorporations, or a custodian can provide them with a nominee shareholder. These nominee shareholders will hold the shares in trust for the beneficial owners, and it is the nominee shareholders that are identified on the register of shareholders.

Each nominee shareholder appointed will sign a declaration of trust to the beneficial owner that they are holding the shares on behalf of the beneficial owner and will return the shares into the name of the beneficial owner or will transfer them to another party as requested. A nominee shareholder is normally a company created for the purpose of holding shares and other securities on behalf of investors.

Institutional investors employing professional investment management firms to manage their assets are highly unlikely to hold these securities in their own name (name on register). The reason for this is simple: the person whose name appears on the share register receives every piece of documentation sent out by the company and is obliged to sign all share transfers and other relevant forms such as instructions for rights issues and other corporate events. To ensure safe custody of assets and remove this administrative burden from the investor, thus allowing the speedy processing of transfers, institutional (and, increasingly, private client) shareholdings are held in the names of 'nominee' companies.

Nominee companies have long been established as the mechanism by which asset managers and custodians can process transactions on behalf of their clients. Given that many investment management firms have outsourced some or all of their investment administration activities to the specialist custodians, the vast majority of institutional shareholdings in fact now reside in nominee accounts overseen by those specialist custodians.

As far as the company is concerned, the nominee name appearing on its share register is the legal owner of the shares for the purposes of benefits and for voting. However, beneficial ownership continues to reside with the underlying client, who is entitled to receive dividends and the capital growth of the shares but does not retain the automatic right to attend company meetings.

It is this separation of ownership which allows the custodians, under proper client authorities, to transfer shares to meet market transactions and to conduct other functions, without the registrar requiring sight of the signature or seal of the underlying client.

5.3 Types of Nominee Companies

Nominee companies can be classified into three types:

- **Pooled** (or omnibus), whereby individual clients are grouped together within a single nominee registration.
- **Designated**, where the nominee name includes unique identifiers for each individual client, eg, XYZ Nominees Account 1, Account 2, Account 3.
- **Sole**, where a single nominee name is used for a specific client, eg, ABC Pension Fund Nominees ltd.

How the shareholdings are registered is of vital importance when it comes to voting.

It is now generally accepted that there are no real advantages, from a security point of view, no matter which type of nominee arrangement is used to register the shares. However, clients brought together with others in a pooled nominee have no visibility to the company: it is the single nominee name, covering multiple clients, which the company recognises. Importantly, from a voting perspective it is only the single bulk nominee that is entitled to vote; no separate entitlement accrues from the registrar's standpoint to each individual client making up the total holding.

Some companies offer their shareholders certain benefits, such as discounts on their products. By using a nominee (either a designated or a pooled structure), the shareholder benefits may not be available to the individual investor. This is simply because the stockbrokers may be unwilling to undertake the necessary administration to facilitate the provision of these benefits.

One reason for registering shares in a designated or sole nominee name would be that, if the underlying investor requires dividends to be mandated to a particular bank account rather than being collected by the custodian, registration in an omnibus account is not practicable.

Designation or individual registration can also help some aspects of auditing and it affords a good control mechanism when identical bargains may have been executed for different clients (for example on the same date, for the same number of shares and for the same settlement consideration).

One reason frequently cited by custodians for insisting on pooled nominee arrangements is the vexed question of **costs**. Operating a designated nominee account should give rise to few additional costs from the custodian's point of view, as the existing nominee name can easily be used, with the addition of a unique designation. While there may be a small amount of extra work involved, eg, in the receipt of separate income payments, the actual procedures are identical and should be capable of being easily absorbed into the existing administration and processing routines.

If the client insists on using a sole nominee name to register the shareholdings, this may involve some costs for the custodian connected with the establishment of a nameplate nominee company, the requisite appointment of directors and the completion of annual returns. The custodian may seek to pass these comparatively meagre costs on to the client, but more usually they will be absorbed within the standard custody tariff.

5.4 The Corporate Nominee

A corporate nominee (alternatively referred to as a **corporate sponsored nominee**) is when the issuing company itself provides a facility for its smaller shareholders to hold their shares within a single corporate nominee.

The corporate nominee is a halfway house between the pooled and the designated nominee structures offered by stockbrokers. It will result in a single entry for all the shareholders together in the company's register (like the pooled nominee) but beneath this the issuing company (or its registrar) will be aware of the individual holdings that make up the nominee. In a similar way to the designated nominee structure, the company will be able to forward separate dividend payments to each of the individual shareholders, as well as voting rights and other potential shareholder perks. Shares held within a corporate nominee in **dematerialised** form enable quick and easy transfer through the settlement system.

5.5 Summary

Custodians and their nominees now control the majority of share registrations for institutional investors, even for clients who may not have directly appointed custodians but whose asset management firms have outsourced their investment administration to these providers.

Custodians uniquely identify their clients' holdings by segregating these in their computer systems, as it is largely these systems which drive the calculation and application of dividends and other entitlements. However, this segregation is not the same as having an individually identifiable holding for a particular client on company share registers.

It is largely impractical for an institutional investor to achieve **name on register**, so the recognised practice is to use nominee names whereby the custodian, or other duly authorised agent, is legally entitled to perform the transfer and administration of the assets on behalf of, and under the authority of, the underlying beneficial owner.

Many custodians prefer to pool all their clients into one single nominee registration, known as an omnibus account. However, this does remove the visibility of the underlying investor and makes individual client voting much more cumbersome.

Clients can request their custodian to adopt an individual registration solely for their particular shareholdings. Typically this takes the form of a standard nominee name with a unique designation for each client. The costs of such separate registration and its ongoing maintenance are minimal, relative to overall custody and securities lending charges and are often absorbed by the custodians.

6. Cum- and Ex-Dividend

Learning Objective

6.1.6 Understand the concepts, requirements, benefits and disadvantages of deals executed cum, ex, special cum and special ex: timetable; effect of deals on the underlying right; effect on the share price before and after a dividend; the meaning of 'books closed', 'ex-div' and 'cum div', cum and ex-rights; effect of late registration; benefits that may be achieved; disadvantages/ risks; when dealing is permitted

Cum-dividend means 'with the dividend'. Shares are normally traded cum-dividend, meaning that buyers of the shares have the right to the next dividend paid by the company. However, there are brief periods when the share becomes ex-dividend, meaning that they would be sold without the right to receive the next dividend payment. The ex-dividend period occurs in the period just prior to a dividend payment, as detailed below.

The sequence of events that is typically adopted in the developed markets leading up to the dividend payment is as follows:

1. **Dividend declared** – on this date the company announces its intention to pay a specified dividend on a specified future date. The declaration usually occurs well before this date (perhaps a month or two earlier).
2. **Record or books-closed date** – the record, or books-closed date is the date on which a copy of the shareholders' register is taken. The people on the share register at the end of this day will be paid the next dividend. In many markets, the books-closed date is normally a Friday, except where the Friday is a public holiday, in which case the books-closed date is the next available business day.
3. **Ex-dividend date** – the ex-dividend date is typically a Thursday: the business day before the record date.
4. **Dividend paid** – this date is determined by the company, and is typically within 30 business days of the record date. The dividend is paid to those shareholders who were on the register on the record/ books-closed date.
5. **Ex-dividend period** – the period from the ex-dividend date up to the dividend payment date is the ex-dividend period. Throughout this period the shares trade without entitlement to the next dividend.

The relationship between the ex-dividend date and the books-closed date is easily explained. Since the equity settlement process in most equity markets takes two business days, for a new shareholder to appear on the register on the Friday they would have to buy the shares on Wednesday at the latest. Wednesday is the last day when the shares trade cum-dividend, because new shareholders will be reflected in the register before the end of the books-closed date. A new shareholder buying their shares on the Thursday will not be entered into the register until the following week – too late for the books-closed date and therefore ex-dividend.

On the Thursday when the shares first trade without the dividend (ex-dividend), the share price will fall to reflect the fact that if an investor buys the share he will not be entitled to the impending dividend.

At all times other than during ex-dividend periods, shares trade cum-dividend, ie, if an investor purchases shares at this time, they will be entitled to all of the future dividends paid by the company for as long as they keep the shares.

During the ex-dividend period, it is possible to arrange a special cum-trade. That is when, by special arrangement, the buyer of the share during the ex-dividend period does receive the next dividend. These trades can be executed up to and including the day before the dividend payment date, but not on or after the dividend payment date.

In a similar manner to a special cum-trade, an investor can also arrange a special ex-trade. This is generally only possible in the ten business days before the ex-date. If an investor buys a share during the cum-dividend period, but buys it special ex, they will not receive the next dividend.

Using special cum or special ex transactions enables the sellers or buyers to avoid the receipt of a dividend – essentially deciding whether or not they want to collect their right to the dividend. The motivation for investors buying or selling with or without the dividend entitlement tends to be related to tax. Dividend income is normally subject to income tax, so selling the right to the dividend may avoid some income tax.

The inherent disadvantage of special cum trades and special ex trades is that they will, potentially, result in dividends from the company being paid to the wrong person. Equally a trade that settles later than usual could mean that the correct owner is not reflected in the shareholders' register on the books-closed date – and the dividend is paid by the company to the wrong person. In such situations, it is the broker acting for the buyers (or seller, as appropriate) that will need to make a claim for the dividend.

In such situations, if the dividend was paid to the wrong person in a special cum-trade, then it is the broker acting for the buyers that should make a claim for the dividend. In contrast, when the dividend has been paid to the wrong person, following a special ex-trade, it is the seller's broker who will have to make the claim for their client to receive their rightful dividend payment.

7. Continuous Linked Settlement (CLS)

Learning Objective

6.1.7 Understand what continuous linked settlement (CLS) is and its purpose: the settlement of currencies across time zones; receiving and matching instructions; advantages; how it reduces settlement risk (Herstatt risk)

As international trade and investment has increased, so has the foreign exchange (FX) market. The average daily volume in the global FX market, and related markets, has grown enormously and was reported to be over US$5 trillion in April 2016 by the BIS (the most recent of the BIS triennial surveys published at the time of writing).

Continuous linked settlement (CLS) is a process by which most of the world's largest banks manage FX settlement among themselves (and their customers and other third parties). The process is managed by CLS Group Holdings and regulated by the Federal Reserve Board of New York.

CLS settles transactions on a payment versus payment (PvP) basis. The two parties to an FX transaction will buy and sell the respective currencies exchanged and the payments made will occur simultaneously. Unless such simultaneity in payments is ensured, there is a possibility of settlement risk which is also often referred to as Herstatt risk. Before the establishment of CLS, FX transactions were settled by each side of a trade making separate payments. The risks implicit in this approach became clear in 1974, when the German banking regulators withdrew the banking licence of Bankhaus Herstatt, putting it into liquidation at the close of business on 26 June. Bankhaus Herstatt had been active in the FX markets and had received currency from counterparties during the day, but had not yet made any payments, when its licence was withdrawn and it was declared bankrupt. Several banks had irrevocably paid over deutschmarks to Herstatt during the day, but had not received the anticipated currency in exchange. In addition, banks had entered into forward trades that were not yet due for settlement, and some lost money replacing the contracts. In short, there were serious repercussions in the FX market after the Bankhaus Herstatt default, thus the intra-day settlement risk highlighted was thereafter termed Herstatt risk.

The result was the impetus to set up a more robust and reliable system that ensured payment from one party was only made if there was a payment coming in the opposite direction to fulfil the other side of the FX deal – PvP. CLS was the result that solved the PVP problem, despite the counterparties potentially being in different parts of the world and time zones.

The CLS process is focused on a five-hour window each business day from 7.00am to 12 midday in Central European Time (CET). This window was created to provide an overlap across the business days in all parts of the world and facilitate global trading.

By 6.30am CET the settlement members must submit their settlement instructions for transactions to settle that day. At 6.30am each settlement member receives a schedule of what monies need to be paid in that day. From 7.00am the settlement members pay in the net funds that are due to settle in each currency to their central banks, and CLS will then begin to attempt to settle deals. In the event that CLS Bank's strict settlement criteria are not met for each side of a trade, then no funds are exchanged. This achieves the PvP system that removes the so-called Herstatt risk. Those trades that can be settled are settled and money is paid out via the central banks.

As outlined above, the payments made to CLS Bank are made via the central banks.

8. Stock Lending and Borrowing

Learning Objective

6.2.1 Know the uses of, requirements and implications of stock lending: what is stock lending; stock lending versus repo; purpose for the borrower; purpose for the lender; risk

6.2.2 Understand the function of stock borrowing and lending intermediaries (SBLIs), including: use of custodian banks; administration, including collateral; regulation; effect on the lender's rights; lender retains the right to sell

Stock lending is the temporary transfer of securities, by a lender to a borrower, with agreement by the borrower to return equivalent securities to the lender at a pre-agreed time. It is commonly seen in the more developed markets where it is exclusively made available to institutional, rather than retail, investors.

There are two main motivations for stock lending: securities-driven, and cash-driven. In securities-driven transactions, borrowing firms seek specific securities (equities or bonds), perhaps to facilitate their trading operations. In the cash-driven trades, the lender is able to increase the returns on an underlying portfolio, by receiving a fee for making its investments available to the borrower. Such transactions may boost overall income returns, enhancing, for example, returns on a pension fund.

The terms of the securities loan will be governed by a securities lending agreement, which requires that the borrower provide the lender with collateral, in the form of cash, government securities, or a letter of credit of value equal to or greater than the loaned securities. As payment for the loan, the parties negotiate a fee, quoted as an annualised percentage of the value of the loaned securities. If the agreed form of collateral is cash, then the fee may be quoted as a rebate, meaning that the lender will earn all of the interest that accrues on the cash collateral, and will rebate an agreed rate of interest to the borrower.

8.1   Benefits of Stock Lending

The initial driver for the securities lending business was to cover settlement failure. If one party fails to deliver stock to you, it can mean that you are unable to deliver stock that you have already sold to another party. In order to avoid the costs and penalties that can arise from settlement failure, stock can be borrowed at a fee, and delivered to the second party. When your initial stock finally arrives (or is obtained from another source) the lender will receive back the same number of shares they originally loaned.

So, the principal reason for borrowing securities is to cover a short position. As you are obliged to deliver the securities that you do not currently hold, you will have to borrow them. At the end of the agreement, you will have to return the equivalent quantity of securities to the lender. Equivalent in this context means fungible, ie, the securities have to be completely interchangeable. Compare this with lending a ten euro note. You do not expect exactly the same note back, as any ten euro note will do.

Securities lending and borrowing is often required, by matter of law, in order to engage in short selling. In fact, regulations enacted in 2008 in the US, Australia and the UK, among other jurisdictions, required that, before short sales were executed for specific stocks, especially banks and financial services companies, the sellers first pre-borrowed shares in those issues.

There is an ongoing debate among global policymakers and regulators about how to impose new restrictions on short selling and in June 2010, during a period of turbulence for the eurozone, Germany took a unilateral step in banning the naked short selling of credit default swaps (CDSs) (ie, when the short seller had no interest in the underlying security for the CDS).

The following are generally considered to be positive aspects of stock lending:

- It can increase the liquidity of the securities market by allowing securities to be borrowed temporarily, thus reducing the potential for failed settlements and the penalties this may incur.
- It can provide extra security to lenders through the collateralisation of a loan.
- It can support many trading and investment strategies that otherwise would be extremely difficult to execute.
- It allows investors to earn income by lending their securities on to third parties.
- It facilitates the **hedging** and arbitraging of price differentials.

8.2   Risks of Stock Lending

Many feel that securities lending can aid market manipulation through short selling, which can potentially influence market prices. Short selling itself is not wrong, but market manipulation certainly is.

The debate about the merits and validity of short selling is sometimes emotion-charged, and features in the rhetoric of politicians in populist attacks on the financial services profession. It is probably fair to say that for most investment professionals who actually work in the financial markets, the notion that short selling in itself is an abusive practice is not palatable. There may be times when the activity can be disruptive, but markets have a tendency to overreact in either direction and the periodic focus given to short selling when a market is moving down should be counterbalanced by the tendency for markets to become too frothy and for long investors to become exuberant when markets are going up.

Furthermore, while securities lending may be a useful tool, it presents associated risks to both the borrower and the lender. The securities on loan, or the collateral, may not be returned on the agreed date, whether because of settlement delays or liquidity problems in the market concerned or the more intimidating prospect of counterparty default or legal challenge. Those securities will then need to be acquired in the market, potentially at a high cost.

In order to mitigate the risk of such failures, lenders are advised to employ a range of precautions to ensure the safe return of the securities and to ensure that the loss is fully compensated in the event that the securities are not returned. These include:

- employing detailed credit evaluations on the borrower
- setting limits on the lender's credit exposure to any individual borrower
- collateralising loan exposures against cash or securities (the lender will decide what quality of collateral it will accept)
- marking exposures and collateral to market (ie, ensuring that exposures and collateral are valued at current market prices) on a daily basis and making margin calls to bring collateral and exposure into line
- employing master legal agreements that set out clear legal parameters that dictate the structure and process of the lending arrangements, and how the lender will be compensated in the event of default or systemic crisis.

When collateral is taken in securities lending arrangements, its value will typically exceed the market value of the borrowed assets by an agreed percentage, known as a 'haircut'. This protects the lender from adverse price movements of the collateral held.

8.3 Stock Borrowing and Lending Intermediaries (SBLIs)

Securities lending has increasingly become a volume business which has encouraged the proliferation of various specialist intermediaries to undertake principal and/or agency roles in this field. These stock borrowing and lending intermediaries (SBLIs) provide a service in separating out the underlying owners of securities – which are typically large pension funds or insurance companies – from those who would be borrowers of those securities, typically hedge funds and other asset managers, and liaising with both sides. The economy of scale offered by SBLIs in pooling together securities of different clients has also enabled smaller asset holders to participate in this market.

Asset managers and custodian banks have added securities lending to the other services they offer. Owners and SBLIs will often split revenues from securities lending at commercial rates. The split will be determined by many factors, including the service level and provision by the agent of any risk mitigation, such as an indemnity. Securities lending is often part of a much bigger relationship and therefore the split negotiation can become part of a bundled approach to the pricing of a wide range of services.

8.3.1 Custodian Banks

Since custody is a highly competitive business, for many providers it is often run as a loss-making activity. Supplementing their custodian role by acting as an SBLI can add a new level of revenue generation for custodian banks. Many large custodian banks have therefore added securities lending to their core custody businesses.

From the perspective of the custodian, the advantages of acting as an SBLI are that they already have:

- an existing banking relationship with their customers
- investment in technology and global coverage of markets arising from their custody businesses
- the ability to pool assets from many smaller underlying funds, insulating borrowers from the administrative inconvenience of dealing with many small funds
- experience in local operations in developing as well as developed markets
- the capability to provide indemnities and manage cash collateral efficiently.

8.3.2 Administration

For SBLIs it is important that there is adequate documentation in place with borrowing counterparties, which sets out the terms and conditions of the service being provided and the risks involved.

If assets are pooled within an SBLI, the SBLI must ensure that only assets belonging to customers who have consented to securities lending are lent out. The SBLI should maintain a separate account or be able to demonstrate that it maintains adequate systems to differentiate between the safe custody investments of those customers who have not consented to stock lending activity and those that have consented.

If collateral is required from the borrower, the SBLI must consider whether that collateral should be provided in advance of the lending, given the risks of the transaction and normal practice in the relevant market. The level and type of collateral should take account of the creditworthiness of the borrower and the risks associated with the collateral being offered.

Cash or assets held in favour of a customer for stock lending activity must be held in accordance with the appropriate custody rules. This includes dividends, stock lending fees and any other payments received in relation to stock lending.

8.4   Legalities

Securities lending is legal and clearly regulated in most of the world's major securities markets. Most markets mandate that the borrowing of securities be conducted only for specifically permitted purposes, which generally include to:

- facilitate settlement of a trade
- facilitate delivery of a short sale
- finance the security, or
- facilitate a loan to another borrower who is motivated by one of these permitted purposes.

Effect on a Lender's Rights and Corporate Actions

When a security is loaned, the title of the security transfers to the borrower. This means that the borrower has the advantages of holding the security, just as though they owned it. Specifically, the borrower will receive all coupon and/or dividend payments, and any other rights such as voting rights. These dividends or coupons must be passed back to the lender in the form of what is referred to as a manufactured dividend.

If the lender wants to exercise its right to vote, it should recall the stock in good time so that a proxy voting form can be completed and returned to the registrar by the required deadline. Similar issues are involved in other corporate actions such as capitalisation issues. Technically, the consequences arising from any corporate action by the issuer of a security, such as a capitalisation or rights issue, when that security has been lent to another would, *prima facie*, be to the benefit/cost of the borrower. Under the terms of the loan, it is customary that these costs/benefits flow back to the lender, and the exact manner in which this is implemented should be reflected in the securities lending agreement.

The parties to a stock lending transaction generally operate under a legal agreement, which sets out the obligations of the borrower and lender. In securities lending, the lender effectively retains all the benefits of ownership. The borrower can use the securities as required – perhaps by lending them on to another party – but is liable to the lender for all the benefits such as dividends, interest and stock splits.

The Global Master Securities Lending Agreement (GMSLA) has been developed as a market standard for securities lending. It covers the matters which a legal agreement ought to cover for securities lending transactions. This agreement is kept under review, and amendments are made from time to time, although parties to an existing agreement will need to agree that any amendments will apply to their agreement.

Stock Lending Versus Repo

Stock lending and sale/repurchase agreements (repos) are similar; however, the key difference is that a stock lender charges a fee to the borrower, whereas a repo counterparty pays (or receives) a rate of interest.

A repurchase agreement, or repo, is a method of secured lending, whereby securities are sold to a counterparty against payment of cash and then repurchased at a later date, with interest being paid to the cash lender. A repo may be employed, for example, to raise the funds necessary to cover the cash leg of a securities transaction. This mode of financing will typically be cheaper than seeking unsecured funding and may be particularly well suited for trading companies that hold a large inventory of stock that may otherwise be unutilised.

For the cash borrower, a key feature of repo transaction is that it provides a method of funding that is significantly cheaper than borrowing on an unsecured basis. The cash lender receives securities as collateral throughout the loan period and is free to utilise these securities if the cash borrower fails to repay cash plus interest (or cash plus fee) to the lender.

For the cash lender, a repo provides an avenue through which it can generate income on its cash balance. Although it could potentially earn more income by lending this cash on an unsecured basis, a repo affords additional security to the lender by ensuring that it holds collateral that it will inherit if the borrowing counterparty defaults on its obligations.

The collateral will be marked-to-market on a daily basis throughout the repo period to reflect current market rates. If the value of the collateral rises or falls outside of a pre-agreed band (known as the variation margin), a margin call will be made (ie, collateral is requested from, or returned to, the lender) to ensure that the value of the collateral remains aligned to the cash sum borrowed through the repo agreement.

The types of securities that will be acceptable as collateral will usually be dependent on the risk appetite of the collateral-taker (ie, the cash lender). Government debt securities (German Bunds, UK gilts, US Treasuries and selected other G10 government bonds) typically represent premium-quality collateral. However, each collateral-taker will apply its own collateral eligibility criteria when specifying the types of collateral that it will accept in repo transactions and other forms of secured lending. These criteria may include asset type, credit rating of issuer, currency, duration and average daily traded volume (ie, a measure of the security's liquidity).

Some collateral-takers will be willing to accept lower-quality collateral in repo arrangements. The motivation for doing so is twofold:

1. Accepting lower-quality collateral will typically yield a better return for the collateral-taker (the lender).
2. Top-grade collateral (eg, high-quality government debt, such as German bunds) is often in short supply and may be expensive to borrow.

As such, some counterparties may accept asset-backed securities (ABSs), high-grade corporate debt and, in some instances, equities as collateral.

Lenders can specify their eligibility criteria for collateral that they are willing to accept.

End of Chapter Questions

1. What are the three stages of clearing and settlement?
   Answer reference: Section 1

2. What are the three models for DvP settlement systems identified by the BIS?
   Answer reference: Section 2

3. What is regarded as the primary role of a custodian?
   Answer reference: Section 3.2

4. What is sub-custody and why is it used?
   Answer reference: Section 3.3.2

5. What is meant if a person owns registered title to an asset?
   Answer reference: Section 4

6. Who is the legal owner of the shares if held by a nominee company?
   Answer reference: Section 5.2

7. What is meant by a pooled nominee'?
   Answer reference: Section 5.3

8. What is the date on which a copy of the shareholders' register is taken known as?
   Answer reference: Section 6

9. What is Herstatt risk and how is it eliminated by CLS?
   Answer reference: Section 7

10. Who has the right to vote when stock is loaned?
    Answer reference: Section 8.4

Chapter Seven
Accounting Analysis

1. Basic Principles   195

2. The Statement of Financial Position   199

3. The Income Statement   205

4. The Statement of Cash Flows   209

5. Financial Statement Analysis   216

7

This syllabus area will provide approximately 13 of the 100 examination questions

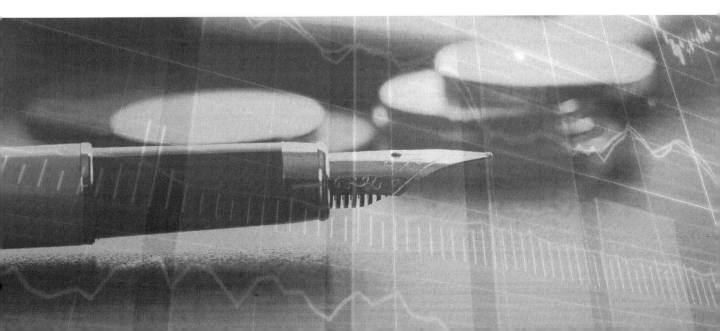

1. Basic Principles

1.1 The Purpose of Financial Statements

Learning Objective

7.1.1 Understand the purpose of financial statements

Accounting can be defined as the recording, measuring and reporting of economic events, or activities, to interested parties in a usable form. It is about providing information relating to the financial and economic activities of a business in the form of a set of accounts. This set of accounts is alternatively referred to as the financial statements of the business.

Accounting information must be prepared and produced in the form of financial statements to provide stakeholders with information about the company in a standard format. This enables stakeholders to objectively compare the information against previous periods (quarters, half-years or years) for the same company, as well as against other companies. Stakeholders include owners, creditors, prospective investors, employees, financial analysts and institutional investors, stock exchanges, as well as governments, consumers and environmental groups.

The directors of a company are required to prepare financial statements and make other disclosures within an annual report and accounts. These set out the results of the company's activities during its most recent accounting period and its financial position as at the end of the period. The accounting period typically spans a 12-month period.

Broadly, these financial statements comprise three major statements:

1. **A statement of financial position/balance sheet** – this provides a snapshot of the company's financial position as of a given date, usually at the company's accounting year-end. The assets it owns and how they are financed (liabilities and shareholders' equity) are displayed on opposite sides of the sheet, and must balance each other (assets = equity + liabilities).
2. **An income statement** – this statement summarises income (or revenue) that has been earned and the expenses incurred by the company over the accounting period. Broadly it is a summary of the trading activities of the company over the year. If income exceeds expenses, the company has made a profit; if expenses exceed income the company has made a loss. The income statement is sometimes referred to as the profit and loss statement.

The income statement links the company's previous statement of financial position with its current one. This relationship is depicted below.

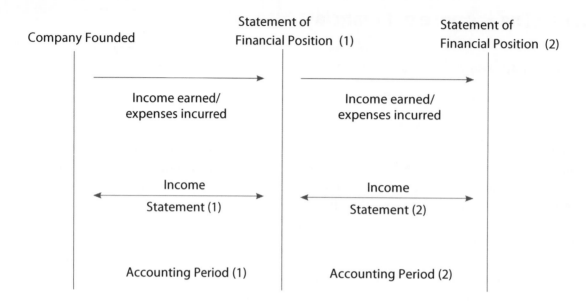

3. **A cash flow statement**. Companies must also publish a cash flow statement within their annual report and accounts. This financial statement identifies how much cash the company generated over the accounting period and how much cash has been spent. The cash flow statement is also referred to as a statement of cash flows.

The financial statements also include certain additional disclosures, such as a statement of other comprehensive income, a statement of changes in equity, comparative figures from the previous year's financial statements, explanatory notes to accompany certain individual statements of financial position and profit and loss account items, and disclosure of the company's accounting policies. The accounting policies are the basis on which the accounts have been prepared.

The information contained in the company's report and accounts is also required to be independently verified, or audited. An audit is an independent assessment of the company's accounts that have been prepared by the directors. This audit is concluded with an auditor's report to the members, or shareholders, of the company confirming whether or not the accounts give a true and fair view of the company's activities and financial position and whether they have been prepared in accordance with the law and other regulations. If they have, an unqualified audit report is issued. If they have not the auditor must issue a qualified report and state the reason for this qualification.

1.2   Accounting Regulations

Learning Objective

7.1.2   Understand the requirements for companies and groups to prepare accounts in accordance with applicable accounting standards and the difficulties encountered when comparing companies using different standards: accounting principles; International Financial Reporting Standards; International Accounting Standards

The form and content of all company financial statements and their respective disclosures are prescribed by the law and by mandatory accounting standards set by the accountancy profession. Accounting standards are authoritative statements of how particular types of transaction and other events should be reflected in financial statements.

The combination of accounting regulations is often referred to as the generally accepted accounting principles (GAAP). There are efforts being made to harmonise GAAP throughout the world, spearheaded by the International Accounting Standards Board (IASB). The IASB is an independent, privately funded accounting standard-setter based in London. The board members include a chair and an internationally diverse set of members with a variety of functional backgrounds. To ensure a broad international diversity, there will normally be members from:

- the Asia/Oceania region
- Europe
- North America
- Africa, and
- South America.

The IASB is committed to developing, in the public interest, a single set of high-quality, understandable and enforceable global accounting standards that require transparent and comparable information in general purpose financial statements. In addition, the IASB cooperates with national accounting standard-setters to achieve convergence in accounting standards around the world.

Standards issued by the IASB are designated International Financial Reporting Standards (IFRSs). There were also standards issued by the IASB's predecessor (the International Accounting Standards Committee) that continue to be designated International Accounting Standards (IASs). The IASB has retained the IASs and also issues IFRSs.

Many developed countries require the IASB's standards to be used for listed companies; however, the US still retains its own 'US GAAP' that is gradually converging with IFRSs. Until fully converged, companies' financial statements prepared under IFRSs will vary to some extent with US GAAP. This means it is not simply the case of judging whether one company has performed better than another by looking at the amount of profit made by a European-listed company using IFRSs and a US competitor preparing accounts under US GAAP – adjustments are required to make the accounting principles adopted compatible.

1.3 Group Versus Company Accounts

Learning Objective

7.1.3 Understand the differences between group accounts and company accounts and why companies are required to prepare group accounts (candidates should understand the concept of goodwill and minority interests but will not be required to calculate them)

If a company invests in another company, all that appears in the accounts of the investing company is the original cost of the investment (in the statement of financial position), and the dividends received (if there are any) appear in the investing company's income statement.

This treatment is fine when the investment is a small minority shareholding in another company. However, in instances when the investment is so significant that the investing company controls the other company, another accounting treatment is required – the preparation of group financial statements (known as group accounts or consolidated financial statements). The investing company is described as the parent and the company or companies that the parent company controls are described as subsidiaries. As long as a parent/subsidiary relationship exists, the parent company should prepare and present a set of group accounts in addition to its individual company financial statements.

These group accounts present the financial statements as if the parent and the subsidiaries were a single entity, rather than distinct individual companies. This entails the addition of the assets of the parent plus all of the subsidiaries' assets to arrive at the group assets, and similar additions to arrive at the group's liabilities, revenues, expenses and cash flows.

Two particular issues can crop up when amalgamating the figures for the parent company and its subsidiaries:

1. **Goodwill** – when presenting the group accounts as a single entity, the assets and liabilities of the subsidiaries are added to those of the parent company. This replaces the original cost of investment in the group statement of financial position. If the cost of investment exceeded the net assets (assets less liabilities) of the subsidiary, the excess is described as goodwill and appears as an asset in the consolidated statement of financial position in the group accounts.
2. **Minority interests** – in circumstances when the parent company owns a majority of the shares in a subsidiary, but not all of the shares, there will be minority interests. These minority interests are commonly referred to as non-controlling interests. For example, if a parent owned 75% of the shares of a subsidiary, the minority interest/non-controlling interest would be 25%; if it owned 51% of the shares, the non-controlling interest would be 49%. As the presentation of the group accounts adds together all of the assets and liabilities of the subsidiaries, it includes some net assets that belong to the minority interests. These are reflected by detailing the extent to which the net assets and net income belong to the non-controlling interests in the consolidated statement of financial position and the group income statement.

2. The Statement of Financial Position

2.1 Purpose, Format and Main Contents

Learning Objective

7.2.1 Know the purpose of the statement of financial position, its format and main contents

The statement of financial position or balance sheet is a snapshot of a company's financial position at a particular moment. It is split into two halves that must always balance each other exactly, hence the term 'balance sheet'. The key information it provides to shareholders, customers and other interested parties is what the company owns (its assets), what the company owes others (its liabilities, or creditors) and the extent to which shareholders are providing finance to the company (the equity). The assets and liabilities are also divided into current and non-current in order to provide additional context as to how liquid or permanent the assets are, and how immediately the liabilities are due.

The balance sheet should reflect all of the reporting company's assets and liabilities, but over time companies and their advisers developed creative structures to enable items to remain off-balance-sheet rather than on-balance-sheet. The IASB and the adoption of its accounting standards should ensure that everything that should appear on the balance sheet is categorised as on-balance-sheet, and those items that are legitimately not assets or liabilities of the company should remain off-balance-sheet.

The typical format of a statement of financial position, with example figures, is provided below, followed by an explanation of each of the headings:

Example statement of financial position as at 31 December 2017	
€000	2017
Assets	
Non-current assets	
Property, plant and equipment	8,900
Intangible assets	2,100
Investments	300
	11,300
Current assets	
Inventories	3,600
Trade and other receivables	2,600
Prepayments	120
Cash	860
	7,180
Total assets	**18,480**
Equity and liabilities	
Capital and reserves	
Share capital – 10m 50c ordinary shares	5,000
Share capital – preference shares	100
Share premium account	120
Revaluation reserve	180
Retained earnings	6,880
Total equity	12,280
Non-current liabilities	
Bank loans	2,000
Provisions	2,000
Current liabilities	
Trade and other payables	2,200
Total liabilities	6,200
Total equity and liabilities	**18,480**

2.2   Assets

An asset is anything that is owned and controlled by the company and confers the right to future economic benefits. Statement of financial position assets are categorised as either non-current assets or current assets.

2.2.1   Non-Current Assets

Non-current assets are those in long-term, continuing use by the company. They represent the major investments from which the company hopes to make money. Non-current assets are categorised as:

- tangible
- intangible.

Tangible Non-Current Assets

A company's tangible non-current assets are those that have physical substance, such as land and buildings and plant and machinery, and indeed are often referred to as plant, property and equipment (PPE). Tangible non-current assets are initially recorded in the statement of financial position at their actual cost, or book value. However, in order to reflect the fact that the asset will generate benefits for the company over several accounting periods, not just in the accounting period in which it was purchased, all tangible non-current assets with a limited economic life are required to be depreciated. The concept of depreciation will be covered in more detail in section 2.3.

Intangible Non-Current Assets

Intangible non-current assets are those assets that are expected to generate economic benefits over a number of accounting periods but are without physical substance. These often take the form of intellectual property and can give a company a competitive advantage over its peers. Commonly quoted examples include computer software, patents, trademarks, capitalised development costs and purchased goodwill.

Purchased goodwill arises in group accounts when the consideration, or price, paid by an acquiring company for a target subsidiary company, exceeds the fair value of the target's separable, or individually identifiable, net assets. This is not necessarily the same as the book, or statement of financial position, value of these net assets:

Purchased goodwill = (price paid for company – fair value of separable net tangible and intangible assets)

Investments

Non-current asset investments are long-term investments held in other companies. These investments might be equity investments or investments in debt instruments. They are recorded in the statement of financial position at cost, less any impairment to their value.

2.2.2 Current Assets

Current assets are those assets purchased with the intention of resale or conversion into cash, usually within a 12-month period. They include stocks (or inventories) of finished goods and work in progress, the debtor balances that arise from the company providing its customers with credit (trade receivables), and any short-term investments held. Current assets also include cash balances held by the company and prepayments. Prepayments are simply when the company has prepaid an expense, as illustrated by the following example:

Example

A company, XYZ, draws up its statement of financial position on 31 December each year. Just prior to the year-end XYZ pays €25,000 to its landlord for the next three months' rental on its offices (to the end of March in the next calendar year).

This €25,000 is not an expense for the current year – it represents a prepayment towards the following year's expenses and is, therefore, shown as a prepayment within current assets in XYZ's statement of financial position.

Current assets are typically listed in the statement of financial position in ascending order of liquidity and appear in the statement of financial position at the lower of cost or net realisable value (NRV).

2.3 Depreciation and Amortisation

Learning Objective

7.2.2 Understand the concept of depreciation and amortisation

Depreciation is applied to tangible, non-current assets such as plant and machinery. An annual depreciation charge is made in the year's income statement. The depreciation charge allocates the fall in the book value of the asset over its useful economic life. This requirement does not, however, apply to freehold land and non-current asset investments which, not having a limited economic life, are not usually depreciated.

To calculate the annual depreciation charge to be applied to a tangible asset, the difference between its cost and estimated disposal value, termed the depreciable amount, must first be established. This value is then written off, over the asset's useful economic life, by employing the most appropriate depreciation method. The most common depreciation method is the straight line method. The straight line method simply spreads the depreciable amount equally over the economic life of the asset. The straight line method is given by the following formula:

$$\text{Straight line depreciation} = \frac{(\text{cost} - \text{disposal value})}{\text{useful economic life in years}}$$

One thing to recognise about the annual depreciation charge is that it is an accounting book entry, or a non-cash charge. That is, no cash flows from the business as a result of making the charge: it is simply an accounting entry made against the income statement to reflect the estimated cost of resources used over an accounting period. The statement of financial position value of the asset is given by its cost, less the accumulated depreciation to date, and is termed the net book value (NBV). This NBV does not necessarily equal the market value of the asset.

Example

Depreciation

A machine purchased for €25,000 has an estimated useful economic life of six years and an estimated disposal value after six years of €1,000. Calculate the depreciation that should be charged to this asset and its NBV in years one to six, using the straight line depreciation method.

Solution

Straight depreciation

$$\text{Straight line depreciation} = \frac{(\text{cost} - \text{disposal value})}{\text{useful economic life (years)}}$$

$$= \frac{(€25,000 - €1,000)}{6} = €4,000 \text{ per annum}$$

Year	Opening net book value	Depreciation	Closing net book value
1	25,000	4,000	21,000
2	21,000	4,000	17,000
3	17,000	4,000	13,000
4	13,000	4,000	9,000
5	9,000	4,000	5,000
6	5,000	4,000	1,000

By reducing the book value of tangible non-current assets over their useful economic lives, depreciation matches the cost of the asset against the periods from which the company benefits from its use.

On occasion, tangible assets, such as land, are not depreciated but periodically revalued. This is done on the basis of providing the user of the accounts with a truer and fairer view of the assets, or capital, employed by the company. To ensure the statement of financial position still balances (total assets = equity and liabilities), the increase in the asset's value arising on revaluation is reflected in a revaluation reserve, which forms part of the equity.

Closely linked to the idea of depreciating the value of a tangible asset over its useful economic life is the potential need for intangible assets to be amortised over their useful economic lives. **Amortisation**, like depreciation, is simply a book entry whose impact is felt in the company's reported income and financial position but does not impact its cash position. Most intangible assets are amortised each year.

Purchased goodwill is accounted for in a slightly different manner to most other intangible non-current assets. Purchased goodwill is capitalised and included in the statement of financial position; it is not amortised and, once capitalised, cannot be revalued but may suffer impairment in value.

2.4 Equity

Learning Objective

7.2.3   Understand the difference between share capital, capital reserves and revenue reserves

Equity is referred to in a number of ways, such as shareholders' funds, owners' equity or capital. Equity usually consists of three sub-elements: share capital, capital reserves and revenue reserves. Additionally, when group accounts are presented, there may be minority or non-controlling interests within the group equity figure.

- **Share capital** – this is the nominal value of equity and preference share capital the company has in issue and has called up.
- **Capital reserves** – capital reserves include revaluation reserves and the share premium account. The revaluation reserve arises from the upward revaluation of non-current assets, and the share premium reserve arises when the company issues shares at a price above their nominal value. Capital reserves are not distributable to the company's shareholders in the form of dividends, as they form part of the company's capital base, although they can be converted into a bonus issue of ordinary shares.
- **Revenue reserves** – the major revenue reserve is the accumulated retained earnings of the company. This represents the accumulation of the company's distributable profits that have not been paid to the company's shareholders as dividends, but have been retained in the business. The retained earnings should not be confused with the amount of cash the company holds or with the income statement that shows how the retained, or undistributed, profit in a single accounting period was arrived at.
- **Non-controlling interests or minority interests** – these arise when a parent company controls one or more subsidiary companies, but does not own all of the share capital. The equity attributable to the remaining shareholders is the minority or non-controlling interests and this is reflected in the statement of financial position within the equity section.

In total, equity is the sum of the called-up share capital, all of the capital reserves and the revenue reserves:

Equity = share capital + reserves

2.5 Liabilities

Learning Objective

7.2.4   Know how loans and indebtedness are included within a statement of financial position

A liability is an obligation to transfer future economic benefits as a result of past transactions or events; more simply, it could be described as money owed to someone else. Liabilities are categorised according to whether they are to be paid within, or after more than, one year:

- **Non-current liabilities** – this comprises the company's borrowing not repayable within the next 12 months. This could include bond issues as well as longer-term bank borrowing. In addition, there is a separate subheading for those liabilities that have resulted from past events or transactions and for which there is an obligation to make a payment, but the exact amount or timing of the expenditure has yet to be established. These are commonly referred to as provisions. Such provisions may arise as a result of the company undergoing a restructuring, for example. Given the uncertainty surrounding the extent of such liabilities, companies are required to create a realistic and prudent estimate of the monetary amount of the obligation, once it is committed to taking a certain course of action.
- **Current liabilities** – this includes the amount the company owes to its suppliers, or trade payables, as a result of buying goods and/or services on credit, any bank overdraft, and any other payables, such as tax, that fall due for payment within 12 months of the date of the statement of financial position.

3.   The Income Statement

3.1   Purpose and Contents

Learning Objective

7.3.1   Know the purpose of the income statement, its format and main contents

The income statement summarises the company's income earned and expenditure incurred over the accounting period. The income statement is alternatively referred to as the statement of profit and loss. The function of this financial statement is to detail how much profit has been earned and how the company's reported profit (or loss) was arrived at.

The amount of profit earned over the accounting period will impact the company's ability to pay dividends and how much can be retained to finance the growth of the business from internal resources.

Like the statement of financial position, the format of the income statement is governed by the law and underpinned by the requirements of various accounting standards. The following table shows a simplified example of an income statement. Under IFRSs, there is some flexibility about the precise format that is presented.

Example income statement for the year end 31 December 2017			
	Notes	2017	2016
		€000	€000
Revenue		9,500	8,750
Cost of sales		(7,000)	(6,600)
Gross profit		2,500	2,150
Distribution costs		(110)	(90)
Administrative expenses		(30)	(20)
Loss on disposal of plant		(260)	
Operating profit		2,100	2,040
Financial costs		(230)	(250)
Financial income		120	112
Profit before taxation		1,990	1,902
Taxation		(555)	(548)
Net income		1,435	1,354
Earnings per share (cents)		16.1c	15.9c

3.1.1 Revenue

The income statement starts with one of the most important things in any company's accounts: its sales revenues. In accounts, sales revenues are generally referred to as revenue, or sometimes turnover. It is simply everything that the company has sold during the year, regardless of whether it has received the cash or not. For a manufacturer, revenue is the sales of the products that it has made. For a company in the service industry, it is the consulting fees earned, or perhaps commissions earned on financial transactions.

3.1.2 Costs of Sales

The costs of sales are the costs to the company of generating the sales made in the financial year. These items are also sometimes known as the cost of goods sold (COGS). They typically include the costs directly associated with producing the goods that are sold, such as of the raw materials used to make a product and the costs of converting those raw materials into their finished state, including the wages of the staff making the products. COGS does not include indirect expenses such as the costs of distribution or selling the goods that are sold.

3.1.3 Gross Profit

Total sales, less the costs of those sales, results in the gross profit for the year.

3.1.4 Operating Profit

Operating profit is also referred to as profit on operating activities. It is the gross profit, less other operating expenses that the company has incurred. These other operating expenses might include costs incurred distributing products (distribution costs) and administrative expenses such as management salaries, auditors' fees and legal fees. Administrative expenses would also include depreciation and amortisation charges. Additional items may be separately disclosed before arriving at operating profit, such as the profit or loss made on selling a non-current asset. When a non-current asset, such as an item of machinery, is disposed of at a price significantly different from its statement of financial position value, the profit or loss when compared to this net book value (NBV) should be separately disclosed if material to the information conveyed by the accounts.

Operating profit is the profit before considering finance costs (interest) and any tax payable – so it can also be described as profit before interest and tax (PBIT).

3.1.5 Finance Costs/Finance Income

Finance costs are generally the interest that the company has incurred on its borrowings – that may be in the form of bonds or may be bank loans and overdrafts.

Finance income is typically the interest earned on surplus funds, such as from deposit accounts.

3.1.6 Profit Before Tax

This is the profit made by the company in the period, before considering any tax that may be payable on that profit.

3.1.7 Corporation Tax Payable

This is simply the corporation tax charge that the company has incurred for the period.

3.1.8 Net Income

Once tax and financing costs have been deducted, the income statement reaches a vital figure: net income, net profit or the profit for the period. Net income reflects all of the revenues earned during the period, less all of the expenditures incurred. This net income is also the profit attributable to the shareholders of the company because, in theory, it could all be distributed to shareholders as dividends.

3.1.9 Earnings Per Share (EPS)

This is an important figure for readers of the financial statements as it displays the company's profit expressed on a per-share basis. This is always reflected at the bottom of the income statement. Earnings per share (EPS) is the amount of profit after tax that has been earned per ordinary share. EPS is calculated as follows:

$$\text{EPS} = \frac{\text{Net income for the financial year} - \text{Dividends on preferred shares}}{\text{Number of ordinary shares in issue}}$$

3.1.10 Dividends

Some, or all, of the profit for the financial year can be distributed as dividends. Dividends to any preference shareholders are paid out first, followed by dividends to ordinary shareholders at an amount set by the board. The dividends for most listed companies are either paid in two or four instalments: either a single interim dividend paid after the half-year stage or three quarterly dividends, and a final dividend to be paid after the accounts have been approved.

The dividends are shown in the accounts in another of the required disclosures under the IFRS – the statement of changes in equity – that reconciles the movement in equity from one statement of financial position to another.

Example statement of changes in equity for the year ended 31 December 2017						
	Ord share capital	Pref share capital	Share premium account	Revaluation reserve	Retained earnings	Total
As at 1 January 2017	4,470	100		100	5,040	9,710
Gain on revaluation				80		80
Issue of shares	530		120			650
Net income for the year					1,435	1,435
Preference dividends paid					(5)	(5)
Ordinary dividends paid					(400)	(400)
As at 31 December 2017	5,000	100	120	180	6,070	11,470

3.2   Capital Versus Revenue Expenditure

Learning Objective

7.3.2   Understand the difference between capital and revenue expenditure

Money spent by a company will usually fall into one of two possible forms: capital expenditure or revenue expenditure.

- **Capital expenditure** is money spent to buy non-current assets, such as plant, property and equipment. It is reflected on the statement of financial position.
- **Revenue expenditure** is money spent that immediately impacts the income statement. Examples of revenue expenditure include wages paid to staff, rent paid on property and professional fees, like audit fees.

4.   The Statement of Cash Flows

4.1   Purpose of the Statement of Cash Flows

Learning Objective

7.4.1   Know the purpose of the cash flow statement, its format as set out in IAS 7

The statement of cash flows or, as it is often termed, the cash flow statement, is basically a summary of all the payments and receipts that have occurred over the course of the year, the total reflecting the inflow (or outflow) of cash over the year.

A statement of cash flows is required by accounting standard IAS 7.

The logic of adding a cash flow statement to a set of financial statements is that it enables the readers of the accounts to see clearly how cash has been generated and/or used over the course of the year. This is considered to provide relatively easily understood information to the users of the accounts that supplements the performance figures provided by the income statement, and the statement of financial position given by the statement of financial position.

IAS 7 cash flow statements require a company's cash flows to be broken down into particular headings, as illustrated in the following example:

Example cash flow statement for the year ended 31 December 2017	
Operating activities	
Cash receipts from customers	4,528
Cash paid to suppliers and employees	(2,441)
Cash generated from operations	2,527
Tax paid	–
Interest paid	(150)
Net cash from operating activities	**4,464**
Investing activities	
Interest received	80
Dividends received	40
Purchase of plant, property and equipment	(1,890)
Proceeds on sale of investments	120
Net cash used in investing activities	**(1,650)**
Financing activities	
Dividends paid	(435)
Repayments of borrowings	(200)
Proceeds on issue of shares	650
Net cash generated from financing activities	**15**
Net increase in cash and cash equivalents	2,829
Cash and cash equivalents at the beginning of the year	425
Cash and cash equivalents at the end of the year	3,254

Looking at the key cash flow statement headings in turn:

- **Operating activities** is the cash that has been generated from the trading activities of the company, excluding financing cost (interest).

- **Investing activities** details the investment income (dividends and interest) that has been received in the form of cash during the year and the cash paid to purchase new non-current assets, less the cash received from the sale of non-current assets during the year.
- **Financing activities** includes the cash spent during the year on paying dividends to shareholders, borrowing on a long-term basis or the cash raised from issuing shares, less the cash spent repaying debt or buying back shares.

The resultant total should explain the changes in cash (and cash equivalents) between the statement of financial positions. Many short-term investments are classified as cash equivalents, such as Treasury bills (T-bills).

4.2   Profit Versus Cash

Learning Objective

7.4.2   Understand the difference between profit and cash and their impact on the long-term future of the business

Profit appears in the income statement and is the excess of revenues earned over the period, over the expenses incurred in that same period. Obviously, generating profits is necessary for the long-term survival of any business, although companies can (and many do) exhibit losses for a number of years. Without profit, that business is unlikely to survive indefinitely.

The extent to which a company has generated (or used up) cash is detailed in the cash flow statement. Cash is generated when cash received exceeds cash paid out, and cash is used up when the cash paid out exceeds the cash received. Cash is often described as the lifeblood of the company. Without it the company will not survive. If a company does not have the cash to pay a liability when it is due, there is a possibility of the company being forced to close down.

When comparing profit against cash, there are some key differences. Because profit is based on revenues earned, not cash received, there is a possibility that the two figures for a company could be very different. For example, a company may make sales on credit and, therefore, recognise the revenues at the point of sale in the income statement. The cash for those sales could be received significantly later.

Similarly, profit is based on expenditure incurred, not cash paid, and there can be significant differences between the two. A key example of the potential for difference is in the different treatments of the purchase of a non-current tangible asset, like a machine. In the income statement, the impact will be a gradual expense incurred each year for the depreciation of the machine. In the cash flow statement, the full cost will be paid in cash at the time of purchase.

Example operating cash flow statement for year ending 31 December 2017			
All figures are in €			
Net income after tax		240,000	
Other additions to cash			
Depreciation and amortisation	35,000		Depreciation is not a cash expense; it is added back into net income for calculating cash flow
Decrease in accounts receivable	17,000		If accounts receivable decreases, then more cash has entered the company from customers paying off their accounts – the amount by which accounts receivable has decreased is an addition to cash
Decrease in inventory			A decrease in inventory signals that a company has spent less money to purchase more raw materials. The decrease in the value of inventory is an addition to cash
Decrease in other current assets	19,000		Similar reasoning to above for other current assets
Increase in accounts payable	26,000		If accounts payable increases it suggests more cash has been retained by the company through not paying some bills – the amount by which accounts payable has increased is an addition to cash
Increase in accrued expenses			For example deferring payment of some salaries will add to cash
Increase in other current liabilities			Similar reasoning to above for increase in taxes payable
Total additions to cash from operations		97,000	
Subtractions from cash			
Increase in accounts receivable			If accounts receivable increases, then less cash has entered the company from customers paying their accounts – the amount by which accounts receivable has increased is a subtraction of cash
Increase in inventory	−33,000		An increase in inventory signals that a company has spent more money to purchase more raw materials. If the inventory was paid with cash, the increase in the value of inventory is a subtraction of cash

Increase in other current assets			Similar reasoning to above for other current assets
Decrease in accounts payable			If accounts payable decreases it suggests more cash has been used by the company to pay its bills – the amount by which accounts payable decreased is a subtraction from cash
Decrease in accrued expenses	−19,000		For example an increase in prepaid expenses results in a subtraction of cash
Decrease in other current liabilities	−23,000		Similar reasoning to above for decrease in taxes payable
Total subtractions from cash from operations		−75,000	
Total operating cash flow		262,000	= net income after tax + total additions to cash from operations + total subtractions from cash from operations

4.3   Free Cash Flow

Learning Objective

7.4.3   Understand the purpose of free cash flow and the difference between enterprise cash flow and equity cash flow

There is no single definition of free cash flow. Logically, it perhaps should be drawn from the cash flow statement and represent the amount of cash that has been generated and that the company can choose what to do with. This might be the operating cash flow less the extent to which the company has to spend cash to maintain the operating capacity of the business. It is the latter figure that is difficult to isolate, and is likely to be a subjective judgement by the user of the accounts. The resultant figure might be adjusted further depending on whether the calculation is for free cash flow to the firm (enterprise cash flow), or just free cash flow to the shareholders (equity cash flow). This will be explored in more detail below.

Because of the difficulty in arriving at free cash flow from the cash flow statement, many users calculate a free cash flow figure from the income statement. This is generally arrived at by taking the net income from the income statement, adding back the charges for depreciation and amortisation and deducting capital expenditure. The capital expenditure is used as a best estimate of the capital spend required to maintain the operating capacity of the business. The use of the income statement figure for operating cash flow presents a smoother, potentially more representative figure for cash generation than the figure in the cash flow statement as it removes the inconsistencies that payments in advance or in arrears create.

As well as there being two potentially different sources for free cash flow (the cash flow statement or the income statement), there are further adjustments that might be made depending on whether the free cash flow is being calculated for the whole enterprise (the enterprise cash flow) or is being calculated for the equity holders only (the equity cash flow).

The enterprise cash flow is the free cash flow before considering payments made to any of the providers of finance to the firm. The providers of finance to the firm are both the lenders and the equity holders. The enterprise cash flow will, therefore, be the free cash flow before considering any financing costs.

In contrast the equity cash flow is the free cash flow to the shareholders, so it will be after any financing costs to the lenders, but before any dividend payments to the shareholders.

Example cash flow statement for year ending 31 December 2017			
All figures are in €			
Total operating cash flow	262,000		= net income after tax + total additions to cash from operations + total subtractions from cash from operations
Investment/capital expenditures			
Additions to cash from investments			
Decrease in plant, property and equipment	150,000		The sale of a building, for example, will lead to an addition to cash
Decrease in notes receivable	12,000		A reduction in notes receivable indicates that cash will have been received
Decrease in securities, investments			Securities will have been sold thereby raising cash
Decrease in intangible, non-current assets			Sale of a patent or copyright will lead to an addition of cash
Total additions to cash from investments	162,000		
Subtractions from cash for investments			
Increase in plant, property and equipment			Purchase of a building will lead to a subtraction from cash
Increase in notes receivable			An increase in notes receivable indicates that cash has not yet been received
Increase in securities, investments	−64,000		Securities will have been purchased thereby reducing cash
Increase in intangible, non-current assets	−250,000		Purchase of a copyright will lead to a reduction of cash

Total subtractions from cash for investments		−314,000	
Total enterprise cash flow		110,000	= total operating cash flow + additions to cash from capital investments − subtractions from cash from capital investments
Financing activities			
Additions to cash from financing			
Increase in borrowings	50,000		Additional net borrowing will lead to an addition of cash
Increase in capital stock			Additional net equity capital paid in will lead to an addition of cash
Total additions to cash from financing		50,000	
Subtractions from cash for financing			
Decrease in borrowings			Net reduction in borrowing will lead to a subtraction of cash
Decrease in capital Stock			Retirement of net equity capital paid in, such as share buybacks, will lead to a subtraction of cash
Total subtractions from cash for financing			
Total equity cash flow		160,000	= total enterprise cash flow + additions to cash from financing + subtractions from cash from financing
Subtractions from cash for dividends			
Dividends paid		−100,000	
Total free cash flow		60,000	= total equity cash flow − dividends paid out
Cash at beginning of period		450,000	
Cash at end of period		510,000	

5. Financial Statement Analysis

5.1 Introduction

Learning Objective

7.5.1 Understand the purpose of ratio analysis and its limitations

The three principal financial statements and associated explanatory notes published by companies in their report and accounts furnish the user with a considerable amount of information. However, the needs of the user can be met more precisely by employing ratio analysis, as key relationships can be established and trends identified by consolidating information into a more readily usable form. Ratios are commonly employed by analysts to assess the prospects for a particular company and, therefore, the investment potential of the shares of that company, as well as assisting other interested parties in assessing the company such as the board, suppliers, competitors and employees.

The purpose of ratio analysis is:

1. To assist in assessing business performance, by identifying meaningful relationships between numbers contained within company financial statements, that may not be immediately apparent. Although there are no statutory rules as to how ratios should be calculated, there should be logic in the numbers being related to each other.
2. To summarise financial information into an easily understandable form.
3. To identify trends, strengths and weaknesses by comparing the ratios to those of the same company in prior periods, other similar companies, sector averages and market averages.

However, ratio analysis does have its limitations:

1. As financial statements contain historic data, ratios are not predictive; indeed, occasionally, historic figures can be restated in later periods, making comparison difficult.
2. The use of alternative accounting methods and differences in international accounting practices may make it difficult to draw comparisons.
3. Significant judgement is needed when performing ratio analysis, which naturally leads to divergence.

The ratios required for the examination follow, firstly, an explanation of each of the key subsets of the ratios to meet the examiner's requirement that the candidate understands the ratios, followed by the formulae so that the candidate can also calculate the specified ratios.

5.2 Return on Capital Employed (ROCE) and Profitability Ratios

Learning Objective

7.5.2   Understand the following key ratios: profitability ratios (gross profit and operating profit margins); return on capital employed

5.2.1 ROCE and Profitability Ratios Explained

Profitability ratios look at the percentage return that the company generates relative to its revenues. The gross profit looks at the percentage of revenues that the company earns after considering the costs of sales. The operating profit margin looks at the percentage of revenues that the company earns after considering costs of sales and other operating costs (such as distribution costs and administrative expenses). Clearly, all other things being equal, a greater profit margin is preferable to a lesser profit margin.

Return on capital employed (ROCE) is widely seen as the best ratio for measuring overall management performance, in relation to the capital that has been paid into the business. It looks at the amount of return (profit) that is being generated as a percentage of the finance put into the business (the capital employed). The amount of capital employed is the equity plus the long-term debt. This is the money that the company holds from shareholders and debt providers, and it is from this money that the management should be able to generate profits.

5.2.2 ROCE and Profitability Ratios: Calculations

Effectively, the ROCE gives a yield for the entire company. It compares the money invested in the company with the generated return. This annual return can then be compared to other companies, or less risky investments.

The formula is:

$$\text{ROCE} = \frac{\text{Operating profit}}{\text{Capital employed}} \times 100$$

where operating profit is the profit before financing and tax on the income statement, and capital employed is the total for equity on the statement of financial position, plus the total for non-current liabilities from the statement of financial position.

Using the example accounts encountered earlier:

$$\text{ROCE} = 2,100 / (12,280 + 2,000) \times 100 = 14.7\%$$

The figures for the profitability ratios are drawn from the income statement. The formulae for the profitability ratios are:

$$\text{Gross profit margin (\%)} = (\text{Gross profit} / \text{Revenues}) \times 100$$

$$\text{Operating profit margin (\%)} = (\text{Operating profit} / \text{Revenues}) \times 100$$

Using the example from earlier:

$$\text{Gross profit margin (\%)} = (2{,}500 / 9{,}500) \times 100 = 26.3\%$$

$$\text{Operating profit margin (\%)} = (2{,}100 / 9{,}500) \times 100 = 22\%$$

5.3 Financial Gearing Ratios

Learning Objective

7.5.3 Understand the following financial gearing ratios: investors' debt to equity ratio; net debt to equity ratio; interest cover

5.3.1 Financial Gearing Ratios Explained

Financial gearing is a measure of risk within a company. Financial gearing is also called 'financial leverage', and the ratios are also referred to as 'financial leverage ratios'. Financial gearing or leverage is determined by examining the amount of a company's financing that comes from debt, and the amount that comes from shareholders' funds or equity – the debt to equity ratio.

The higher the proportion of debt finance, the higher the risk that the company will not be able to meet its financing commitments. This is because interest on debt must be paid every year and the debt must be repaid at some point, whereas dividends on shares need only be paid in profitable years and share capital never has to be repaid. It is the inability to service and repay debt that brings about company failure. However, high levels of borrowing in some circumstances can be positive for the shareholders because, if the debt interest is fixed, what is left after paying debt interest is the entitlement of the equity holders so, in years when the firm earns substantial returns, all of the excess belongs to the equity holders.

Whether debt levels are excessive is a matter of judgement, but gearing ratios tend to look at the total debt compared to equity. Sometimes this ratio may be less useful because, as well as holding substantial amounts of debt, the company also holds substantial cash and short-term investments that could be used to repay the debt – it is in these circumstances when net debt to equity is used.

Another way to assess whether debt levels are excessive is to look at the extent to which profits are being made to cover the interest burden on that debt – the interest cover.

5.3.2   Financial Gearing Ratios: Calculations

Debt to Equity = Debt/Equity

Both figures for debt and equity are drawn from the statement of financial position of a company. All non-current liabilities are generally considered to be debt, and the total of the equity portion of the statement of financial position is considered to be equity. The ratio is either stated as a simple proportion: debt to equity is 0.6; or, as a percentage: debt is 60% of the equity.

Using the example encountered earlier:

$$\text{Debt to equity} = 2{,}000 / 12{,}280 = 0.163 \text{ or } 16.3\%$$

Net Debt to Equity = (Debt less cash and short-term investments)/Equity

Net debt is simply the debt as in the debt-to-equity ratio, less the cash and short-term investments that are within the current assets on the statement of financial position.

Using the example:

$$\text{Net debt to equity} = (2{,}000 - 860) / 12{,}280 = 0.093 \text{ or } 9.3\%$$

Interest Cover = Operating Profit/Interest Costs

Interest cover figures are drawn from the income statement. The operating profit is simply divided by the interest costs (the financing costs line on the income statement).

Using the example:

$$\text{Interest cover} = 2{,}100 / 230 = 9.13 \text{ times}$$

5.4   Investors' Ratios Explained

Learning Objective

7.5.4   Understand the following investors' ratios: enterprise value to EBIT; enterprise value to EBITDA; earnings per share; diluted earnings per share

7.5.5   Be able to calculate the following investors' ratios: earnings per share; price earnings ratio (both historic and prospective); gross dividend yield; gross dividend cover

Existing and potential investors look at a variety of ratios to assess whether or not a company is likely to be a good investment. These ratios look to establish how:

- expensive the shares are, in order to reach a conclusion on the likelihood of capital growth
- much in dividends the shares pay, and how easily the company is able to bear the payment of those dividends, to reach a conclusion on the income those shares are likely to generate.

5.4.1 Earnings Per Share (EPS)

The earnings per share (EPS) ratio is one of the most useful and often-cited ratios used in the investment world. It is used universally and more or less has the same meaning in most jurisdictions, but is one ratio for which there are prescribed rules regarding its calculation. These are laid out in IAS 33, which essentially defines the EPS as follows:

$$EPS = \frac{\text{Net profit / loss attributable to ordinary shareholders}}{\text{Average weighted number of ordinary shares outstanding in a period}}$$

The EPS reveals how much profit was made during the year that is available to be paid out to each share. As a figure for profit per share, it can be divided into the current share price to assess how many times the profit per share must be paid to buy a share – in effect, how expensive (or cheap) those shares are. This is the price earnings ratio (P/E).

Furthermore, investors are particularly interested in the earnings each share will generate in the future, rather than how much they have generated in the past. As a result, stockbrokers' research departments will endeavour to anticipate what the EPS will be – the prospective EPS – rather than what the EPS was in the last reported set of results – the historic EPS.

To calculate the EPS, one simply divides the value of net income or earnings (which is the net income for the financial year) by the number of ordinary shares in issue.

$$EPS = \frac{\text{Net income for the financial year – Dividends on preferred shares}}{\text{Number of ordinary shares in issue}}$$

Note that if the company has preference shares in issue, the earnings are after the preference shareholders' dividend but before the ordinary shareholders' dividend. For a group of companies preparing consolidated accounts, the earning line will also be after any minority/non-controlling interests. Minority interests are the profits that belong to shareholders of any subsidiary companies that are not shareholders in the parent company.

The following illustration shows how to calculate the earnings per share.

Illustration

XYZ has net income or earnings of €898,000 for its most recent **fiscal year** and, at the time of preparing the EPS estimate, has 5 million outstanding ordinary shares.

The EPS is €898,000 / 5,000,000 shares = 18c per share.

5.4.2 Diluted Earnings Per Share

The purpose of publishing a separate figure for diluted EPS is to warn shareholders of potential future changes in the EPS figure as a result of events that actually may have, or theoretically could take place.

The EPS, as defined in section 5.4.1, is potentially misleading if the company has substantial quantities of instruments in issue that are convertible into shares. These may be convertible bonds or share options issued to the senior management of the company. If the EPS is calculated in the usual way – by simply dividing the net income for the period by the number of issued shares – the users of the accounts are not incorporating the impact that convertible instruments may have – in particular their dilutive impact on the EPS. The issuance of more shares will mean a lower EPS. As a result, for companies with significant convertible instruments in issue, an adjusted figure for the EPS is required to be disclosed that takes this into account. This ratio is called the diluted EPS.

The reason why the term theoretically is used in this context is because there is only a possibility – legally certain rights have been granted which could be exercised and require further issues of shares – and the prudent method of accounting is to assume, from the point of view of share dilution, the worst case scenario.

There are two broad forms of securities that could cause share dilution and which need to be incorporated into calculating a diluted EPS. A company may have either or both of the following kinds of securities outstanding:

- issued convertible loan stock or convertible preference shares
- issued options or warrants.

Each of these circumstances may potentially result in more shares being issued, and thereby qualifying for a dividend in future years, which may have a material effect in diluting the current EPS.

The diluted EPS figure is considered of such importance to the reader of the accounts, and a potential investor, that its calculation and disclosure is required by IAS 33 – Earnings Per Share.

The following illustration for the same imaginary company shows how to calculate the diluted EPS.

Illustration

The debt financing of XYZ at the year-end includes €250,000 of 10% convertible loan stock, which was issued some years earlier. The terms of conversion for every €100 nominal value of loan stock is for 115 ordinary shares, and the convertible stockholders have not taken the option of converting, so the €250,000 of convertible loan stock is still in issue at year-end.

Basic earnings for the year to 31 December is €898,000.

If the convertible loan stock had been converted, interest would have been saved of €250,000 @ 10% = €25,000.

However, assuming a corporation tax rate of 30% this would have increased the tax payable by €25,000 x 30% = €7,500.

So, the fully diluted earnings, assuming the conversion had occurred = (€898,000 + €25,000 – €7,500) = €915,500.

Number of shares pre-dilution for the period is 5,000,000.

The option remains for the loan stock to be converted at a rate of 115 shares. So, the maximum number of new ordinary shares that could be issued is [250,000 / 100] x 115 = 287,500 shares.

So the fully diluted number of ordinary shares is 5,287,500.

Pre-dilution, the basic EPS is €898,000 / 5,000,000 shares = 18c per share.

The fully diluted EPS is €915,500 / 5,287,500 shares = 17.3c.

5.4.3 Price Earnings (P/E) Ratio

The price earnings (P/E) ratio is calculated as follows:

$$P/E\ Ratio = \frac{Current\ market\ price\ per\ share}{Earnings\ per\ share}$$

Let us suppose that the ordinary shares for a company are currently trading at €2.50 per share and that the EPS is 20c: the P/E ratio is €2.50/€0.20 = 12.5.

The P/E ratio can be thought of as the number of years of earnings at the current level to generate the share price, and in this case it is 12.5 years.

The price per share in the numerator is the market price of a single share of the stock. The EPS in the denominator of the formula can vary according to the type of P/E that is being offered for consideration.

Essentially, analysts will tend to look at two types of earnings for the denominator – backward-looking and forward-looking. Forward-looking EPS requires forecasting, which can be unreliable and is often based on a company's own projections.

Trailing (P/E)

Also known as P/E trailing twelve months (ttm), this is the backward-looking version that has already been described in the formula. It can be updated between annual reports using half-yearly or quarterly figures and it is customary in the analyst community to take for earnings the net income of the company for the most recent 12-month period divided by the number of shares outstanding. This is the most common meaning of P/E if no other qualifier is specified.

Forward P/E

This is also known as P/E or estimated P/E, and is based on estimation of net earnings over the next 12 months. Estimates are typically derived as the mean of a select group of analysts. In times of rapid economic dislocation, such estimates become less relevant as the macroenvironment changes (eg, new economic data is published and/or the basis of the analysts' forecasts becomes obsolete) occur ahead of the analysts adjusting their forecasts.

Companies with losses (negative earnings) or no profit have an undefined P/E ratio (usually shown as not applicable (N/A)).

Illustration

Continuing with the illustration from above of XYZ, if the ordinary shares are currently trading at €1.60 each, and there is a forecast EPS for the next fiscal year for XYZ of 17 cents per share, the P/E ratios for the company will be as follows:

Historic P/E = 160 / 18 = 8.89 (this is based on the pre-diluted EPS of 18 cents)

Prospective P/E = 160 / 17 = 9.41 (this is based on the forecast EPS of 17 cents)

Uses of the P/E Ratio

By comparing price and EPS, one can analyse the market's stock valuation of a company and its shares, relative to the income the company is actually generating. Stocks with higher (and/or more certain) forecast earnings growth will usually have a higher P/E, and those expected to have lower (and/or riskier) earnings growth will, in most cases, have a lower P/E.

Investors can use the P/E ratio to compare the relative valuations of stocks. If one stock has a P/E twice that of another stock, all things being equal, it is a less attractive investment. However, companies are rarely equal and comparisons between industries, companies, and time periods can be misleading.

P/E ratios are closely followed by the investment community and financial analysts. Indeed, the P/E ratios of stock market indices or averages are often used to determine whether or not the overall market is considered to be expensive, is priced in line with historical norms, or is cheap. For example, in the US the S&P 500 Index has a mean historical P/E ratio, over the last 50 years, of approximately 18, but has fluctuated rather considerably from that mean. When analysing the ratio it is customary to use the last 12 months of earnings of the constituent stocks of the index, and this is referred to as the trailing average.

Companies in different sectors of the economy will also tend to exhibit different P/E ratios. This will itself be largely based upon the market's expectations as to future earnings growth in different sectors. For example, a relatively young technology company which has bright prospects will often be rewarded by investors with a relatively high P/E ratio as the earnings are expected to grow dynamically. On the other hand a mature utility company which has fairly predictable future earnings potential will tend to have a relatively lower P/E ratio based on more conservative growth estimations.

At times during the recession in the early 1980s, the trailing P/E ratio for the S&P Index reached below eight and, in the early part of 2000 just prior to the collapse of the dot com stocks, the P/E ratio reached above 40, measured on a trailing 12-month basis.

One factor which can influence the criterion used to assess whether the overall market is overpriced, fairly priced or underpriced is the interest rate environment as well as the annual rate of inflation. During periods when short-term interest rates are relatively low, and inflation is considered to be benign, a larger P/E ratio is supportable as there is less competition for equities coming from the income obtainable from fixed-income securities and vice versa.

Another useful application of the P/E ratio is to consider the relationship between it on an individual company's security and the P/E ratio of the stock market average or of the sector average. Some investors will be attracted to companies with a low P/E ratio as it suggests that the company may be undervalued.

5.4.4   Enterprise Value (EV) to Earnings Before Interest and Tax (EBIT)

This ratio consists of two other metrics – enterprise value (EV), and EBIT (earnings before interest and tax).

EV is a measure of a company's value and is often used as an alternative to straightforward market capitalisation. A firm's EV is calculated as its market capitalisation plus all of its outstanding debt, minority interests and preferred shares, minus all of the cash and cash equivalents.

From a slightly different perspective, EV is the sum of the claims of all of a company's security holders, which includes all of the debt holders, preferred shareholders, minority shareholders, common equity holders, and others. EV is one of the fundamental metrics used in business valuation, financial modelling, accounting and portfolio analysis.

A simplified and intuitive way to understand EV is to consider it as the cost of purchasing an entire business. If you settle with all the security holders, you have essentially purchased the company at its EV.

EBIT is the same as profit before interest and tax (PBIT) and is another fairly widely used indicator of a company's financial performance, calculated as:

EBIT = Revenue less expenses (excluding tax and interest)

Comparison of EV/EBIT with P/E Ratio

Price earnings ratios provide a measure of the expensiveness, or cheapness, of a particular company's shares. As an alternative, EV multiples look at the whole company, incorporating both the equity and the debt. Simplistically, the smaller the EV to EBIT, the cheaper the company is, which could highlight a buying opportunity for investors.

5.4.5   Enterprise Value (EV) to Earnings Before Interest Tax, Depreciation and Amortisation (EBITDA)

This ratio, once again, is used as a measure of the relative expensiveness (or cheapness) of a business and also uses the EV as the numerator in the ratio.

EBITDA is essentially income before interest and tax, but with depreciation, and amortisation reversed and added back. It can be considered as a simplistic operating cash flow from the business, as depreciation and amortisation do not involve the movement of cash. However, it must be clearly understood that this is a non-GAAP measure. This means that companies can, and often do change the items included in their EBITDA calculation from one reporting period to the next.

Care must be taken as EBITDA does not truly represent cash earnings: it leaves out the cash required to fund working capital and the replacement of old equipment, which can be significant.

EBITDA = Revenue less expenses (excluding tax, interest, depreciation and amortisation)

5.4.6 Gross Dividend Yield

The gross dividend yield expresses the total dividends per share paid out over the last year as a percentage of the current share price.

To calculate gross dividend yield, simply divide the dividend per share by the current share price and multiply it by 100:

$$\text{Gross dividend yield} = \frac{\text{Dividend}}{\text{Current share price}} \times 100$$

For XYZ, let us assume that the board of directors decides to distribute €400,000 to shareholders in the form of a dividend and retain the rest of net income on its statement of financial position. The dividend per share will be €400,000 divided by five million shares = 8c.

The gross dividend yield will be:

$$\text{Gross dividend yield} = \frac{8}{160} \times 100 = 5\%$$

A high yield may indicate that the share price is relatively low in comparison with the return it offers. This suggests that the market does not have confidence that the dividends paid in the past will continue to be paid in the future. Conversely, a low dividend yield indicates high market confidence in the company's ability to increase dividends.

5.4.7 Gross Dividend Cover

The dividend cover can be used to assess how well a company covered its dividend payout with the profits it made. In other words, how easy was it for the company to pay these dividends?

Dividend cover compares the earnings of the company (net income in relation to the year's activity) with the dividends paid in the year. This also reveals the proportion of profits that were reinvested in the company. If dividend cover was two times, then half of the profits are paid out to shareholders and half are retained.

A dividend cover of less than one is known as an uncovered dividend, meaning the year's profits were not enough to cover the dividend.

To calculate the dividend cover for XYZ, take the company's EPS and divide it by the dividends per share:

$$\text{Dividend cover} = \frac{\text{EPS}}{\text{Dividends per share}}$$

Using the figures from above, the dividend cover for XYZ will be 18 / 8 = 2.25 times.

End of Chapter Questions

1. What is the alternative name for the financial accounts of a business?
   Answer reference: Section 1.1

2. What is the basic description of a statement of financial position?
   Answer reference: Section 2.1

3. What is meant by non-current assets?
   Answer reference: Section 2.2.1

4. What is meant by intangible non-current assets?
   Answer reference: Section 2.2.1

5. What is depreciation generally applied to?
   Answer reference: Section 2.3

6. What are the two typical types of capital reserves and how do they arise?
   Answer reference: Section 2.4

7. How does a minority interest arise?
   Answer reference: Section 2.4

8. What is the purpose of an income statement?
   Answer reference: Section 3.1

9. What is meant by operating profit?
   Answer reference: Section 3.1.4

10. How is the dividend yield calculated?
    Answer reference: Section 5.4.6

Chapter Eight
Risk and Reward

1.	Investment Management	229
2.	Institutional Investment Advice	252

This syllabus area will provide approximately 12 of the 100 examination questions

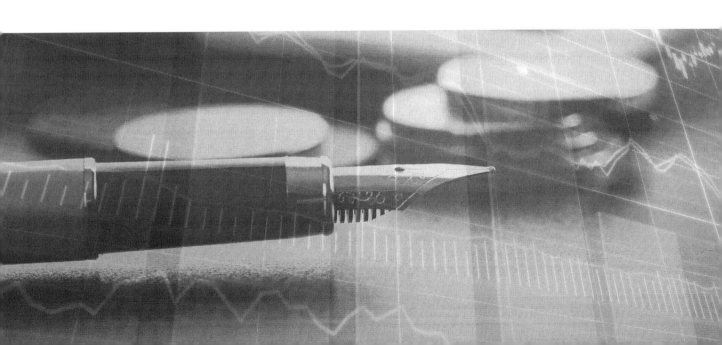

1. Investment Management

1.1 Risk and Reward

Learning Objective

8.1.1   Know the basics of risk and reward: assessment of returns; types of risk; quantifying risk

In general terms, when choosing between investments across the various asset classes, the returns achieved will depend on a variety of factors, including how the economy in general performs, what events are taking place in the geographical location of the investment (political, economic) and how the sector of the economy in which the company operates behaves. The decisions which need to be made with respect to investment management are very much concerned with a balancing (or, as it is sometimes expressed, a trade-off) between the likely rewards and potential returns from the chosen investment given the associated risks, and then considering the impact of those risks on the overall portfolio.

Let us consider the situation of a fund manager who is concerned about how the economy will behave and is trying to put together an overall assessment of the expected returns (ERs) on a portfolio of investments depending upon the future growth of the economy. In the illustration below, the economic outlook is quite uncertain.

The table shows three different scenarios with their association probabilities and ERs. The first row of the table considers that the economy will be in a recession with overall contraction. The fund manager gives that a probability of 20% and a return for that scenario of negative 10% for the assets under consideration. The second scenario is for a growth rate between just above zero up to 3% per annum (based upon gross domestic product (GDP) for example) and this is assumed to have a 50% probability with an associated annual return of 8%. The most upbeat scenario is for growth above 3% and the fund manager's assessment is that there is a 30% probability of this and an appealing 15% return for this scenario.

Future Growth of Economy	Probability P	Scenario Return SR	Probability * Scenario Return P*SR	Scenario Variance SV [SR−ER]2	Probability * Scenario Variance SV*P
Contraction < 0%	20%	−10.0%	−2.0%	0.027225	0.005445
> 0% Growth < 3%	50%	8.0%	4.0%	0.000225	0.0001125
Growth > 3%	30%	15.0%	4.5%	0.007225	0.0021675
	100%	Expected Return (ER)	6.5%	σ2	0.77%
		Standard Deviation √σ2		σ	8.79%

The overall ER from these scenarios is calculated by taking the probability of each and multiplying that by the scenario return (SR) and summing the results. Under the conditions in the table, the expected return is 6.5%.

The manner in which the risks are associated with the different scenarios can be determined by calculating the variance. The variance measures the extent to which returns 'vary' from the average (or expected) return. As can be seen from the right-hand column of the table, the total of each variance can be calculated and, from this, we can derive the standard deviation. The standard deviation is the square root of variance, and is used as a statistical measure of risk that depicts the likely variation from ER levels.

In essence the cornerstones of investment theory require calculations similar to the above in many instances. First, what is the expected return? Often based upon a probability study, and, just as important, what is the notion of the risk associated with achieving that return? From the point of view of investment management, the risk reflects the variability or deviation of the likely returns from the ER and reflects the uncertainty of the likely outcomes.

1.1.1 Types of Risk

Risk arises from the uncertainty of outcomes. Each time an investor decides to purchase a security or invest in an opportunity, the outcome is uncertain in the same way that any future event is. The investor may incur a loss if the opportunity has been miscalculated, or they may not realise, fully or even partially, the ER.

At the macro level, investors may be concerned about the risks of market crashes, terrorist incidents that cause markets to plunge and other critical events. At the micro level, investors are concerned with internal or external events that may impact the company (or the creditworthiness/solvency of the company) invested in. All of these contribute to the potential for profit from investment and speculation and the accompanying uneasiness felt about the possibility of losses or adverse consequences from investment or speculative activities. This is the general notion of risk.

There are a number of types of risk faced by investors that are difficult to avoid, and the main categories can be identified in overview under the following headings.

Market or Systematic Risk

This is the risk that the overall market in general, or the relevant part of the capital markets for investors wanting exposure to specific sectors, will rise or fall, as economic conditions and other market factors change. This may affect returns over a period of time, or it may have a more immediate impact if an investor buys at the top of the market or sells at the bottom.

Inflation Risk

Inflation will erode returns or purchasing power and even if the investor has taken account of inflation in their analysis the actual and expected inflation may be different from that assumed in calculating ERs.

Interest Rate Risk

Changes in interest rates will affect prices; this is possibly a sub category of market risk.

In addition, there are a number of risks, specific to particular companies or sectors, which can be avoided by diversification or by ignoring an investment altogether.

Exchange Rate Risk

Any investor who purchases securities which are denominated in a foreign currency may suffer (or benefit) from changes in the exchange rates between the home or base currency or the other currency. In addition, it is important to consider the risk that an investor's base or home currency may fall against other currencies, thereby diminishing the purchasing power for global assets.

Default Risk

An investor may find that a company from which they have purchased a security could become insolvent due to a harsh operating environment, high levels of borrowing, poor management and other financial miscalculations. Fixed-income investors, who purchase the bonds of companies, have some access to alerts of possible credit defaults through the credit ratings agencies, such as Standard & Poor's (S&P), Moody's and Fitch Ratings.

Liquidity Risk

The risk that an investor will not be able to obtain the price they want for a security when buying or selling due to limited quantity or trading activity. Generally, the larger capital markets, such as those of New York, London and Tokyo, among others, provide sufficient liquidity for investors to sell a security easily with a narrow spread between the ask and the bid prices. During stressful periods, however, this liquidity can diminish and it can become much harder to sell a security readily.

1.1.2 Quantifying Risk

How can we quantify the risk and expected return of any investment?

In order to assess the risk and expected returns from particular opportunities, an investor needs to conduct an analysis of the forecasts for the economy and the forecasts for particular companies and/or sectors and undertake a risk analysis of the possible outcomes, and their likelihood, which could adversely affect these forecasts. This can be summarised as both forward- and backward-looking:

- **Forward-looking** forecasts and probabilities assess the likelihood of each possible state of the world occurring and estimate the returns and values arising given that particular outcome.
- **Backward-looking** analyses tend to study historically observed returns and associated frequencies on the assumption that this past data will be representative of the future.

In both cases, assessing the likelihood or probability of certain outcomes becomes the central task and it is necessary to consider the probability of returns and their associated risks from a broad perspective.

Risk and reward are important aspects of investment decisions. Risk and potential reward are generally positively correlated: investments with a higher potential return generally carry a higher risk of loss. High-risk investments generally have potential for a higher reward, plus a greater possibility of loss. Low-risk investments generally have a lower reward, with a lower possibility of loss.

1.2 Equities

Learning Objective

8.1.2 Understand the risk and reward of investment in equities: risk profile; effect of longer term; can offer income and capital appreciation; purpose and use of dividends

Equities are shares in companies that give the investor an ownership stake in the company, alongside the attraction of limited liability. If the issuing company collapses, the shareholders' loss is simply the amount paid for the shares. As a part-owner of the company, the investor has the opportunity to share in the company's profits and vote at general meetings. Indeed, most investors are attracted to equities in the hope that the value of the shares increases (capital appreciation), and this may be combined with income in the form of regular, and perhaps increasing, dividends.

Risk Profile for Equities

Equity investments are generally considered to be risky, relative to other investments, such as bonds and money market instruments. Medium levels of risk are attached to larger, well-established company shares, and high levels of risk attached to smaller company shares and start-up company shares. However, equity investments offer the potential to deliver high returns if held long-term.

Equity Risk Premium

For equity investors there is an equity risk premium, which effectively is a higher rate of return that is required to entice investors to take on the risk of owning shares or equity, as opposed to holding a more secure asset such as a bond. If one is seeking the most secure form of investment this will usually be available in the form of a government bond or short-term instrument. The risk-free rate is the rate on government bonds and short-term debts, because of the low chance that the government will default on its loans. An investment in stocks or equities has far more risk associated with it, as it is a non-secured asset and companies can suffer from adverse business conditions or go bankrupt, in which case shareholders often receive no residual value.

As an example, if the total return on a stock is 10% over a given period and the risk-free rate over the same period is 4%, the equity-risk premium is 6%.

1.3 Money Market Instruments

Learning Objective

8.1.3 Understand the risk and reward of investment in money market instruments: risk profile; use as short-term investment

For investment horizons that are very short (eg, the next six months rather than the next 20 years), there is the potential for investors to keep their funds in cash and place them on interest-earning deposit, or to invest in short-term money market instruments, like Treasury bills (T-bills). These investments are low-risk, relatively secure and deliver income, but provide little scope for capital growth. For investors that do not want their money tied up for long periods, however, the predictable value and liquidity of these short-term investments is important.

Prices of money market instruments fluctuate and can, in moments of financial crisis, become quite erratic. Many investors will want to hold the shortest-term instruments such as T-bills during periods when the money markets are not functioning normally. During the financial crisis, which became especially acute in September and October of 2008, many institutions wanted to replace all of their other money market holdings with the shortest-duration T-bills. This can have the perverse consequence, on extreme occasions, of making such instruments, which are priced on a discount basis, yield a negative return or at a rate which is far below that which would normally be expected. The desire to move into such short-term paper during moments of crisis is referred to as a flight to safety.

While some institutional investors, such as pension funds, seek out longer-dated maturities in fixed-income markets, there are many that prefer shorter- and medium-term assets.

There is often a trade-off and calculation to be made between the value of a long-term income stream from such instruments versus the greater volatility in the prevailing prices of longer-dated paper.

1.4   Debt Instruments

Learning Objective

8.1.4   Understand the risk/reward of investments in debt (fixed-interest, floating-rate and index-linked): compared to equities; effect of holding to maturity; can combine low risk and certain return; can provide a fixed income; inflation risk; interest rate risk; default risk

Bonds are fixed-interest loan instruments, predominantly issued by companies, governments, government agencies and supranationals like the World Bank, providing the issuer with debt finance. Their attractiveness to investors is driven by the fixed income that they offer from regular, pre-determined coupons, combined with the relative certainty of the principal amount to be repaid at redemption.

The coupons can be fixed (at a percentage of nominal value), they can float depending upon a published interest rate such as the London Interbank Offered Rate (LIBOR), or they can be tied to inflation by being index-linked (eg, to the consumer prices index (CPI)). The principal amount paid at maturity is generally the par or nominal value, although with index-linked bonds it will be uplifted for inflation. They are generally less risky than equities, but offer less potential for substantial returns. Indeed, for highly rated bonds, where the risk of default is low, investors can be virtually certain of the yield that their investment will deliver, as long as they hold their bonds to maturity. If the bonds are sold before they reach maturity, however, there is a danger that their market value may be below their nominal value, bringing about a capital loss and the potential to impact the investor's yield adversely.

As explained in section 1.1.1, interest rate risk is the risk that an interest rate movement brings about an adverse movement in the value of an investment. It is particularly acute when the investment is a fixed-interest bond and the interest rate rises. Because of the inverse relationship between bonds and interest rates, the value of the bond will fall. Interest rate risk is largely removed if the bond is floating-rate, since the coupon will be reset in line with the higher market interest rate.

Inflation risk arises when inflation is more substantial than the investor expected, and the value of the investments held may fall. Generally, bonds will suffer because the fixed cash payments that they deliver are less valuable. Floating-rate bonds will suffer less because the higher inflation will bring about a higher interest rate, but the real value of the principal at redemption will fall. Inflation-protected securities will not suffer. The coupon and the principal are linked to a measure of inflation (eg, increases in the CPI) so the investor will not lose out.

In contrast to debt instruments, equities and property cope reasonably well with unexpected inflation. Companies are able to increase their prices and deliver larger dividends, and the property market as a whole tends to reflect the inflationary increases.

Investors in bonds face default risk. This is the risk of the issuer defaulting on their payment obligations. The probability of default (often referred to as credit risk) is measured by various independent credit rating agencies, mainly S&P, Moody's and Fitch Ratings. These rating agencies divide issuers into two distinct classes: investment grade (alternatively referred to as prime) and sub-investment grade (alternatively referred to as speculative, non-prime or junk).

The largest three rating agencies apply similar criteria to assess whether the issuer will be able to service the required payments on the debt. The bonds are then categorised according to their reliability, payment history and current financial situation. Triple A is the best and the next best is double A (although the rating agencies can have lesser notches such as pluses and minuses).

Very few organisations, except a very select group of companies, some western governments and supranational agencies, have triple A ratings, but most large companies boast an investment grade rating. An investment grade rating is one that is at least BBB (from S&P or Fitch Ratings), or at least Baa from Moody's. Issues of bonds categorised as sub-investment grade are alternatively known as junk bonds because of the high levels of credit risk.

If the rating agencies downgrade the issuer of a bond, potential investors will look to compensate for the increased risk by demanding a greater yield on the issuer's bonds. This will inevitably result in a lower price for the bond. Some issuers of bonds utilise credit enhancements to enable their bonds to be rated more highly by the credit rating agencies. Examples of credit enhancements are bonds guaranteed by another group company, or bonds with a fixed charge over particular assets.

1.5 Overseas Equities and Bonds

Learning Objective

8.1.5 Understand risk profile of investment in overseas shares and debt: country risk; exchange rate risk

To lessen the risk that a particular company, or issuer of a bond, delivers poor returns due to problems in the domestic economy, investors can invest in overseas companies' equities, or overseas bond issues. Like domestic equities and bonds, these overseas investments may offer the possibilities of income and capital appreciation.

However, the investor may be less knowledgeable about the overseas company/issuer and there may be particular idiosyncrasies in some overseas markets; for example, local custodians may not be required to give the holder access to corporate actions.

Currency (or Exchange Rate) Risk

These overseas investments are also higher-risk than their domestic equivalents because of the additional risk that is created by the possibility of exchange rates moving against the investor. For investments that are denominated in a currency other than the home currency of the investor, an adverse exchange rate movement will create an adverse movement in the value of the investment. Clearly, this is particularly relevant for overseas investments. It can also be problematic if the investment is in a local company that has substantial overseas business interests.

1.6 Types of Risk

Learning Objective

8.1.6 Understand the risks facing the investor: specific/unsystematic; market/systematic; interest rate risk; inflation risk

Risk can be categorised in a number of different ways, but the overriding rule for investment is that the potential for spectacular return can only arise if the investor takes a large amount of risk: the risk-return relationship.

Market (or Systematic) Risk

This is the risk that the whole market moves in a particular direction. It is typically applied to equities and brought about by economic and political factors. It cannot be diversified away. For example, political crises or general recessions will tend to bring about falls in the market value of all shares, although they may affect different company shares to different degrees.

Specific (or Unsystematic) Risk

This is the risk that something adverse impacts the value of a particular investment, but the adverse impact is not market-wide. An obvious example is a company's management making some sort of error – perhaps producing a defective product with resultant impact on profits and customer goodwill. Specific risk can be diversified away by holding many investments.

Interest Rate Risk

As seen earlier in this chapter, changes in interest rates will affect prices, and interest rate risk is in essence a sub category of market risk.

Inflation Risk

Inflation risk is possibly another sub category of market risk. Inflation will erode returns and, even if the investor has taken account of inflation in their analysis, the actual and expected inflation may be different from that assumed in calculating expected returns.

1.7 Correlation and Diversification

Learning Objective

8.1.7 Understand how to optimise the risk/reward relationship through the use of: correlation; diversification; use of different asset classes

Investors generally choose to avoid unnecessary risk in their portfolios by holding appropriate proportions of each class of investment. The more conservative investor will hold a greater proportion of low-risk bonds and money market instruments. These lower-risk investments are likely to give rise to lower, but more predictable, returns. The more adventurous investor will hold a greater proportion of medium- and high-risk equity investments, because higher risk means greater potential for higher returns. Essentially, the choice of investments is driven by the investor's attitude to risk and the fact that there is a trade-off between risk and return.

However, diversification can remove some of the market risk without having to remove all high-risk investments from a portfolio. This is done by combining securities that are not perfectly positively correlated into a portfolio, which will remove some of the unsystematic risk in that portfolio. Unsystematic risk affects certain sectors of the market, but not the market as a whole. So, by reducing the concentration in certain sectors (with diversification), the portfolio risk will be reduced with the addition of additional uncorrelated securities.

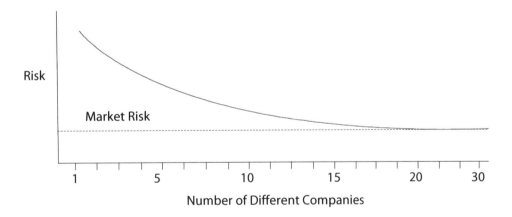

For example, an investor's portfolio might contain high-risk equity investments but as the portfolio diversifies, ie, as the investor includes a wider range of companies' shares, risk diminishes, because unexpected losses made on one investment are offset by unexpected gains on another.

1.7.1 Correlation

From an investment perspective the statistical notion of correlation is fundamental to portfolio theory. The very simplest idea is that, if one is seeking diversification in the holdings of a portfolio, one would like to have, say, two assets where there is a low degree of association between the movements in price and returns of each asset. The degree of association can also be expressed in terms of the extent to which directional changes in each asset's returns, or their co-movement, are related.

If assets A and B have a tendency to react to the same kinds of business conditions in a very simple and predictable manner they could be said to be strongly correlated. Let us assume that a certain kind of regular release of economic data (for example the monthly CPI data) is announced and company A's shares move up by 3% and company B's shares move up by 2.5% when the data is below expectations, and that the inverse pattern of price movement is seen when the data is above expectations. In such a case there is a strong correlation between the movements (or changes) in the performance returns of A and B and this is expressed as strong positive correlation.

1.7.2 Diversification

Diversification benefits are maximised by holding investments with uncorrelated returns (when the returns do not tend to move in the same direction and to the same degree). It is not necessary for the investments to be wholly negatively correlated, as combinations of investments that are positively correlated do still provide diversification benefits. It is only a combination of investments that are perfectly positively correlated that will offer no diversification benefits.

However, diversification cannot remove all of the risk. There are certain things, such as economic news, that tend to impact the whole market. The risk that can be removed is known as the specific or unsystematic risk, and the risk that cannot be diversified away is the market or systematic risk.

Diversification by Asset Class

This is achieved by holding a combination of different kinds of asset within a portfolio, possibly spread across cash, fixed-interest securities, equity investments, property-based investments, and other assets.

Cash can be useful as an emergency fund or for instantly accessible money. At times when the future for interest rates is uncertain, it may be wise to hold some cash in variable-rate deposits, in the hope of a rate rise, and some in fixed-rate deposits as a hedge against a possible fall in the rate.

Fixed-interest securities, such as government bonds, give a secure income and known redemption value at a fixed future date.

Equities can be used to produce a potentially increasing dividend income and capital growth. For example, a share yielding 3% income plus capital growth of 6% gives an overall return of 9% compared with a bank deposit account yielding, say, 4%.

Collective investments, such as mutual funds, spread the risk still further. In this case, the client is participating in a pool of investments. The client may choose a fund investing in a number of different economies, thereby reducing risk still further. Pooled investments may be a sensible method of obtaining exposure to some of the less sophisticated world markets where there is a high risk in holding just one company's shares.

The use of property, whether residential or commercial and other types of assets such as antiques, coins or stamps might help to spread risk further.

1.8 Active and Passive Investment Management Methodologies

Learning Objective

8.1.8 Understand active investment management methodologies and strategies, and their advantages and disadvantages

---

1.8.1 Active Management

Active management (also called active investing) refers to a method of portfolio management where the manager's strategy is designed to outperform the returns available from an investment benchmark index. For example, an active portfolio manager focused on investing in large-cap UK equities will be seeking to realise returns superior to those available from a simple method/strategy of buying and holding all of the constituents of the FTSE 100.

It is worth pointing out that purchasing a simple derivative, such as a FTSE 100 futures contract, will not reflect the total returns available to an investor in the actual index, as it will only capture changes in the price level of the index and not the dividend income. More complex derivative products can emulate the total returns without requiring an outright purchase of all 100 stocks in the index.

Active portfolio managers can use various strategies to construct their portfolios with a view to superior performance than that available from index tracking. For example, the manager could focus on selecting securities based on research and quantitative analysis focused on measures such as P/E ratios and price earnings growth (PEG) ratios, sector investments that attempt to anticipate long-term macro-economic trends (such as a focus on energy or technology stocks), and purchasing stocks of companies that are temporarily out of favour or selling at a discount to their intrinsic value. Certain actively managed funds will also pursue more specialised strategies, such as merger arbitrage, option writing, and forms of statistical arbitrage, involving more exotic securities, such as derivatives and convertible securities.

The effectiveness of an actively managed investment portfolio will clearly depend on the skill (or good fortune) of the manager and research staff. In reality, the majority of actively managed funds rarely outperform their index counterparts over an extended period of time, assuming that they are benchmarked correctly. For example, research covering managed active funds established in the US (mostly retail US equity and global equity in the form of Standard & Poor's Index Versus Active (SPIVA) scorecards), demonstrates that only a minority of actively managed mutual funds have gains better than the S&P Index benchmark. As the time period for comparison increases, the percentage of actively managed funds whose gains exceed the S&P benchmark declines further.

1.8.2   Advantages of Active Management

The primary attraction of active management is that it allows selection of a variety of investments instead of investing in the market as a whole. Investors may have a number of reasons for not wanting to simply track an index. They may, for example, be sceptical of the efficient market hypothesis (EMH), or believe that some market segments are less efficient than others. They may also want to reduce volatility by investing in less risky, high-quality companies, rather than in the market as a whole, even at the cost of slightly lower returns. Conversely, some investors may want to take on additional risk in exchange for the opportunity of obtaining higher-than-market returns. Investments that are not highly correlated to the market are useful as a portfolio diversifier and may reduce overall portfolio volatility.

Some investors may also wish to follow a strategy that avoids or underweights certain industries compared to the market as a whole, for instance, an employee of a high-technology growth company who receives company stock or stock options as a benefit might prefer not to have additional funds invested in the same industry.

1.8.3   Disadvantages of Active Management

The most obvious disadvantage of active management is that the fund manager may make bad investment choices or follow an unsound theory in managing the portfolio. The fees associated with active management are also higher than those associated with **passive management**, even if frequent trading is not undertaken. Those who are considering investing in an actively managed fund should evaluate the fund's prospectus carefully.

Active fund management strategies that involve frequent trading generate higher transaction costs which diminish the fund's return. In addition, the short-term capital gains resulting from frequent trades often have an unfavourable income tax impact when such funds are held in a taxable account.

More specialised tracker funds can also be linked to the performance of securities in emerging markets, and specific industry sectors. Increasingly the proliferation of exchange-traded funds (ETFs), allows investors to purchase shares in a fund which trades actively on a major exchange and which provides exposure to certain kinds of securities and where the minimal management fees are incorporated into the actual price of the shares of the ETF. The benefits to an investor purchasing such ETFs is that there is usually a high degree of liquidity, the asset values of the fund constituents as well as the price of the ETF shares are updated on a real-time basis, and the costs for the packaging of the securities are minimal.

When the assortment of assets of an actively managed fund becomes too large, it inevitably begins to take on index-like characteristics as it must invest in an increasingly broad selection of securities which will tend to perform exactly in line with the overall market. In such a situation, the fund becomes a pseudo-tracker, and an investor in the fund is paying active management fees when the actual style is effectively passive. This last factor is why some fund managers close their funds to new investors after the fund reaches a certain size, so that they can avoid having to be so broadly diversified as to deviate from their original selection criteria underlying their active strategic focus.

1.8.4 Active Management with Manager Participation

One meaning sometimes given to active management is when the managers/directors have a vested interest in the success of the fund. Many funds do not have either the manager or directors with an equity stake in the fund that the manager is running. In contrast, private equity funds and hedge funds often provide real active management. In private equity, this is because there are usually only a small number of shareholders in the privately owned companies, and a significant stakeholder like the private equity fund will contribute to the strategic decisions. In hedge funds, it is usual to see and expect the managers to include their own money in the fund.

The advantage to an investor in a fund where the management is personally at risk by holding a stake in the fund under management is that the manager's interests will be aligned with those of the investors. The manager has what is known as skin in the game.

1.8.5 Active Bond Strategies

Generally speaking, active strategies are used by those portfolio managers who believe the bond market is not perfectly efficient and therefore is subject to mispricing. If a bond is considered mispriced, then active management strategies can be employed to capitalise upon this perceived pricing anomaly.

Bond switching, or bond swapping, is used by those portfolio managers who believe they can outperform a buy-and-hold passive policy, by actively exchanging bonds perceived to be overpriced for those perceived to be underpriced.

Bond switching takes three forms:

- **Anomaly switching** – this involves moving between two bonds similar in all respects apart from the yield and price on which each trades. This pricing anomaly is exploited by switching away from the more to the less highly priced bond.
- **Policy switching** – when an interest rate cut is expected but not implied by the yield curve, shorter-dated, low-duration bonds are sold in favour of longer-dated, high-duration bonds. By pre-empting the rate cut, the holder can subsequently benefit from the greater price volatility of the latter bonds.
- **Inter-market spread switch** – when it is believed that the difference in the yield being offered between corporate bonds and comparable government bonds, for example, is excessive given the perceived risk differential between these two markets, an inter-market spread switch will be undertaken from the gilt to the corporate bond market. Conversely, if an event that lowers the risk appetite of bond investors is expected to result in a flight to quality, government bonds will be purchased in favour of corporate bonds.

Active management policies are also employed if it is believed the market's view on future interest rate movements, implied by the yield curve, are incorrect or have failed to be anticipated. This is known as market timing.

Riding the yield curve is an active bond strategy that does not involve seeking out price anomalies, but instead takes advantage of an upward-sloping yield curve.

Example

If a portfolio manager has a two-year investment horizon then a bond with a two-year maturity could be purchased and held until redemption. Alternatively, if the yield curve is upward-sloping and the manager expects it to remain upward-sloping without any intervening or anticipated interest rate rises over the next two years, a five-year bond could be purchased, and sold two years later when the bond has a remaining life of three years.

As long as the yield curve remains static over this period, the manager could generate a better return than would have been generated by purchasing a two-year maturity bond.

1.9 Passive Management

Learning Objective

8.1.9 Understand passive investment management methodologies and strategies and their advantages and disadvantages

Passive managers are those that do not aspire to create a return in excess of a benchmark index. They often follow exactly the course just outlined and invest in an index fund or derivative that replicates as closely as possible the investment weighting and returns of a selected benchmark index, such as the FTSE 100 in the UK market or, if they seek to match the returns of the US market, they may invest in an instrument which exactly tracks the total returns of the S&P 500 Index.

1.9.1 Advantages of Passive Management

To a large extent, the advantages and disadvantages of a passive approach to portfolio management will tend to be the converse of the respective positions with respect to active management that have just been covered.

Indeed, the most frequently cited advantage of a passive approach to asset management is that the performance of the fund is not dependent on the manager's ability to make investment choices which, it is contended by the active manager, will outperform the broad market, but which in fact may well prove not to be the case and will lead to a less rewarding performance than simply investing in a tracker fund.

Subscribers to the EMH will tend to favour the use of index trackers if they are seeking out a risk/reward ratio which is in accordance with the overall performance of the market. By investing in a fund which tracks a broad benchmark, such as the S&P 500 Index or FTSE 100 Index, the investor is only exposed to the systematic risk within the market and can avoid the risks (and potential rewards) of non-systematic risk.

Several research studies have provided evidence that the majority of actively managed large- and mid-cap stock funds in the US have failed to outperform their passive index counterparts.

Investors in a passively managed fund can also avoid incurring the fees associated with active management. A passive fund management strategy can avoid the frequent trading which is more likely under an active management approach, and transaction costs will be lower which, relatively speaking, will enhance the fund's return. Also, a strategy of buy-and-hold, which is typically the outcome of a passive strategy, is far less likely to incur frequent short-term capital gains resulting from the greater focus on short-term trading activities of active management, and to that extent will also be able to avoid the unfavourable income tax impact when such funds are held in a taxable account.

Another significant advantage of a passive management style is the fact that the total expense ratio will be considerably lower than for many actively managed funds, such as hedge funds which operate with fees charged for funds under management and also incentive fees. With regard to unit trusts and mutual funds, it is also the case that index tracker funds will have lower expense ratios and, somewhat ironically, they may not differ significantly in their performance and fund composition from the actively managed funds. As mentioned, this can arise when the asset composition of an actively managed fund becomes so large that it begins to take on index-like characteristics. In such cases, the actively managed fund, while it may not have set out with the intention, becomes, in effect, a closet index tracker.

Passive management has recently become more appealing to a broad range of investors because innovative investment products, introduced in recent years, now allow investors to invest in sector trackers and so-called smart beta ETFs (further considered below). For example, specialised ETFs can be linked to the performance of securities in emerging markets and specific industry sectors or use alternative index construction methods taking in factors other than market capitalisation, such as cash flow and profitability. Increasingly, the proliferation of ETFs allows investors to purchase shares in a fund which trades regularly on a major exchange and which provides exposure to certain kinds of securities with minimal management fees.

1.9.2   Disadvantages of Passive Management

Disadvantages of passive management include the fact that performance is always dictated by a benchmark or index, meaning that investors must be satisfied with the index returns. In addition, the inherent lack of control dictated by being passive prevents defensive measures if it appears that a certain class of asset prices, specifically equities, may be heading for turbulent trading conditions and possible capital losses.

The investor in a passively managed fund should only expect to realise similar returns to those that are available from the index upon which the passively managed fund is based. So, while the investor's returns will be acceptable from a relative perspective, ie, they will be highly correlated with the market return, they may still be unacceptable from an absolute perspective in the sense that losses will arise if the market sustains losses.

The main disadvantage of passive management is that it lacks the potential to generate **alpha** or above-market returns. The investor in a passively managed fund forgoes the opportunity to have exposure to a variety of investments which could outperform a broad benchmark index and which may have other desirable attributes providing diversification and lower correlation elements than simply investing in the market as a whole.

Investors may have a variety of reasons for not wanting to simply track an index. Those opposed to passive management may have serious reservations regarding the validity of the EMH and believe that some market segments are more efficient in creating profits than others. They may also want to reduce volatility by investing in less risky, high-quality companies rather than in the market as a whole, even at the cost of slightly lower returns. Conversely, some investors may want to take on additional risk in exchange for the opportunity of obtaining higher-than-market returns, and such investors will be willing to seek out higher **beta** stocks (by definition a broad benchmark-based portfolio should have a beta of approximately one) in exchange for the possibility of above-average potential gains (and losses). Investments that are not highly correlated to the market, eg, certain commodities such as gold, are useful as a portfolio diversifier and may reduce overall portfolio volatility.

Some investors may also wish to follow a strategy that avoids or underweights certain industries compared to the market as a whole, as part of a deliberate diversification strategy. For example, someone employed in the financial services profession whose own compensation is closely tied to company stock or the stock options of their employer may prefer not to have any additional funds invested in the same sector.

1.9.3   Smart Beta

Beta is a measure of the sensitivity of an investment's movements in relation to the overall market. The market has a beta of precisely one, and an index that tracks the market exactly would also have a beta of one. A security with a beta greater than one would be more volatile (risky) than the overall market, and a beta with less than one would be less volatile (risky). However, tracking a market capitalisation-weighted index has the inherent disadvantage of going overweight in those stocks that are overvalued, and underweight in those stocks that are undervalued. Smart beta is a potential solution to this.

Smart beta is the term for an investment strategy that does not use the traditional market capitalisation weighting system, but instead uses alternative weighting systems, for example weighting constituents equally, or based on dividends paid, sales revenues or cash flow generation. Smart beta can be thought of as taking the key advantage of active investment management by introducing the possibility of outperformance, and combining it with the key advantages of passive index tracking by creating a well-diversified portfolio at a lower cost than active management.

1.9.4   Passive Bond Strategies

Passive bond strategies are employed either when the market is believed to be efficient, in which case a buy-and-hold strategy is used, or when a bond portfolio is constructed around meeting a future liability fixed in nominal terms.

Immunisation is a passive management technique employed by those bond portfolio managers with a known future liability to meet. An immunised bond portfolio is one that is insulated from the effect of future interest rate changes. Immunisation can be performed by using either of the following techniques.

- **Cash matching** involves constructing a bond portfolio whose coupon and redemption payment cash flows are synchronised to match those of the liabilities to be met.
- **Duration-based immunisation** involves constructing a bond portfolio with the same initial value as the present value of the liability it is designed to meet and the same duration as this liability. A portfolio that contains bonds that are closely aligned in this way is known as a bullet portfolio.

Alternatively, a barbell strategy can be adopted. If a bullet portfolio holds bonds with durations as close as possible to ten years to match a liability with ten-year duration, a barbell strategy may be to hold bonds with a durations of five and 15 years. Barbell portfolios necessarily require more frequent rebalancing than bullet portfolios.

Finally, a ladder portfolio is one constructed around equal amounts invested in bonds with different durations. So, for a liability with a ten-year duration, an appropriate ladder strategy may be to hold equal amounts in bonds with a one-year duration, two-year duration and so on right through to 20 years.

1.9.5 Management Strategy and the Efficient Markets Hypothesis (EMH)

The efficient markets hypothesis (EMH) is an investment theory stating that it is impossible to beat the market because stock market efficiency causes existing share prices to always incorporate and reflect all relevant information. According to the EMH, this means that stocks always trade at their fair value on stock exchanges, making it impossible for investors to either purchase undervalued stocks or sell stocks for inflated prices. As such, it should be impossible to outperform the overall market through expert stock selection, technical analysis or market timing, and the only way an investor can possibly obtain higher returns is by purchasing riskier investments.

Passive fund management is consistent with the idea that markets are efficient and that no mispricing exists. If the EMH is an accurate account of the way that capital markets work, then there is no benefit to be had from active trading. Such trading will simply incur dealing and management costs for no benefit. Investors who do not believe that they can identify active fund managers who they are confident can produce returns above the level of charges for active management will often elect to invest in passive funds or index trackers.

An active manager will try to achieve the desired goal of outperforming a designated benchmark by seeking out market inefficiencies and by purchasing securities that are undervalued, or by short-selling securities that are overvalued. Either of these methods may be used alone or in combination. Depending on the goals of the specific investment portfolio, active fund management may also serve to create less volatility (or risk) than the benchmark index. The reduction of risk may be instead of, or in addition to, the goal of creating an investment return greater than the benchmark.

1.10 Hedging

Learning Objective

8.1.10 Know the role of hedging in the management of investment risk and how to achieve it: futures; options; CFDs

The risks that are inevitable when investing in shares, bonds and money market instruments can be largely removed by entering into hedging. Unfortunately, the hedging strategies will have a cost that inevitably impacts investment performance.

Hedging is the attempt to reduce risk, usually achieved by using derivatives, for example, options, futures and forwards. The objective is to buy or sell derivatives that reduce the exposure to market fluctuations that would take place in the portfolio. This is done by taking the opposite position of what is in the portfolio with the derivative. For example, buying put options (the right to sell) on investments held in the portfolio will enable the investor to remove the risk of a fall in value. However, the investor will have to pay a premium to buy the options.

Futures, such as stock index futures, can be used to hedge against equity prices falling – but the future will remove any upside as well as downside.

Forwards, such as currency forwards, can be used to eliminate exchange rate risk – but, like futures, the upside potential will be lost in order to hedge against the downside risk.

1.10.1 Hedging with Futures Contracts

One of the most commonly used techniques for hedging a portfolio is through selling futures contracts to control the level of exposure that one has from ownership of equities.

Example

A UK-based pension fund which has a large exposure to large-capitalisation equities traded on the London Stock Exchange (LSE) could use the FTSE 100 futures contract as a hedging instrument

Calculating the number of futures contracts to sell for hedging purposes can be a formidable challenge. The simplest case is when the cash portfolio has similar characteristics to an available futures contract such as the FTSE 100 contract. In such a case, one simply divides the cash value of the portfolio by the nominal size of the futures contract and then sells that number of contracts. If the extent to which the cash portfolio moves in relation to the benchmark index, which is known as the portfolio's beta, can be measured with some precision, then the number of contracts sold needs to be prorated by the ratio between the portfolio's beta and the beta of the index which, since it is the benchmark reference, is given a beta value of one.

The use of futures has the advantages of lower cost, greater efficiency and less portfolio disruption. The shortcomings of selling futures contracts are as follows.

The exact risk characteristics, ie, the beta value of the portfolio, may not be emulated by the performance of any index or instrument which is available as a futures contract. For example, a portfolio which has a combination of small-capitalisation stocks and emerging market exchange-traded funds will be difficult to hedge by selling a broad-based futures contract on, say, the FTSE 100 index or the S&P 500.

Also, the key issue is one of knowing when to enter the futures hedge trade and when to exit the trade. If the short sale of an index future is not settled before the market has completed a correction and is starting to rise again, the continued ownership of a short position in an index futures position will offset the gains being made in the cash portfolio.

1.10.2 Hedging with Options

An alternative way of implementing a hedge strategy for a fund manager is to continue to hold the investments, such as individual equities, in the portfolio, and to purchase put options on those positions (or on an index where the performance of an index closely matches the overall portfolio). This combination of being long on both the investment(s) and the puts enables the holder to continue to participate in any upside potential of the investments, while enjoying the right to sell the investment at a pre-determined level (as set out in the put contract) if the investments do not perform. This provides the protection from excessive loss, which is the primary objective of the hedging exercise. As the holder (buyer) of the put, the manager has the right, but not the obligation to exercise the ability to sell at the strike price.

Being long a put option is thus motivated by a view that an asset's price will fall; it is a hedging move or can be used as an outright bearish strategy, which will enable the option buyer to benefit should the price of the underlying instrument or equity fall.

On the other side of the trade, the seller is said to be 'short' the put option and expects the market to either rise or not fall sufficiently for the option to be exercised. Known as the 'writer', the seller seeks for the option not to be exercised and to profit from the premium paid by the buyer.

Example – Hedging with a Put Option

Assume that in December an investor holds 1,000 shares in XYZ, the current price is $110 and the investor has a bearish view of the price development in the intermediate term – let us assume six months forward in June. The investor can buy put options in XYZ with a strike of $110, an expiry of June and a premium of $6. This means that they have the right (but not the obligation) to sell the XYZ shares for $110 in June.

Model of Option Payoffs and Profits			Action	Buy	Put
Exercise Price	110.00	Premium Paid	6.00	Strategy	Long

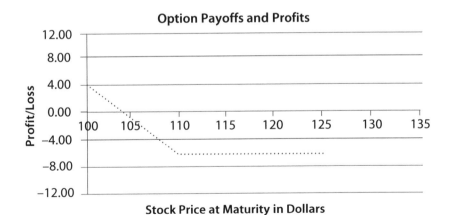

Option Payoffs and Profits

.... Option Profit

Stock	95	100	105	110	115	120	125	130	135
Intrinsic Value	15.00	10.00	5.00	0.00	0.00	0.00	0.00	0.00	0.00
Profit/Loss	9.00	4.00	−1.00	−6.00	−6.00	−6.00	−6.00	−6.00	−6.00

The break-even point for this option is calculated by deducting the premium from the exercise price, eg, $110 – $6 = $104. The premium needs to be recovered before any profit or hedge protection is made.

However, the maximum profit will occur if the share price falls to zero, meaning that the shares can (theoretically) be bought for nothing and sold for $110. With the premium of $6 deducted, the maximum profit will be $104, the same as the break-even point.

In a hedging exercise it must obviously be recalled that the profit seen from this option payoff diagram is only going to cover the losses which are incurred from holding the underlying shares of XYZ. But the option does provide the portfolio manager with protection all the way down to the worst-case scenario of the shares going to zero.

The risks taken by the purchaser of a put option are limited to the premium paid and this is illustrated in the diagram as the extended horizontal line showing a return of minus six dollars per share.

The motivation behind buying a put option will be to protect against a fall in the share price. The holder of a put obtains the right, but not the obligation, to sell at a fixed price. The value of this right will become increasingly valuable as the asset price falls. The greatest profit that will arise from buying a put will be achieved if the asset price falls to zero.

The purchase of put options is an added expense for a fund manager and, in the nature of all options contracts, the premium paid for the put option is known as a wasting asset as it is subject to decay as the expiration of the option period approaches. If a fund manager wishes to continue to protect a portfolio with put options, which have definite maturity dates, then a process of rolling over the options contracts can be employed. This will further add to the costs, and the least advantageous position from the point of view of the overall returns to the fund manager is the situation when portfolio insurance has been purchased through extended use of put options, the cash value of the portfolio continues to rise as the insurance is not required, and the cost of the premiums has to be charged against the earnings of the cash portfolio.

1.10.3 Hedging with Contracts for Differences (CFDs)

Contracts for differences (CFDs) were originally developed in the early 1990s and were initially used by institutional investors to hedge their exposure to stocks in a cost-effective way.

CFDs are different from traditional cash-traded instruments (such as equities, bonds, commodities and currencies) in that they do not confer ownership of the underlying asset. Investors can take positions on the price of a great number of different instruments.

Along with futures and options, CFDs are derivatives. The price of the CFD tracks the price of the underlying asset, and so the holder of a CFD benefits, or loses, from the price movement in the stock, bond, currency, commodity or index. But the CFD holder does not take ownership of the underlying asset.

CFDs are margin-traded, meaning that the investor does not have to deposit the full value of the underlying asset with the CFD provider. Thus, an investor or fund manager can use CFDs to buy exposure to market movements, using only a fraction of the capital they would require in the cash market. The investor then has a geared position relative to the capital deposited.

Since CFDs allow an investor to benefit from downward movements in an equity position or index, they are useful for hedging purposes. They enable the fund manager to retain a position in the cash instrument but have a derivative position which is equivalent to that of short-selling the stock. This flexibility, and the possibility of margin trading, means that CFDs can be used flexibly either for hedging or speculation.

The costs of CFDs comprise commissions for each deal, plus a cost built into the spread of the CFD price, together with a funding/financing charge. CFD contracts are subject to a daily financing charge, usually applied at a previously agreed rate linked to LIBOR. The parties to a CFD pay to finance long positions and may receive funding on short positions in lieu of deferring sale proceeds. The contracts are settled for the cash differential between the price of the opening and closing trades.

CFDs are subject to a commission charge on equities that is a percentage of the size of the position for each trade.

Investors in CFDs are required to maintain a certain amount of margin as defined by the brokerage – usually ranging from 1% to 30%. One advantage to investors of not having to put up as collateral the full notional value of the CFD is that a given quantity of capital can control a larger position, amplifying the potential for profit or loss. On the other hand, a leveraged position in a volatile CFD can expose the buyer to further margin calls in a downturn, which will fund what may crystallise as a substantial loss.

As with many leveraged products, maximum exposure is not limited to the initial investment; it is possible that an investor loses more than the margin put in, with additional money paid in the form of subsequent 'margin calls' to cover losses.

Example

Suppose you wish to hedge 10,000 shares in XYZ plc which are held in a portfolio and are currently trading at 99p each. CFDs are available at a quoted price of 98.5p/99.5p. To achieve this hedge you could sell the equivalent of 10,000 shares locking in the current CFD price of 98.5p, and then if the price declines the returns from the CFD position will be similar to those available if you had a short position in the stock selling 10,000 shares for 98.5p each – a total position of £9,850.

Using CFDs, assuming a 5% margin, you will only need an initial deposit of £492.50 (£9,850 x 5%). As the price decreases the returns from the CFD will compensate for the loss incurred on the actual long holding of the stock.

Assume a month later the price of XYZ plc shares has declined to 84p, and the CFDs are now quoted at 83.5p/84.5p.

The loss on the shares within the portfolio amounts to £1,500. Initially they were worth 10,000 x 99p = £9,900 and now they are only worth 10,000 x 84p = £8,400.

The gain on the CFDs (before considering any commissions on the sale and purchase and ignoring any funding charges) is £1,400. The CFDs were initially sold for 10,000 x 98.5p = £9,850 and then bought for 10,000 x 84.5p = £8,450.

So, ignoring funding charges and commissions, the hedge had managed to remove £1,400 of the £1,500 loss on the shares. Given that this is a short sale, the funding charges can be considered negligible. Commissions would be payable on the initial sale of CFDs and the subsequent purchase of CFDs at say 0.15%, so in total would be £27.45 (£9,850 x 0.15%) + (£8,450 x 0.15%). So overall, the hedge is marginally less efficient, but still very worthwhile.

However, it is important to emphasise that had the shares risen over the period, the CFD hedge would have lost money, removed the gain on the portfolio and (after costs) turned it into a net loss. The failure of the short position to make money in such circumstances is commonly referred to as a 'short squeeze'.

CFDs allow a trader to go short or long on any position using margin. There are always two types of margin with a CFD trade:

- **Initial margin** – normally between 5% and 30% for shares/stocks and 1% for indices and foreign exchange. In the above example, 5% of the contract price was assumed.
- **Variation or maintenance margin** – the CFD will be marked to the market at currently prevailing prices and if the position has moved beyond the amount taken as initial margin – ie, the position has moved adversely – additional margin would be required. This is termed variation or maintenance margin.

1.11 Company Liquidations

Learning Objective

8.1.11 Understand the general concept of ranking in respect of shares and corporate bonds in the event of a company's liquidation

In the case of the winding-up or liquidation of a company, the priority and manner in which the owners of different tiers of the capital structure of that company are dealt with is referred to as the liquidation ranking.

The basic rule is that all shareholders or equity participants are subordinate to debt holders. There are separate provisions for the priority of debt holders, based upon the seniority of the debt, whether there is a fixed charge associated with the debt or a floating charge, and other covenants that were granted at the time of debt issuance.

Once the obligations to the debt holders have been discharged, preference shareholders will take priority over the ordinary shareholders in a liquidation. From the proceeds following a liquidation event (which may be defined to include events other than the winding-up of the company), the preference shareholders will receive the par value of their shares before there is any distribution to the ordinary shareholders.

There is one further consideration which relates to the issuance of preference shares as part of early-stage or venture funding of a start-up company; this is often referred to as liquidation preference.

The liquidation preference is the amount that must be paid to the preference shareholders, such as venture capital or angel investors, before distributions may be made to common stockholders. The liquidation preference is payable on either the liquidation of a company, asset sale, merger, consolidation or any other reorganisation resulting in the change of control of the start-up. It is usually expressed as a multiple of the original purchase price of the preferred, such as 2x. Thus, if the purchase price of the preferred is $2 per share, a liquidation preference of 2x will be $4 per share. In effect, the preference shareholders will receive twice the nominal value of their shares upon liquidation before the proceeds (if any) are distributed to the ordinary shareholders.

1.11.1 Debt Seniority

Debt issued by companies can come in a variety of forms including bonds and bank borrowing. When there are multiple forms of debt, the issuer will have to establish some sort of order as to which debt will be serviced and repaid first, in the event of the company's encountering financial difficulties. In broad terms, the seniority of the debt falls into three main headings:

- **Senior** – senior debt or bonds have a claim that is above that of the more junior forms of borrowing and the equity of the issuer in the event of liquidation.
- **Subordinated** – subordinated debt or bondholders have accepted that their claim to the issuer's assets ranks below that of the senior debt in the event of a liquidation. As a result of accepting a greater risk than the senior debt, the subordinated borrowing will be entitled to a greater rate of interest than that available on the senior debt.
- **Mezzanine and payment-in-kind (PIK)** – the mezzanine level of debt, if it exists at all, will be even more risky than the subordinated debt. It will rank below other forms of debt but above the equity in a liquidation. As the most risky debt, the mezzanine debt will offer a greater rate of interest than the subordinated and senior levels of debt. Mezzanine borrowing can be raised in a variety of ways – one example is the issue of PIK notes. PIK notes are simply zero coupon bonds (ZCBs) that are issued at a substantial discount to their face value. When they are repaid, the difference between the redemption value and the purchase cost provides the investor's return.

It should be noted that each of the three main categories can themselves contain subcategories such as senior secured, senior unsecured, senior subordinated and junior subordinated. In practice, the various rating agencies look at debt structures in these narrower terms. Seniority can be contractual as the result of the terms of the issue, or based on the corporate structure of the issuer.

2. Institutional Investment Advice

2.1 Institutional Client Profiles

Learning Objective

8.2.1 Know the differences between institutional client profiles including: pension funds; life and general insurance funds; hedge funds; regulated mutual funds; banks

2.1.1 Institutional Investors

There are a number of institutional investors, including pension funds, the providers of life assurance, the providers of general insurance and banks.

Pension funds are set up with the aim of providing retirement funds for the beneficiaries. They may be sponsored by an employer, be solely dependent on contributions from the workforce, or a combination of the two. Pension funds tend to be approved by tax authorities and can then accumulate income and capital gains tax-free. The money in the fund is invested by fund managers and, because pension funds have a relatively long investment horizon, they can take risks and have tended to invest heavily in equities.

Pension funds can be divided into two broad classes: those that define the benefits they will pay out (defined benefit schemes or final salary schemes), and those where the benefit is driven by the contributions made and the investment performance (defined contribution schemes).

Life assurance business arises from insurance contracts written by an insurance company on the life of an individual. They mainly comprise:

* **term assurance policies** which, in exchange for a regular premium, only pay out if the individual dies before the end of a set policy term
* **whole of life policies** which simply pay out on death in exchange for regular premiums
* **endowment policies** which are term assurance policies with a significant investment element that depends on the performance of the insurance company's fund
* **single premium life assurance bonds** which are single premium endowments; again they have a significant investment element.

Like pension funds, because of the long-term nature of life assurance business, the funds tend to be willing to invest in higher-risk investments involving a heavy weighting in equity investments. Unlike pension funds, the income and the gains made within life assurance funds are typically subject to tax.

General insurance is when insurance is written by an insurance company against short-term personal and commercial risks, such as car or household contents insurance. Because of the short-term nature of the liabilities, the funds from the premiums tend to be invested in low-risk, liquid, short-term assets such as money market instruments. Like life assurance funds, general insurance funds are subject to tax on the income and gains within the fund.

If banks hold surplus cash at the end of each business day, they will place the funds on deposit with other banks (in the interbank market) and invest in eligible money market instruments (such as Treasury bills and commercial paper (CP)) – relatively risk-free investments to cover the short-term nature of the banks' liabilities to depositors. An eligible money market instrument means that the BoE will accept it as collateral against loans. As with insurance companies, banks are taxed on income and gains they generate from their investments.

The following table provides a summary of the key distinctions and similarities across the institutional investors:

Institution	Investment horizon	Proportion of equity investments	Proportion of money market investments	Relative risk profile
Pension fund	Long-term*	High	Low	High
Life assurance fund	Long-term	High	Low	High
General insurance fund	Short-term	Low	High	Low
Bank	Short-term	Low	High	Low

* Clearly, this depends on the maturity profile of the pension scheme; a scheme with the bulk of members nearing retirement would take a shorter-term view.

2.1.2   Regulated Mutual Funds

Diversification of shareholdings reduces risk, but for a private client with a relatively modest amount to invest this would be prohibitively expensive. One way of avoiding the high cost of investing in many different companies is to invest in a pooled fund where a fund manager handles the money of a group of investors. As a result, the portfolio is conveniently and cheaply diversified.

Collective investment vehicles are either regulated or unregulated. This refers to authorisation by the regulator, such as the Securities and Exchange Commission (SEC) in the US. Regulated schemes can be freely marketed; unregulated schemes cannot be freely marketed.

An unauthorised collective investment scheme can still be marketed but with restrictions, eg, only to relatively large customers, more sophisticated investors or those who already hold such an investment.

2.1.3   Hedge Funds

Hedge funds are unauthorised investment vehicles that are free to invest in high-risk strategies, including highly geared derivatives and arbitrage, such as going long in some investments and short in others (a long/short strategy). Most hedge funds are offshore investments, with the fund domiciled in the most tax-efficient location.

Unlike most of the conventional collective investment vehicles that are restricted to a long-only investment strategy, hedge funds can be more flexible and take substantial short positions.

The term hedge fund comes from the fact that the unconventional nature of their investments means they can produce positive returns when the general market is suffering. For example, a long/short strategy will potentially generate positive returns regardless of the general market – it is described as a market-neutral strategy.

Due to their unauthorised nature, nothing prevents hedge funds from borrowing money and gearing up the returns for their shareholders. Indeed, many hedge funds have substantial amounts of borrowed funds and are highly geared.

As hedge funds are not authorised, they cannot be freely marketed. This, combined with the requirement to invest substantial minimum amounts, means that hedge funds tend to be accessible only to institutional investors and high net worth individuals.

2.2   Regulatory Information and Financial Communications

Learning Objective

8.2.2   Understand the need for the publication of regulatory information and financial communications and the types of entity through which publication is achieved: PIPs; RNS; SIPs; Bloomberg; Reuters; analyst research

Listed companies that have their shares traded on exchanges need to keep market participants posted on any price-sensitive information that may arise. For example, if a company has won a significant, new contract or simply announced its most recent set of results, it needs to inform the market participants in an orderly manner. In Europe, this is a requirement of the European Union's (EU's) Transparency Directive, and companies typically satisfy this by notifying primary information providers (PIPs). An example of a primary information provider is the LSE's Regulatory New Service (RNS).

RNS is a leading service for regulatory news announcements in the UK. It helps companies and their intermediaries fulfill their UK, and other global, regulatory disclosure obligations in an efficient manner.

Almost 300,000 announcements are processed by RNS each year, with over 70% of all regulatory and potentially price-sensitive UK company announcements originating from RNS. Releasing announcements through RNS ensures company information is distributed immediately and accurately. Announcements are visible on over two million market professional terminals, databases and financial websites across the world, including key vendor services, such as Reuters, Bloomberg and the Dow Jones.

PIPs simply offer a service that receives regulatory information from listed companies, processes that information and disseminates it by circulating it to secondary information providers (SIPs). Examples of SIPs include Bloomberg, Reuters and the Dow Jones. The SIPs disseminate the information to the wider financial community, such as stockbrokers and research analysts.

The information that reaches the financial community via the PIPs and SIPs is used to inform and update research reports written by research analysts that comment on the likely future movements in the companies' share prices.

End of Chapter Questions

1. What is liquidity risk?
   Answer reference: Section 1.1.1

2. What is meant by backward-looking analyses?
   Answer reference: Section 1.1.2

3. What is the equity risk premium?
   Answer reference: Section 1.2

4. What is meant by strongly correlated assets?
   Answer reference: Section 1.7.1

5. How do active and passive investment methodologies differ?
   Answer reference: Sections 1.8 and 1.9

6. What is the motivation for buying an equity put option when holding the underlying shares?
   Answer reference: Section 1.10.2

7. Who takes priority in a company liquidation?
   Answer reference: Section 1.11

8. What are the three main types of debt seniority?
   Answer reference: Section 1.11.1

9. What is the basic definition of a hedge fund?
   Answer reference: Section 2.1.3

10. What are PIPs and what service do they offer?
    Answer reference: Section 2.2

Glossary

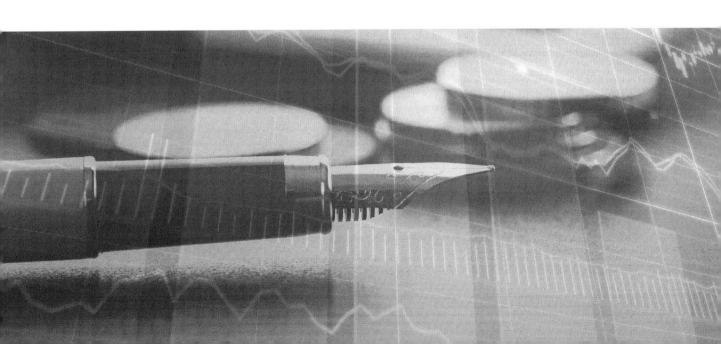

Active Management

A type of investment approach employed to generate returns in excess of an investment benchmark index. Active management is employed to exploit pricing anomalies in those securities markets that are believed to be subject to mispricing by utilising fundamental analysis and/or technical analysis to assist in the forecasting of future events and the timing of purchases and sales of securities.

Alpha

The return from a security or a portfolio in excess of a risk-adjusted benchmark return.

AIM

The London Stock Exchange's (LSE) market for smaller UK public limited companies (PLCs). AIM has less demanding admission requirements and places less onerous continuing obligation requirements upon those companies admitted to the market than those applying for a full list on the LSE.

American Depositary Receipt (ADR)

An ADR is a security that represents securities of a non-US company that trades in the US financial markets.

Amortisation

The depreciation charge applied in company accounts against capitalised intangible assets.

Annual General Meeting (AGM)

The annual meeting of directors and ordinary shareholders of a company. All companies are obliged to hold an AGM at which the shareholders receive the company's report and accounts and have the opportunity to vote on the appointment of the company's directors and auditors and the payment of a final dividend recommended by the directors. Also referred to as an Annual General Assembly in some jurisdictions.

Arbitrage

The process of deriving a risk-free profit by simultaneously buying and selling the same asset in two related markets where a pricing anomaly exists.

Asset Allocation

The process of deciding on the division of a portfolio's assets between asset classes and geographically before deciding upon which particular securities to buy.

Auction

System used to issue securities where the successful applicants pay the price that they bid. Examples of its use include the UK Debt Management Office when it issues gilts. Auctions are also used by the London Stock Exchange to establish prices, such as opening and closing auctions on SETS.

Base Currency

The currency against which the value of a quoted currency is expressed. The base currency is currency X for the X/Y exchange rate.

Bear Market

A negative move in a securities market, conventionally defined as a 20%+ decline. The duration of the market move is immaterial.

Bearer Securities

Those whose ownership is evidenced by the mere possession of a certificate. Ownership can, therefore, pass from hand to hand without any formalities.

Beta

The relationship between the returns on a stock and returns on the market. Beta is a measure of the systematic risk of a security or a portfolio in comparison to the market as a whole.

Bonus Issue

The free issue of new ordinary shares to a company's ordinary shareholders, in proportion to their existing shareholdings through the conversion, or capitalisation, of the company's reserves. By proportionately reducing the market value of each existing share, a bonus issue makes the shares more marketable. Also known as a capitalisation issue or scrip issue.

Broker-Dealer

An exchange member firm that can act in a dual capacity both as a broker acting on behalf of clients and as a dealer dealing in securities on their own account.

Captive Insurance

The creation of a specialist insurance entity to provide insurance to other companies within the same group.

Central Bank

Central banks typically have responsibility for setting a country's or a region's short-term interest rate, controlling the money supply, acting as banker and lender of last resort to the banking system and managing the national debt.

Circuit Breaker

An automated suspension of trading on an exchange when prices move by more than a predetermined amount to enable market participants to reflect and prevent panic buying or selling.

Clean Price

The quoted price of a bond. The clean price excludes accrued interest to be added or to be deducted, as appropriate.

Closed-Ended

Organisations such as companies which are a fixed size as determined by their share capital. Commonly used to distinguish investment trusts (closed-ended) from unit trusts and OEICs (open-ended).

Collective Investment Scheme (CIS)

A collective investment scheme is essentially a way of investing money with other people to participate in a wider range of investments than those feasible for most individual investors, and to share the costs of doing so. Terminology varies by country, but collective investments are often referred to as investment funds, managed funds, mutual funds or simply funds.

Commercial Paper (CP)

Money market instrument issued by large corporates.

Commission

Charges for acting as agent or broker.

Commodity

Items including sugar, wheat, oil and copper. Derivatives of commodities are traded on exchanges (eg, oil futures on ICE Futures).

Consumer Prices Index (CPI)

Index that measures the movement of prices faced by a typical consumer.

Convertible Bond

A bond which is convertible, usually at the investor's choice, into a certain number of the issuing company's shares.

Correlation

A statistical measure of how two securities move in relation to each other.

Coupon

The regular amount of interest paid on a bond.

CREST

Electronic settlement system used to settle transactions for shares, gilts and corporate bonds, particularly on behalf of the London Stock Exchange.

Cum-Dividend

The way a financial instrument is described when the buyer will be entitled to the next dividend (on a share) or coupon (on a bond).

Debt Management Office (DMO)

Agency responsible for issuing gilts on behalf of the UK Treasury.

Dematerialised

System where securities are held electronically without certificates.

Derivatives

Instruments where the price or value is derived from another underlying asset. Examples include options, futures and swaps.

Dirty Price

The price of a bond inclusive of accrued interest or exclusive of interest to be deducted, as appropriate.

Diversification

Investment strategy that involves spreading risk by investing in a range of investments.

Dividend

Distribution of profits by a company to shareholders.

Dow Jones Industrial Average (DJIA)

Major share index in the US, based on the prices of 30 major US listed company shares.

Equities

Another name for shares.

Eurobond

An interest-bearing security issued internationally. More strictly a eurobond is an international bond issue denominated in a currency different from that of the financial centre(s) in which the bonds are issued. Most eurobonds are issued in bearer form through bank syndicates.

Euronext

European stock exchange network formed by the merger of the Paris, Brussels, Amsterdam and Lisbon exchanges.

Exchange Rate

The rate at which one currency can be exchanged for another.

Ex-Dividend (xd)

The period during which the purchase of shares or bonds (on which a dividend or coupon payment has been declared) does not entitle the new holder to this next dividend or interest payment.

Exercise Price

The price at which the right conferred by a warrant or an option can be exercised by the holder against the writer.

Fiscal Years

These are the periods for reporting, alternatively referred to as financial years. The term is particularly used by the tax authorities for periods of assessment for tax purposes.

Fixed-Interest Security

A tradeable negotiable instrument, issued by a borrower for a fixed term, during which a regular and predetermined fixed rate of interest based upon a nominal value is paid to the holder until it is redeemed and the principal is repaid.

Flipping

Typically used in the context of an initial public offering (IPO), flipping is where the shares are purchased with the intention of immediately selling at a higher price. Flipping is only successful if the share price rises above the IPO price.

Floating-Rate Notes (FRNs)

Debt securities issued with a coupon periodically referenced to a benchmark interest rate, such as LIBOR.

Forex

Abbreviation for foreign exchange.

Forward

A derivatives contract that creates a legally binding obligation between two parties for one to buy and the other to sell a pre-specified amount of an asset at a pre-specified price on a pre-specified future date. Forward contracts are commonly entered into in the foreign exchange market. As individually negotiated contracts, forwards are not traded on a derivatives exchange.

FTSE 100

Main UK share index of the 100 largest listed company shares measured by market capitalisation. Also referred to as the 'Footsie'.

Fund Manager

Firm or person that makes investment decisions on behalf of clients.

Future

An agreement to buy or sell an item at a future date, at a price agreed today. Differs from a forward in that it is a standardised contract traded on an exchange.

Greenshoe Option

An over-allotment option. It gives the underwriters of an IPO the right to sell additional securities in an offering if demand for the securities is in excess of the original amount offered. It is a strategy that underwriters have developed which enables them to smooth out price fluctuations if demand surges on the one hand, and to help support the IPO if there are adverse market conditions.

Grey Market Trading

Also known as 'pre-release', grey market trading is the purchase and sale of an instrument before its formal release into the market. A key example is a depository bank selling an American depository receipt (ADR) in the three-month period up to its creation.

Gross Domestic Product (GDP)

A measure of a country's output.

Gross Redemption Yield (GRY)

The annual compound return from holding a bond to maturity taking into account both interest payments and any capital gain or loss at maturity. Also referred to as the yield to maturity (YTM). The GRY or YTM is the internal rate of return on the bond based on its trading price.

Harmonised Index of Consumer Prices (HICP)

The way the consumer prices index in the EU was originally described.

Hedging

A technique employed to reduce the impact of adverse price movements on financial assets held.

Index-Linked Gilts

Gilts whose principal and interest payments are linked to the retail prices index (RPI). An example of an inflation-protected security.

Inflation

A persistent increase in the general level of prices. Usually established by reference to consumer prices and the CPI.

Initial Public Offering (IPO)

A new issue of ordinary shares that sees the company gain a stock market listing for the first time, whether made by an offer for sale, an offer for subscription or a placing.

Introduction

In the context of a listing or IPO, an introduction is a company applying for, and gaining a listing for, its securities on a stock market, without raising any funds.

Investment Bank

Firms that specialise in advising companies on M&A (mergers and acquisitions), and corporate finance matters such as raising debt and equity. The larger investment banks are also heavily involved in trading financial instruments.

Investment Trust

Despite the name, an investment trust is a company, not a trust, which invests in a diversified range of investments.

Liquidity

Ease with which an item can be traded on the market. Liquid markets are also described as 'deep'.

Liquidity Risk

The risk that an item, such as a financial instrument, may be difficult to sell at a reasonable price.

Listing

Companies whose securities are listed are available to be traded on an exchange.

London Interbank Offered Rate (LIBOR)

Benchmark money market interest rates published for a number of different currencies over a range of periods. LIBOR, which is the rate at which funds in a particular currency and for a particular maturity, are available to one bank from other banks. LIBORs are gathered and published on a daily basis.

Long Position

The position following the purchase of a security or buying a derivative.

Market Capitalisation

The total market value of a company's shares or other securities in issue. Market capitalisation is calculated by multiplying the number of shares or other securities a company has in issue by the market price of those shares or securities.

Market Maker

A stock exchange member firm registered to quote prices and trade shares throughout the trading day (such as the LSE's mandatory quote period).

Maturity

Date when the principal on a bond is repaid.

Monetary Policy Committee (MPC)

Committee run by the Bank of England that sets UK interest rates.

Multilateral Trading Facilities (MTFs)

Systems that bring together multiple parties that are interested in buying and selling financial instruments including shares, bonds and derivatives.

Net Redemption Yield (NRY)

Similar to the GRY in that it takes both the annual coupons and the profit (or loss) made through to maturity into account, however the NRY looks at the after-tax cash flows rather than the gross cash flows. As a result, it is a useful measure for tax-paying, long-term investors.

Nominal Value

The amount on a bond that will be repaid on maturity. Also known as face or par value. Also applied to shares in some jurisdictions and representing the minimum that the shares are issued for.

Nominee

A nominee is the party holding legal ownership of securities, such as shares, on behalf of another beneficial owner.

Offer Price

Bond and share prices are quoted as bid and offer. The offer is the higher of the two prices and is the one that would be paid by a buyer.

Open-Ended

Type of investment, such as OEICs or unit trusts, which can expand without limit.

Option

A derivative giving the buyer the right, but not the obligation, to buy or sell an asset in the future.

Over-the-Counter (OTC)

Transactions between banks and their counterparties not on a recognised exchange.

Passive Management

In contrast to active management, passive management is an investment approach that does not aspire to create a return in excess of a benchmark index. The approach often involves tracking the benchmark index.

Pre-Emption Rights

The rights accorded to ordinary shareholders to subscribe for new ordinary shares issued by the company in proportion to their current shareholding.

Preference Share

Shares which usually pay fixed dividends but do not have voting rights. Preference shares have preference over ordinary shares in relation to the payment of dividends and in default situations.

Premium

An excess amount being paid, such as the excess paid for a convertible bond over the market value of the underlying shares it can be converted into. The term is also used for the amount of cash paid by the holder of an option or warrant to the writer in exchange for conferring a right.

Prospectus

A detailed document about a company that is issuing securities. If it relates to an initial public offering, it will include all of the information to enable prospective investors to decide on the merit of the company's shares.

Proxy

Appointee who votes on a shareholder's behalf at company meetings.

Real Estate Investment Trust (REIT)

An investment trust that specialises in investing in commercial property.

Redemption

The repayment of principal to the holder of a redeemable security.

Registrar

The official who maintains the share register on behalf of a company.

Reinsurance

Insurance purchased by an insurer against the risks that it may have to pay out on the policies it has underwritten. Effectively enables insurers to transfer some of their risks to other insurers.

Repo

The sale and repurchase of securities between two parties: both the sale and the repurchase agreement are made at the same time, with the purchase price and date fixed in advance.

Rights Issue

The issue of new ordinary shares to a company's shareholders in proportion to each shareholder's existing holding. The issue is made in accordance with the shareholders' pre-emptive rights and the new shares are usually offered at a discounted price to that prevailing in the market. This means that the rights have a value, and can be traded 'nil-paid'.

Scrip Issue

Another term for a bonus or capitalisation issue.

Share Buyback

The purchase and typically the cancellation by a company of a proportion of its ordinary shares.

Share Capital

The nominal value of a company's equity or ordinary shares. A company's authorised share capital is the nominal value of equity the company may issue, while the issued share capital is that which the company has issued. The term share capital is often extended to include a company's preference shares.

Stock Split

A method by which a company can reduce the market price of its shares to make them more marketable without capitalising its reserves. A share split simply entails the company reducing the nominal value of each of its shares in issue while maintaining the overall nominal value of its share capital. A share split should have the same impact on a company's share price as a bonus issue.

Short Position

The position following the sale of a security not owned or selling a derivative.

Special Purpose Vehicle (SPV)

Bankruptcy-remote, off-balance-sheet vehicle set up for a particular purpose such as buying assets from the originator and issuing asset-backed securities.

Special Resolution

Proposal put to shareholders requiring 75% of the votes cast in order to be accepted.

Swap

An over-the-counter (OTC) derivative whereby two parties exchange a series of periodic payments based on a notional principal amount over an agreed term. Swaps can take a number of forms including interest rate swaps, currency swaps, credit default swaps and equity swaps.

Treasury Bills

Short-term (often three months) borrowings of the government. Issued at a discount to the nominal value at which they will mature. Traded in the money market.

Two-Way Price

Prices quoted by a market maker at which they are willing to buy (bid) and sell (offer).

Underwriting

When financial institutions, such as banks, insurers and asset managers, agree to buy securities being issued (for example in an IPO) if demand is otherwise insufficient.

Unit Trust

A vehicle whereby money from investors is pooled together and invested collectively on their behalf. Unit trusts are open-ended vehicles.

Yield

Income from an investment expressed as a percentage of the current price.

Yield Curve

The depiction of the relationship between the yields and the maturity of bonds of the same type.

Zero Coupon Bonds (ZCBs)

Bonds issued at a discount to their nominal value that do not pay a coupon but which are redeemed at par on a pre-specified future date.

Multiple Choice
Questions

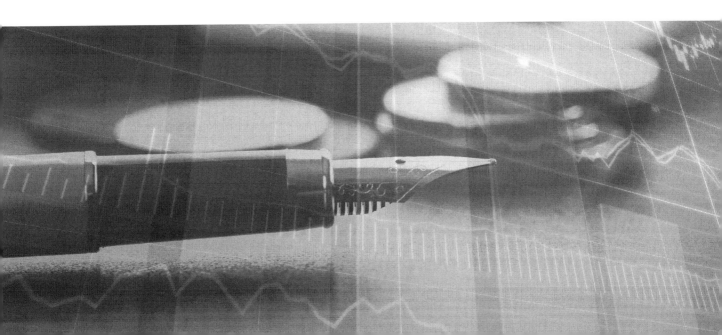

1. A bond with a 4% coupon, redeemable in five years' time, is currently trading at 105. Which of the following is most accurate in terms of the limitation of using the flat yield to assess whether or not to invest in this bond?

   A. The flat yield includes the annualised gain through to redemption of the bond

   B. The flat yield includes the annualised loss through to redemption of the bond

   C. The flat yield ignores the gain through to redemption

   D. The flat yield ignores the loss through to redemption

2. Which best describes the purpose of stabilisation in the conduct of an initial public offering?

   A. To coordinate the marketing activities of the origination syndicate so that they are not disjointed

   B. To ensure that pension funds are treated equally in the numbers of shares offered to them in an initial public offering

   C. To ensure that the prices of the new issue increase after the initial public offering

   D. To prevent a substantial fall in the value of securities by buying back securities in the market

3. The risk-free rate of return is best described as the rate of return:

   A. offered by large corporations which have no previous history of default

   B. on government bonds and short-term debts

   C. from a well-diversified and balanced portfolio

   D. on any investment with a AAA rating (or equivalent) from all three large credit rating agencies

4. What is the maximum period during which a special-ex trade can normally be transacted and who is entitled to receive the dividend?

   A. In the two business days before the ex-dividend date with the seller entitled to the dividend

   B. In the two business days before the ex-dividend date with the buyer entitled to the dividend

   C. In the ten business days before the ex-dividend date with the buyer entitled to the dividend

   D. In the ten business days before the ex-dividend date with the seller entitled to the dividend

5. The exchange rate on which of the following currency pairs is considered a cross rate?

   A. The British pound and the Swiss franc

   B. The British pound and the US dollar

   C. The US dollar and the Australian dollar

   D. The Swiss franc and the US dollar

6. How does CLS reduce the settlement risk for foreign exchange transactions?

A. By adopting a PvP system

B. By collecting margin from both participants to a trade

C. By requiring collateral in the form of investment grade bonds

D. By only allowing the biggest banks to participate

7. Which of the following best distinguishes the operations of the NYSE and the London Stock Exchange?

A. The NYSE is the US listing authority, the LSE is not the UK's listing authority

B. The LSE is primarily quote-driven, the NYSE is primarily order-driven

C. Only the NYSE operates an open-outcry system

D. The presence of dark pools as off-exchange facilities are only provided by the NYSE

8. If interest rates were to rise in the UK, what would one expect to be the effect on the price and yield of gilts?

A. Price and yield would remain the same

B. Price would fall and yield would rise

C. Price would fall and yield would fall

D. Price would rise and yield would fall

9. Which of the following ranks lowest in the order of priority in a liquidation?

A. Senior debt

B. Preferred shares

C. PIK debt

D. Subordinated debt

10. All of the following are true of the foreign exchange market, except:

A. banks are the major market participants

B. spot and forward contracts are available

C. central bank authorisation is required for the acquisition of foreign currencies by local residents

D. deals for delayed settlement are allowed

11. Which of the following measures is used as a target for the UK Monetary Policy Committee in relation to inflation?

A. Retail Prices Index

B. Retail Prices Index excluding mortgage payments

C. Producer Prices Index

D. Consumer Prices Index

12. Under FCA regulations, which of the following is the level at which an investor is first judged to have a notifiable interest in a public company? If they hold voting rights that amount to:

    A. 1%
    B. 3%
    C. 5%
    D. 9.9%

13. Which of the following types of fund typically sees the manager hold a stake in the fund?

    A. Pension fund
    B. Insurance fund
    C. Mutual fund
    D. Hedge fund

14. Which of the following best describes the action that an investor should take in relation to a rights issue if they want to retain influence over the company at the same level?

    A. Take up the rights in full
    B. Sell the rights nil-paid
    C. Sell part of the rights nil-paid and use the proceeds to buy shares
    D. Take no action

15. £100 nominal of a convertible loan stock carries the right to convert into 50 ordinary shares. The current market price of the convertible is £107 and the ordinary share price is £1.85. The conversion premium is therefore:

    A. 15.7%
    B. 16.2%
    C. 10.1%
    D. 13.5%

16. US Treasury-issued long bonds have maturities of:

    A. 10 years
    B. 15 years
    C. 20 years
    D. 30 years

17. Which type of security has the characteristic that it is an anonymous, freely transferable share certificate?

    A. A bearer share
    B. A preference shareholder's certificate
    C. An accumulation share
    D. A share that pays dividends quarterly

18. Private placements which are allowed to proceed without a full prospectus can only be made available to which of the following types of investors?

    A. Member firms of the local stock exchange

    B. Pension funds

    C. Hedge funds

    D. Qualified investors

19. Which of the following best describes the income statement?

    A. A summary statement of generation and spending of cash over the accounting period

    B. A summary of the income earned and expenses incurred over the accounting period

    C. A report from the directors regarding their forecast of the expected revenues in the next fiscal year

    D. A snapshot of the financial position as at the year-end

20. What is the present value of a 4% annual coupon-paying $100 nominal bond with two years to maturity, with a prevailing discount rate of 1%?

    A. $98.73

    B. $100

    C. $105.91

    D. $104.12

21. Which of the following best describes the STRIPS market? It is the market for:

    A. zero coupon bonds

    B. bonds trading cum interest/dividend

    C. bonds trading ex interest/dividend

    D. the individual cash flows on a government bond

22. How does a regulated fund differ from an unregulated fund?

    A. Only regulated funds are legal

    B. Only regulated funds can be marketed

    C. Unregulated funds have marketing restrictions

    D. Unregulated funds are run by unauthorised persons

23. Which of the following order types used for exchange order books provides some of the characteristics now demanded by users of dark pools?

    A. Limit order

    B. Iceberg order

    C. Fill or kill order

    D. Execute and eliminate order

24. A fund wants to invest in bonds that are relatively risky to capture as high a yield as possible, but does not want to venture into 'junk' bond territory. Which of the following credit ratings is likely to be most attractive?

    A. A+

    B. A–

    C. BBB–

    D. BB+

25. A summary statement of payments and receipts over an accounting period is:

    A. a statement of cash flows

    B. a statement of financial position

    C. a report from the directors regarding the financial prospects for the company

    D. an income statement

26. What term is given to the risk that the overall market in general will rise or fall as economic conditions and other market factors change?

    A. Systemic risk

    B. Systematic risk

    C. Liquidity risk

    D. Inflation risk

27. What is a special purpose vehicle?

    A. A totally separate 'off-balance-sheet' entity which does not require the guarantee of the asset's originator

    B. A vehicle which is created offshore to avoid corporate taxation

    C. A special investment vehicle which is underwritten by a sovereign guarantee

    D. An 'off-balance-sheet' entity which would be legally required to be taken back on to the originator's balance sheet in the case of the assets becoming distressed

28. All of the following would be considered examples of capital expenditure, except:

    A. money spent to buy a non-current asset

    B. the purchase of a new office building

    C. the purchase of copyrights from another company

    D. a payment to an investment bank for advice on an acquisition

29. XYZ announces a 1 for 4 rights issue. The cum-rights share price is $4.50 and the right enables shares to be purchased at $3.20 each. What is the theoretical ex-rights price?

    A. $1.04

    B. $1.30

    C. $4.24

    D. $12.80

30. If an investor wishes to avoid the administrative tasks involved with share registration and transfers title to a nominee, which of the following is true?

    A. The nominee becomes the beneficial owner while the investor retains legal ownership

    B. The nominee or custodian will become the beneficial owner of the shares

    C. The nominee will become the legal owner of the shares and keep all dividends

    D. The nominee will become the legal owner but the investor will remain as the beneficial owner and be entitled to receive all dividends

31. How does an open offer differ from a rights issue?

    A. Open offers are free, while rights issues are not

    B. Open offers are only open to the existing shareholders, while rights issues are open to everyone

    C. Open offers cannot be sold nil-paid, while rights can be sold nil-paid

    D. Open offers are made without any advisory involvement, while rights issues use advisers

32. Which of the following correctly identifies the longest-term debt instrument issued by the German Government?

    A. German Treasury Note

    B. Schatz

    C. Bund

    D. Eurobond

33. All of the following major stock indices are capitalisation-weighted, except the:

    A. FTSE 100 Index

    B. Standard & Poor's 500 Index

    C. Dow Jones Industrial Average

    D. Nasdaq Composite Index

34. Which entity is responsible for determining the maturities of debt issued by the UK Government and its date of issuance?

    A. Bank of England

    B. Debt Management Office

    C. HM Revenue & Customs

    D. Financial Conduct Authority

35. Which of the following arranges deals in investments for retail investors without giving any advice?

    A. Investment banks

    B. Insurance companies

    C. Execution-only stockbrokers

    D. Wealth managers

36. An inability for investors to sell a security easily, with a wide spread between bid and ask, is best described as which of the following?

    A. Liquidity risk

    B. Default risk

    C. Inflation risk

    D. Market risk

37. Which of the following would be a reason for holding shares in a designated rather than a pooled nominee account?

    A. The shareholder retains the right to vote

    B. The shareholder requires any dividends to be mandated to a particular bank account

    C. Shareholder benefits are made available to the investor with a designated account

    D. Transaction charges are lower for a designated account

38. Which of the following ratios effectively provides a yield for the whole company being analysed?

    A. Return on capital employed

    B. Debt to equity

    C. Enterprise value to EBIT

    D. Gross dividend yield

39. Which of the following best describes the purpose of the primary market?

    A. To allow providers of capital to purchase new securities which are made available from new issuers

    B. To allow institutional investors to buy shares that they have not previously owned

    C. To allow speculators and traders to provide liquidity for those requiring large-scale portfolio rebalancing

    D. To allow the calculation of the daily value of the stock indices

40. Which of the following measures of profit is stated after deduction of only the cost of goods sold?

    A. Gross profit

    B. Operating profit

    C. Revenue

    D. Net income

41. Which of the following combinations of two shares in a portfolio will give zero diversification benefits? Two shares that are:

    A. perfectly positively correlated

    B. perfectly negatively correlated

    C. positively correlated

    D. negatively correlated

42. Which of the following holds ownership via a nominee name with a unique identifier for each individual client?

    A. Pooled nominee

    B. Omnibus nominee

    C. Designated nominee

    D. Sole nominee

43. Which of the following clearing and settlement models involves gross settlement of securities followed by net settlement of funds?

    A. BIS model 1

    B. BIS model 2

    C. BIS model 3

    D. The sub-custodian model

44. Which of the following best describes the straight line method of depreciation?

    A. An annual charge equal to the cost of a non-current asset

    B. An annual charge to match the cost of a non-current asset in equal amounts over its useful economic life

    C. An annual payment made into a deposit account to cover the deterioration in the performance of a company's asset

    D. An annual charge to represent the opportunity cost of the loss of interest as a result of purchasing a non-current asset

45. Agreeing procedures for settling a transaction typically forms part of which stage of the clearing and settlement process?

    A. Matching

    B. Clearing

    C. Settlement

    D. Post-settlement

46. Which of the following types of corporate debt is likely to offer the highest rate of interest?

    A. Senior unsecured

    B. Mezzanine

    C. Senior secured

    D. Subordinated

47. Which of the following would form part of a passive rather than an active portfolio management strategy?

    A. Short-selling securities that are overvalued

    B. Hedging an existing holding using an OTC forward to take advantage of price movements outside normal trading hours

    C. Selecting securities based on quantitative research and the P/E ratios of companies within selected sectors

    D. Buying index-based equity derivatives to emulate the FTSE 100

48. Which of the following measures is the same as the internal rate of return of a bond?

    A. Modified duration

    B. Convexity

    C. Flat yield

    D. Gross redemption yield

49. Which of the following is the standard settlement timetable for equity transactions in most developed markets?

    A. T+1

    B. T+2

    C. T+3

    D. T+5

50. Becker Inc shares are trading at 90 cents. Becker decides to undertake a reverse stock split with each share representing six of the previously existing shares. What is the new share price likely to be?

    A. $0.15

    B. $1.50

    C. $5.40

    D. $36.00

51. Which of the following is a passive strategy for investing in bonds to meet a future liability?

    A. Riding the yield curve

    B. Anomaly switching

    C. Policy switching

    D. Barbell strategy

52. An investment bank is organising the execution of client orders on its own account on a frequent, systematic and substantial basis. How would the investment bank be described under MiFID?

    A. A regulated market

    B. A multilateral trading facility

    C. A national securities exchange

    D. A systematic internaliser

53. If demand for a new issue is insufficient, who typically buys the remaining shares?

    A. The issuing company

    B. The lead manager

    C. The underwriter

    D. The secondary market

54. A company has a 1 for 3 rights issue at £2.00 per share. Immediately before the announcement the share price was £6. What is the nil-paid value of the rights?

    A. £2

    B. £3

    C. £5

    D. £6

55. How frequently are coupons paid on German Government Bunds?

    A. Never

    B. Quarterly

    C. Semi-annually

    D. Annually

56. The following are reasons for scrip issues, except:

    A. raising money for acquisitions

    B. as a public relations exercise

    C. to reduce the current market price

    D. to tidy up shareholders' funds

57. The following are terms used to describe off-exchange trading venues where stocks are traded in large quantities without prices being displayed until after the trade is done, except:

    A. Dark pools

    B. ATSs

    C. MTFs

    D. MiFIDs

58. When the yield curve is described as inverted, which of the following is most likely to be true?

    A. Long-term corporate bonds are yielding less than the equivalent government bonds

    B. Short-term corporate bonds are yielding less than the equivalent government bonds

    C. Long-term government bond yields are higher than short-term government bond yields

    D. Short-term bond government yields are higher than long-term government bond yields

59. How does the majority of corporate bond secondary market trading take place?

    A. Stock exchange order-driven system

    B. Stock exchange quote-driven system

    C. Decentralised dealer market

    D. The original issuers of the bonds

60. A medium-term note that is sold to an investor after the investor requests a certain quantity and price is generally referred to as:

    A. selective marketing

    B. a reverse inquiry

    C. an auction

    D. a tender offer

61. If a company writes an option to issue more than a base number of shares in an IPO, it is usually called which one of the following?

    A. Greenshoe

    B. Follow-on

    C. Underwriting

    D. Syndication

62. Which government issues BTFs into its money markets?

    A. UK

    B. Germany

    C. US

    D. France

63. Which of the following is a cash flow that impacts the equity, but not the enterprise?

    A. Sale of a building

    B. Receipts from customers

    C. Purchase of an intangible

    D. Payment of interest on borrowings

64. A hybrid system:

    A. includes both buy and sell orders

    B. trades both bonds and equities

    C. involves investment banks and fund managers

    D. combines quote-driven and order-driven trading

65. Which of the following best describes the dirty price of a bond?

    A. The price quoted in the market

    B. The price that ignores any accrued interest

    C. The price that includes any accrued interest

    D. The par value of the bond

66. A bond issued by VPN plc pays a 4% coupon and redeems in five years. It also provides the holder with the right, but not the obligation, to hand back the bond and accept five shares in DEF plc instead. How would the bond be best described?

    A. A convertible bond

    B. An exchangeable bond

    C. A preferred equity

    D. A bond with warrants attached

67. Which of the following is generally considered to be most risky?

    A. Small company shares

    B. Large company shares

    C. Bonds

    D. Money market instruments

68. A preference share that will carry forward the right to dividends unpaid and can also be bought back by the issuing company at particular times, is best described as:

    A. cumulative and convertible

    B. cumulative and participating

    C. cumulative and redeemable

    D. convertible and participating

69. Which of the following is most involved in the due diligence of the prospectus for a new issue of shares?

    A. The corporate broker

    B. The PR consultant

    C. The reporting accountants

    D. The non-executive director

70. What particular issue only crops up in a set of accounts for a group of companies?

    A. Goodwill

    B. Intangible assets

    C. Receivables from other companies

    D. Payables to other companies

71. The lowest yielding bonds are likely to come from an issuer rated at:

    A. Baa3

    B. Caa1

    C. BB+

    D. BBB−

72. A client of a stockbroking firm is considering purchasing shares in an already listed company for the first time. The purchase will most likely be made:

   A. in the primary market

   B. in the secondary market

   C. from the company

   D. from the stockbroking firm

73. A company has a 1 for 5 rights issue at £3.00 per share. Immediately before the announcement the share price was £6.00. What is the theoretical ex-rights price?

   A. £2.50

   B. £3.00

   C. £5.50

   D. £6.00

74. Which of the following is the name of the German Government bond that is issued with a five year maturity?

   A. OAT

   B. BTAN

   C. Bund

   D. Bobl

75. Which of the following best describes stabilisation?

   A. Supporting the price of newly issued securities in the aftermarket

   B. Keeping the price of securities at the same level

   C. Preventing shares from being removed from the stock market index

   D. Selecting a variety of shares from the same industry in a portfolio

76. Dale Inc shares are currently trading at $120 each. Dale decides it is appropriate to split the shares on the basis of three new shares for each share. What is the most likely resultant share price?

   A. $30

   B. $36

   C. $40

   D. $360

77. Which of the following US equity indices would give more influence to a higher-priced stock, regardless of that stock's market capitalisation?

   A. DJIA

   B. S&P 500

   C. Nasdaq Composite

   D. Wilshire 5000

78. Which of the following is true of a trade executed via an IDB?

   A. The deal price is never revealed

   B. The deal is always done via a dark pool

   C. The deal is settled as if the IDB was the principal

   D. The deal involves a large-cap stock

79. A company has two types of share in issue: 'A' and 'B' shares. Both classes of share have voting rights and the right to receive dividends determined by the company. Neither share type has a fixed entitlement to dividends and both classes rank equally in respect of dividend payment priority. The 'A' shares are entitled to ten votes per share and the 'B' shares are entitled to one vote per share. How would the two shares best be described?

   A. As types of ordinary share

   B. As types of preference share

   C. The 'A' shares as preference shares and the 'B' shares as ordinary shares

   D. The 'B' shares as preference shares and the 'A' shares as ordinary shares

80. What is the term typically used for an issue of securities that involves marketing to a preselected group of potential investors, rather than investors generally?

   A. Follow-on offer

   B. IPO

   C. Greenshoe

   D. Placing

81. Spencer plc's 4% ten-year bonds are yielding a 45 basis points spread over the relevant ten-year government bond that is yielding 3.80%. Ten-year swaps are currently 4.15%. What are Spencer's bonds yielding in relation to swaps?

   A. Plus 10 basis points

   B. Minus 15 basis points

   C. Plus 25 basis points

   D. Plus 60 basis points

82. The allocation of the estimated cost of an intangible asset as it is used up over its useful economic life is known as which of the following?

    A. Amortisation

    B. Depreciation

    C. Revaluation

    D. Owners' equity

83. If bond A has a significantly higher modified duration than bond B, which of the following is true?

    A. Bond A has a higher coupon than bond B

    B. Bond A has a shorter maturity than bond B

    C. Bond A has a higher credit rating than bond B

    D. Bond A is more responsive to interest rate changes than bond B

84. A fund manager wishing to hedge exposure to risk arising from long equity positions is most likely to do which of the following?

    A. Buy futures contracts

    B. Buy put options

    C. Buy call options

    D. Effectively buy using CFDs

85. How is cash at the bank normally classified within a company's statement of financial position?

    A. As a non-current asset

    B. As a current asset

    C. As a liability

    D. As part of equity

86. Which of the following types of organisation typically offers corporate finance advice, securities trading and merger and acquisition assistance?

    A. Wealth managers

    B. Financial planners

    C. Investment banks

    D. Custodian banks

87. In a large new listing, which of the following is the term for the firm that book builds?

    A. Syndicate

    B. Lead manager

    C. Issuer

    D. Primary adviser

88. A company has reduced its activities and wants to reorganise its capital structure to include more debt and less equity. Which of the following corporate actions is likely to be most appropriate?

    A. Share buyback

    B. Rights issue

    C. Bonus issue

    D. Placing

89. Which of the following is the type of order that does not specify a price?

    A. Market order

    B. Limit order

    C. Iceberg order

    D. Execute and eliminate order

90. Which of the following best describes the features of subordinated debt?

    A. The yields are higher than senior debt, the bonds rank above equity in a liquidation

    B. The yields are lower than senior debt, the bonds rank above equity in a liquidation

    C. The yields are higher than senior debt, the bonds rank below equity in a liquidation

    D. The yields are lower than senior debt, the bonds rank below equity in a liquidation

91. What is the normal priority that is given to orders on an order-driven trading system?

    A. Price and then time

    B. Time and then price

    C. Quantity and then price

    D. Frequency and then price

92. The foreign exchange market is best described as which of the following?

    A. An over-the-counter market, with no central exchange or clearing house

    B. An exchange-driven market, centred in London, New York and Hong Kong

    C. A market exclusively provided by a small number of major multinational banks

    D. A market that only trades the major currencies – the US dollar, euro, sterling and the yen

93. Which of the following best describes an open offer?

    A. A follow-on issue of new shares to new investors

    B. A follow-on issue of new shares to existing investors

    C. An IPO to institutional investors only

    D. An IPO that does not involve institutional investors

94. Which of the following institutional investors is most likely to hold the highest proportion of money market instruments in its portfolio?

    A. General insurance fund

    B. Defined benefit pension fund

    C. Defined contribution fund

    D. Life assurance fund

95. All of the following are expenses charged in the income statement, except:

    A. corporation tax

    B. costs of sales

    C. finance costs

    D. dividends

96. A share premium account is classed within what sub-element of equity?

    A. Share capital

    B. Capital reserves

    C. Revenue reserves

    D. Minority interests

97. Combining securities with a less than perfect positive correlation in a portfolio will remove some of which of the following risks?

    A. Unsystematic risk

    B. Market risk

    C. Systematic risk

    D. Political risk

98. All of the following are headings within a cash flow statement under IAS 7, except:

    A. operating activities

    B. investing activities

    C. financing activities

    D. depreciating activities

99. A company applies for a listing and becomes listed without selling any shares in the primary or secondary markets. How is this process typically described?

    A. Placing

    B. Reverse takeover

    C. Over-allotment

    D. Introduction

100. All of the following are generally viewed as key benefits of utilising a central counterparty, except:

    A. providing anonymity

    B. avoiding the need for exchange membership

    C. facilitating netting

    D. reducing administration

Answers to Multiple Choice Questions

1.   **D**   **Chapter 2, Section 2.2.1**

The buyer of this bond will suffer a loss through to redemption since the price at 105 is above par. However, the flat yield ignores the loss since it just takes into account the coupon divided by the price.

2.   **D**   **Chapter 3, Section 3.4**

To prevent a substantial fall in the value of securities when a large number of new securities are issued, the lead manager of the issue agrees to support the price by buying back the newly issued securities in the market if they should drop below an agreed-upon minimum price.

3.   **B**   **Chapter 2, Section 3.1**

In standard financial theory it is the rate of return on government bonds and short-term debts because of the low chance that governments will default on their loans.

4.   **D**   **Chapter 6, Section 6**

A special cum-trade can be arranged any time during the ex-dividend period. A special ex-trade, however, is generally only possible in the ten business days before the ex-date.

5.   **A**   **Chapter 2, Section 8.1**

A cross rate is between two currencies that do not include the US dollar.

6.   **A**   **Chapter 6, Section 7**

CLS adopts a system known as payment versus payment.

7.   **C**   **Chapter 4, Section 2.1**

The trading floor at the London Stock Exchange has been closed for decades. A relatively minor part of trading on the NYSE is still operated on an open-outcry basis in Wall Street.

8.   **B**   **Chapter 2, Section 2.2.1**

An interest rate rise will mean that the yield on bonds will need to rise too, and the change in yield is brought about by a reduction in the price of the bond.

9.   **B**   **Chapter 8, Section 1.11**

Preferred shares will rank above ordinary/common shares but below forms of debt in a liquidation.

10.   **C**   **Chapter 2, Section 8**

There is no requirement for central bank authorisation. For example, anyone can buy or sell currencies at a foreign exchange booth in an airport.

11. **D** **Chapter 2, Section 3.2.2**

In December 2003, the UK's Chancellor of the Exchequer changed the inflation target to a new base, the harmonised index of consumer prices (HICP), which has since been renamed the consumer prices index (CPI).

12. **B** **Chapter 5, Section 4.2**

Notifiable interests in the UK begin at 3% or more of the voting rights.

13. **D** **Chapter 8, Section 1.8.4**

Both hedge funds and private equity funds typically see the management having stakes to provide 'skin in the game'.

14. **A** **Chapter 5, Section 3.1**

The investor would have to buy all of their rights in order to retain the same percentage in the enlarged share capital.

15. **A** **Chapter 2, Section 2.3.2**

To calculate the premium, take the value of the bond (£107) and divide it by the value of the shares the bond could be converted into, ie, (50 x 185p) = £92.50. The answer is therefore 107 divided by 92.50 which is 1.157, so the bond is worth 1.157 times the value of the shares into which it could be converted: a 15.7% premium.

16. **D** **Chapter 2, Section 3.4**

The US long bond has a maturity of 30 years.

17. **A** **Chapter 6, Section 4**

Since the issuer maintains no register for bearer shares, it does not record the seller or the buyer.

18. **D** **Chapter 3, Section 2.5.1**

Private placements can only be made available to 'qualified investors' as specified by the financial services regulator.

19. **B** **Chapter 7, Section 1.1**

The income statement summarises the income earned and expenses incurred over the accounting period.

20. **C** **Chapter 2, Section 2.6**

$Y1 = 100 \times 4\% \times (1 \div 1.01) = 3.96$

$Y2 = 104 \times (1 \div 1.01^2) = 101.95$

Present value $= 3.96 + 101.95 = 105.91$

21.   **D**   **Chapter 2, Section 3.3**

STRIPS is an acronym for Separate Trading of Registered Interest and Principal of Securities and enables a bond's individual cash flows – the coupons and the principal – to be traded separately.

22.   **C**   **Chapter 2, Section 9.1**

Authorisation by the regulator removes some of the marketing restrictions that apply to an unregulated or unauthorised fund. Both regulated and unregulated funds are legal, and tend to be run by authorised persons.

23.   **B**   **Chapter 4, Section 3.2**

Iceberg orders enable a market participant with a particularly large order to partially hide the size of their order from the market and reduce the market impact that the large order might otherwise have.

24.   **C**   **Chapter 2, Section 4.3**

The minimum acceptable investment grade from S&P and Fitch is BBB–, and BB+ is below investment grade.

25.   **A**   **Chapter 7, Section 4.1**

The summary statement of payments and receipts over an accounting period is known as the statement of cash flows.

26.   **B**   **Chapter 8, Section 1.6**

Systematic risk or market risk is the risk that the overall market will rise or fall, as economic conditions and other market factors change.

27.   **A**   **Chapter 2, Section 4.1.3**

There is normally no legal requirement for the originator to support the assets in an SPV. However, when the assets become distressed, or if there is no market for determining the value of the assets held in the SPV, as was the case during the 'sub-prime' crisis of 2007/8, the originators of the securitisation instruments have occasionally chosen to fully transfer the troubled assets on to their primary balance sheets for reputational reasons.

28.   **D**   **Chapter 7, Section 3.2**

The payment to the investment bank would be considered as professional fees and not part of the capital expenditure which would be incurred in an acquisition. The consideration paid to the acquired company for an acquisition would, however, be a capital expenditure.

29.   **C**   **Chapter 5, Section 3.1.2**

Theoretical ex-rights price = (4 x 4.50) + (1 x 3.20) ÷ 5 = $4.24.

30.   **D**   **Chapter 6, Section 4**

The nominee will become the legal owner but the investor will remain as the beneficial owner of the shares and be entitled to receive all dividends.

31. **C** **Chapter 3, Section 2.3**

Open offers are the equivalent of a rights issue, without the ability for shareholders to sell their right on in the nil-paid market.

32. **C** **Chapter 2, Section 3.4**

A Bund is the longest-term debt instrument issued by the German Government.

33. **C** **Chapter 4, Section 4.3**

The Dow Jones Industrial Average is not capitalisation-weighted and as an example of a price-weighted average it gives higher-priced stocks more influence than their lower-priced counterparts.

34. **B** **Chapter 3, Section 5.2**

The Debt Management Office, which is an executive agency of HM Treasury, is responsible for deciding on what are the most appropriate maturities for gilts and their dates of issuance.

35. **C** **Chapter 1, Section 3**

Execution-only brokers give no advice, but simply offer trading services to retail clients. They earn their profits by charging commissions on the transactions arranged.

36. **A** **Chapter 8, Section 1.1.1**

Liquidity risk is the inability to sell easily with the market displaying a wide spread between buying and selling prices.

37. **B** **Chapter 6, Section 5**

One reason for registering shares in a designated or sole nominee name would be to enable the underlying investor to have dividends mandated to a particular bank account rather than collected by the custodian.

38. **A** **Chapter 7, Section 5.2**

It is the ROCE that effectively provides a yield – operating profit expressed as a percentage of capital.

39. **A** **Chapter 3, Section 1**

The primary market allows providers of capital to purchase new securities, usually conducted through IPOs, which are made available from new issuers of securities.

40. **A** **Chapter 7, Section 3.1.3**

Gross profit is the profit after deducting the cost of sales or the cost of goods sold.

41. **A** **Chapter 8, Section 1.7.2**

Combining perfectly positively correlated investments gives no diversification benefits.

42.   **C**   **Chapter 6, Section 5.3**

It is the designated nominee that involves a unique identifier rather than the actual client name (which is used in the sole nominee).

43.   **B**   **Chapter 6, Section 2.2**

The three BIS models all provide delivery versus payment terms. Model 1 involves gross simultaneous settlements of securities and funds, Model 2 gross settlement of securities transfers followed by net settlement of funds and Model 3 simultaneous net transfers of securities and funds. There is no sub-custodian model for clearing and settlement.

44.   **B**   **Chapter 7, Section 2.3**

Straight line depreciation is an annual charge to match the cost of a non-current asset and which is applied in equal amounts over the useful economic life of the asset.

45.   **B**   **Chapter 6, Section 1**

Agreeing procedures for settling a transaction is one part of the clearing process, alongside matching and confirming details.

46.   **B**   **Chapter 8, Section 1.11.1**

Mezzanine debt, including PIK notes, ranks below other forms of debt but above equity in the event of a liquidation. As the most risky debt, it will offer a greater rate of interest than the subordinated and senior levels of debt.

47.   **D**   **Chapter 8, Section 1.9**

Passive management requires the construction of an equity portfolio to track, or mimic, the performance of a recognised equity index. Using index-based derivatives can emulate the total returns without requiring an outright purchase of all of the stocks in the index.

48.   **D**   **Chapter 2, Section 2.2.2**

The gross redemption yield provides the 'internal rate of return' of the bond. The internal rate of return is simply the discount rate that, when applied to the future cash flows of the bond, produces the current price of that bond.

49.   **B**   **Chapter 6, Section 2.1**

In most developed equities markets, the settlement of equity trades is T+2.

50.   **C**   **Chapter 5, Section 2.3**

Since 6 x 90 cents shares form each new share, the new share price should be $5.40.

51.   **D**   **Chapter 8, Section 1.9.4**

A barbell strategy is a passive strategy that involves creating a portfolio containing bonds with durations either side of the future liability.

52. **D** **Chapter 4, Section 1.1**

Under MiFID, systematic internalisers are investment firms that execute client orders on their own account on a frequent, systematic and substantial basis.

53. **C** **Chapter 3, Section 2.1**

It is usual for new issues to be underwritten. The underwriter will then buy any unsold shares at a contracted price which may be at a discount to the offer price.

54. **B** **Chapter 5, Section 3.1.3**

	Number of shares	Value	Portfolio value
Starting minimum number of shares at the cum-rights price	3	£6	£18
Rights share at exercise price	1	£2	£2
Resultant portfolio at average, ex-rights price	4	£5	£20

Nil-paid value = theoretical ex-rights price less exercise price = £5 – £2 = £3

55. **D** **Chapter 2, Section 3.4**

German bunds pay coupons once per year.

56. **A** **Chapter 5, Section 2.2.1**

A scrip issue, also known as a bonus issue or capitalisation issue, involves giving shares away for nothing. Scrip issues will not raise any money.

57. **D** **Chapter 4, Section 1.1**

Dark pools are a form of multilateral trading facility and, in Europe, are commonly referred to as alternative trading systems (ATSs). MiFID is an EU directive.

58. **D** **Chapter 2, Section 2.5.2**

The inverted yield curve is where long-term government bond yields are lower than short-term government bond yields and so the yield curve slopes downwards to the right.

59. **C** **Chapter 4, Section 6.1.3**

Secondary market trading of corporate bonds takes place away from the stock exchanges via a decentralised dealer system.

60. **B** **Chapter 3, Section 5.2**

A reverse inquiry is used to describe the situation where a request from an investor results in the issuing company creating new securities (such as medium-term notes).

61.   **A**   **Chapter 3, Section 2.1**

The greenshoe is where the issuing company writes an option to increase the number of shares it issues above a base level. This is in order to stabilise the price in the aftermarket.

62.   **D**   **Chapter 4, Section 5.1**

BTFs are French. The UK has Treasury bills, the US has T-bills and Germany has Bubills.

63.   **D**   **Chapter 7, Section 4.3**

Enterprise cash flow is the cash flow to all of the providers of capital (debt and equity). It does not include cash flows from, or to, the debt holders.

64.   **D**   **Chapter 4, Section 2.1**

Hybrid trading systems are those that combine both order-driven and quote-driven elements.

65.   **C**   **Chapter 2, Section 2.3.4**

The dirty price of a bond can be best described as the price that includes any accrued interest.

66.   **B**   **Chapter 3, Section 2.7**

An exchangeable bond is able to be exchanged for shares in a company that is not the issuer of the bond.

67.   **A**   **Chapter 8, Section 1.2**

Equities are generally considered more risky than bonds and money market instruments, and smaller company shares are more risky than larger, more established company shares.

68.   **C**   **Chapter 2, Section 1.2**

Cumulative preference shares accumulate unpaid dividends and being redeemable means that the issuer has the right to buy the shares back at a specific point (or points) in the future.

69.   **C**   **Chapter 3, Section 3.1**

The reporting accountants will be attesting to the validity of the financial information contained within the prospectus. Alongside the legal advisers, it is the reporting accountants that provide the due diligence.

70.   **A**   **Chapter 7, Section 1.3**

Goodwill only ever appears as an asset in a set of group accounts.

71.   **A**   **Chapter 2, Section 4.3**

All of the credit ratings given are from Moody's, and the best of the given ratings is Baa3 (Moody's lowest investment grade rating). Bonds issued from a company rating at investment grade, rather than junk, are likely to provide a lower yield.

72.   **B**   **Chapter 3, Section 1**

Shares purchased in companies that are already listed are typically arranged by stockbrokers and purchased from other investors who are willing to sell in the secondary market.

73.   **C**   **Chapter 5, Section 3.1.2**

	Number of shares	Value	Portfolio value
Starting minimum number of shares at the cum-rights price	5	£6	£30
Rights share at exercise price	1	£3	£3
Resultant portfolio at average, ex-rights price	6	£5.50	£33

74.   **D**   **Chapter 2, Section 3.4**

The Bobl is issued with a five-year maturity. Bunds are longer-dated German government bonds and OATs and BTANs are French Government bonds.

75.   **A**   **Chapter 3, Section 3.4**

Stabilisation is the process of supporting the price of newly issued securities, usually by the lead manager, for a short period after the issue.

76.   **C**   **Chapter 5, Section 2.3**

If shares were trading at $120, a stock split of three new shares for each share would most likely give a resultant share price of $40.

77.   **A**   **Chapter 4, Section 4.3**

The Dow Jones Industrial Average is price-weighted rather than market-capitalisation-weighted. A price-weighted average gives higher-priced stocks more influence over the average than their lower-priced counterparts, but takes no account of the relative market capitalisation of the components. All of the other options are market-capitalisation-weighted indices.

78.   **C**   **Chapter 4, Section 2.2**

Inter dealer brokers act as agent for dealers but keep the identities secret by settling as if the IDB was the principal to the deal.

79.   **A**   **Chapter 2, Section 1**

Although relatively unusual, some companies issue different classes of ordinary shares with the primary difference being that one class has more voting rights than the other.

80. **D** **Chapter 3, Section 2.5**

A placing is alternatively referred to as a selective marketing. It is where the securities are only offered to a preselected group of potential investors and not investors in general.

81. **A** **Chapter 2, Section 2.4**

Spencer's bonds are yielding 3.80% + 0.45% = 4.25% which is 10 basis points (0.10%) above the 4.15% swap rate.

82. **A** **Chapter 7, Section 2.3**

The annual expense for using up a non-current asset is termed depreciation if the asset is tangible, and amortisation if the asset is intangible.

83. **D** **Chapter 2, Section 2.2.4**

Modified duration provides the approximate price movement brought about by an interest rate change.

84. **B** **Chapter 8, Section 1.10**

Buying futures contracts, call options or buying via CFDs would increase risk by adding more long positions. Buying put options would reduce the risk.

85. **B** **Chapter 7, Section 2.1**

Cash is classified as a current asset within the balance sheet.

86. **C** **Chapter 1, Section 4.1**

Investment banks tend to specialise in corporate finance, securities trading and mergers and acquisitions.

87. **B** **Chapter 3, Section 3.2**

The lead manager of the syndicate will coordinate the overall level of demand and allocate buyers – a process known as bookbuilding.

88. **A** **Chapter 5, Section 4.1**

Share buybacks (a company using its own money to buy back shares from existing investors) are typical in two situations – when the company has reduced its activities (perhaps having sold a major part of its business) and has surplus cash to return to shareholders, and when the company wants to reorganise its capital structure to include more debt and less equity.

89. **A** **Chapter 4, Section 3.2**

Market orders execute at the market price and do not need to specify a price.

90. **A** **Chapter 2, Section 4.2**

Subordinated debt is more risky than senior debt, so it will have a higher yield. All bonds rank above equity in a liquidation.

91.   **A**   **Chapter 4, Section 3.1.1**

Order-driven systems give priority to price first, followed by the time at which the order was submitted.

92.   **A**   **Chapter 1, Section 2.3**

The foreign exchange market is an over-the-counter market with brokers/dealers negotiating directly with one another. It is distributed among all of the major financial centres and includes thousands of banks and many currencies.

93.   **B**   **Chapter 3, Section 2.3**

An open offer is much like a rights issue. It is an offer of shares in a listed company to existing shareholders in proportion to their holdings. It differs from a rights issue in that there is no possibility of selling on the right to purchase the shares nil-paid.

94.   **A**   **Chapter 8, Section 2.1.1**

General insurance is short-term in nature, so tends to hold the greater proportion of money market instruments.

95.   **D**   **Chapter 7, Section 3.1.10**

Dividends are not charged within the income statement. Instead, they are shown in the statement of changes in equity that reconciles the movement in equity from one balance sheet to another.

96.   **B**   **Chapter 7, Section 2.4**

Share premium accounts arise where shares are sold by a company above their nominal value. The excess is treated as a capital reserve.

97.   **A**   **Chapter 8, Section 1.7**

Less than perfect positive correlation between securities in a portfolio will reduce the unsystematic risk.

98.   **D**   **Chapter 7, Section 4.1**

The cash flow statement is split into three headings: cash from operating activities, investing and financing. Depreciation is not a cash flow.

99.   **D**   **Chapter 3, Section 2.6**

An introduction is where a company that already meets the requirements for listing becomes listed without selling any shares.

100.   **B**   **Chapter 4, Section 3.3**

The existence of a central counterparty does not impact the need for brokers and dealers to be members of the exchange. A central counterparty does provide anonymity to both sides of the trade, facilitate netting of transactions in the same security and reduce administration by always settling with the same (central) counterparty.

Syllabus Learning Map

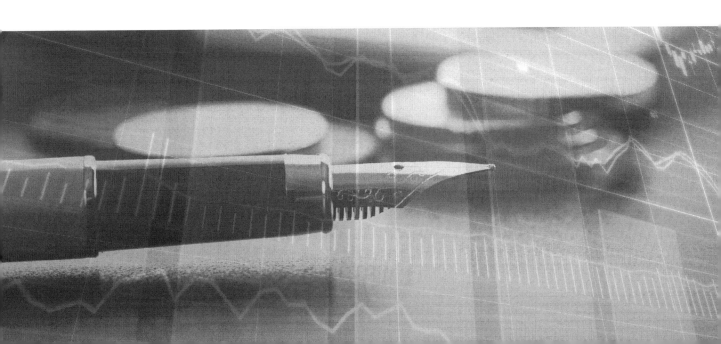

Syllabus Unit/ Element		Chapter/ Section

Element 1	The Financial Services Profession	Chapter 1
1.1	**The Financial Services Profession** On completion, the candidate should:	
1.1.1	know the differences between retail and professional businesses, including: • their clients • equity markets • bond markets • foreign exchange markets	2
1.1.2	know the role of the following within the retail sector of the financial services markets: • banks • pension funds • insurance companies • investment services • financial planning and advice	3
1.1.3	know the role of the following within the wholesale sector of the financial services markets: • investment banks • fund managers • stockbrokers • custodians	4
1.1.4	know the basic differences between equities and bonds	1.1

Element 2	Asset Classes	Chapter 2
2.1	**Cash Assets** On completion, the candidate should:	
2.1.1	understand the uses, advantages and disadvantages of holding cash deposits	5.1
2.1.2	understand the features and characteristics of Treasury bills: • issuer • purpose of issue • minimum denomination • normal life • no coupon and redemption at par	5.2
2.1.3	know the principal features and uses of commercial paper: • issuers, including CP programmes • investors • discount security • unsecured • asset-backed • rating • normal life • method of issuance • role of dealer	5.3

Syllabus Unit/ Element		Chapter/ Section
2.1.4	understand the basic purpose and characteristics of the repo markets: • repo • reverse repo • documentation • benefits of the repo market	5.4
2.2	**Shares** On completion, the candidate should:	
2.2.1	Understand the advantages and disadvantages to issuers and investors of the following investments and their principal features and characteristics: • ordinary shares • non-voting shares • redeemable shares • partly paid shares and calls • and, in respect of these, the generally accepted practice regarding ranking for dividends and voting rights	1
2.2.2	understand the advantages and disadvantages to issuers and investors of the following classes of preference/preferred shares and their principal characteristics: • cumulative • participating • redeemable • convertible	1.2
2.3	**Debt Instruments** On completion, the candidate should:	
2.3.1	know the principal features and characteristics of debt instruments	2.1
2.3.2	understand the uses and limitations of the following: • flat yield • gross redemption yield (using internal rate of return) • net redemption yield • modified duration in the calculation of price change	2.2
2.3.3	be able to calculate: • simple interest income on corporate debt • conversion premiums on convertible bonds and whether it is worth converting • flat yield • accrued interest (given details of the day count conventions)	2.3
2.3.4	understand the concept of spreads: • spread over a government bond benchmark • spread over/under swap	2.4
2.3.5	understand the role of the yield curve and the relationship between price and yield with reference to the yield curve (normal and inverted)	2.5
2.3.6	be able to calculate the present value of a bond (maximum two years) with annual coupon and interest income	2.6

Syllabus Unit/ Element		Chapter/ Section
2.4	**Government Debt** On completion, the candidate should:	
2.4.1	understand the following features and characteristics of conventional government debt: • redemption price • interest payable • accrued interest • effect of changes in interest rates • concept of risk-free	3.1
2.4.2	understand the following features and characteristics of index-linked debt: • inflation – effects and measurement • index-linking • effect of the index on price, interest and redemption • return during a period of zero inflation and, in some economies, deflation	3.2
2.4.3	understand the purpose and characteristics of the strip market: • advantages, disadvantages and uses • result of stripping a bond • zero coupon securities	3.3
2.4.4	understand the characteristics and purpose of government bonds in developed, undeveloped and emerging markets: • settlement periods • coupon payment frequency • terms and maturities • currency, credit and inflation risks	3.4
2.5	**Corporate Debt** On completion, the candidate should:	
2.5.1	understand the principal features and uses of secured debt: • fixed charges and floating charges • asset-backed securities • mortgage-backed securities • covered bonds • securitisation process • role of the trustee, when involved	4.1
2.5.2	understand the principal features and uses of unsecured debt: • subordinated • guaranteed • convertible bonds	4.2
2.5.3	understand the principal features and uses of credit ratings: • rating agencies • impact on price • uses and risks of credit enhancements • difference between investment grade and sub-investment grade bonds • limitations	4.3

Syllabus Unit/ Element		Chapter/ Section
2.6	**Eurobonds** On completion, the candidate should:	
2.6.1	understand the principal features and uses of eurobonds: • issued through syndicates of international banks • bearer • immobilised in depositories • accrued interest • ex-interest date • interest payments	6
2.7	**Other Securities** On completion, the candidate should:	
2.7.1	know the principal features and characteristics of depositary receipts: • American depositary receipts • global depositary receipts • means of creation including pre-release facility • registration • rights attached • dividends • transfer to underlying shares	7.1
2.7.2	know the rights, uses and differences between warrants and covered warrants	7.2
2.7.3	understand the risks and rewards involved in investment in property and the differences between the different investment routes: • direct investment • Real Estate Investment Trusts • open-ended funds	7.3
2.8	**Foreign Exchange** On completion, the candidate should:	
2.8.1	know the principal features and uses of spot, forward and cross rates: • quotation as bid-offer spreads • forwards quoted as bid-offer margins against the spot • quotation of cross rates	8.1
2.8.2	be able to calculate spot and forward settlement prices using: • adding or subtracting forward adjustments • interest rate parity	8.2
2.8.3	understand the factors that affect foreign exchange rates: • freely floating exchange rates • purchasing power parity • currency demand and supply	8.3
2.8.4	understand the factors that affect foreign exchange trading and speculation	8.3.2

Syllabus Unit/ Element		Chapter/ Section
2.9	**Collective Investments** On completion, the candidate should:	
2.9.1	understand the differences between regulated and unregulated collective investment schemes and their advantages and disadvantages to the issuer and investor	9.1
2.9.2	understand the differences between open-ended and closed-ended collective investment schemes and their advantages and disadvantages to the issuer and investor	9.2
2.9.3	understand the circumstances under which a collective investment scheme may be exchange-traded or offered by a fund manager	9.2
2.9.4	understand the circumstances where a collective investment scheme would be issued under a deed of trust and where it may be company or private equity based	9.2

Element 3	Primary Markets	Chapter 3
3.1	**Principal Characteristics** On completion, the candidate should:	
3.1.1	know the principal characteristics of, and the differences between, the primary and secondary markets. In particular: • the role of the governing authority • users of the primary market • users of the secondary market • uses of primary and secondary markets	1
3.2	**Types of Offer** On completion, the candidate should:	
3.2.1	understand the use of an initial public offering: • why would a company choose an IPO • structure of an IPO – base deal plus greenshoe • stages of an IPO • underwritten versus best efforts	2.1
3.2.2	understand the use of follow-on offerings: • why would a company choose a follow-on offering • structure of a follow-on – base deal plus greenshoe • stages of a follow-on offering • underwritten versus best efforts	2.2
3.2.3	understand the use of open offers and offers for subscription: • why would a company choose an open offer • structure of an offer • stages of an offer • tenders, strike price, who is involved in the offer process	2.3

Syllabus Unit/ Element		Chapter/ Section
3.2.4	understand the use of offers for sale: • why would a company choose an offer for sale • structure of an offer for sale • stages of an offer for sale • tenders, strike price, who may receive an allotment, who is involved in the offer process	2.4
3.2.5	understand the basic process and uses of selective marketing and placing: • advantages to the issuing company • what is a placing • what is selective marketing • how is a placing achieved • how is selective marketing achieved	2.5
3.2.6	understand the use of introductions: • why would a company undertake an introduction • structure of an introduction • stages of an introduction	2.6
3.2.7	understand the use of exchangeable/convertible bond offerings: • the difference between exchangeable and convertible bonds • structure of an offering – base deal plus greenshoe • stages of an offering • underwritten versus best efforts	2.7
3.3	**Participants Involved with Equity Offerings** On completion, the candidate should:	

3.3.1	understand the role of the syndicate group:
	 • different roles within a syndicate:
	   ◦ bookrunner
	   ◦ co-lead
	   ◦ co-manager
	   ◦ marketing and book building
		3.2

3.3.2	know the role of advisers: • listing agent • corporate broker	3.1
3.3.3	know the issuer's obligations: • corporate governance • reporting	3.1
3.3.4	understand the purpose and practice of underwriting, rights and • responsibilities of the underwriter: • benefits to the issuing company • risks and rewards to the underwriter	3.3

Syllabus Unit/ Element		Chapter/ Section
3.3.5	understand stabilisation and its purpose: • governing principles and regulation with regard to stabilisation activity • who is involved in stabilisation • what does stabilisation achieve • benefits to the issuing company and investors	3.4
3.4	**Stock Exchanges** On completion, the candidate should:	
3.4.1	know the role of stock exchanges and their regulatory frameworks	4
3.4.2	understand the purpose of admission criteria for main markets and how they can differ for the other markets dealing with smaller companies: • appointment of advisers and brokers • transferability of shares • trading record • amount raised • percentage in public hands • shareholder approval • market capitalisation	4.1
3.5	**Bond Offerings** On completion, the candidate should:	
3.5.1	know the different types of issuer: • supranationals • governments • agency • municipal • corporate • financial institutions and special purpose vehicles	5.1
3.5.2	know the methods of issuance: • scheduled funding programmes and opportunistic issuance, eg, medium-term notes (MTNs) • auction/tender • reverse inquiry (under MTN)	5.2
3.5.3	understand the role of the origination team including: • pitching • indicative bid • mandate announcement • credit rating • roadshow • listing • syndication	5.3

Syllabus Unit/ Element		Chapter/ Section
Element 4	**Secondary Markets**	**Chapter 4**
4.1	**Trading Venues** On completion, the candidate should:	
4.1.1	understand the main characteristics and practices in the developed markets	1
4.1.2	understand the main characteristics and practices in the undeveloped and emerging markets	1
4.1.3	understand the purpose, role and main features of stock exchanges generally. In particular: • scope • provision of liquidity • price formation • brokers versus dealers	1
4.1.4	understand the purpose, role and main features of alternative trading venues: • off-exchange trades • dark pools • OTC • private transactions • multilateral trading facilities	1
4.2	**Methods of Trading and Participants** On completion, the candidate should:	
4.2.1	understand the differences between quote-driven and order-driven markets and how they operate	2.1
4.2.2	know the functions and obligations of: • market makers • broker-dealers • inter-dealer brokers	2.2
4.2.3	understand high frequency trading: • reasons • consequences for the market (eg, flash crashes) • types of company that pursue this strategy	2.3
4.2.4	understand the main services provided by an equity and fixed income prime broker, including: • securities lending and borrowing • leverage trade execution • cash management • core settlement • custody • rehypothecation	2.4

Syllabus Unit/ Element		Chapter/ Section
4.3	**Stock Exchanges** On completion, the candidate should:	
4.3.1	understand the rules, procedures and requirements applying to dealing through the Stock Exchanges' bespoke electronic systems and hybrid trading systems relating to: • order book features • order management • limitations and benefits of trading through bespoke systems • right to call a halt in trading • liquidity • market makers	3.1
4.3.2	understand the following order types and their differences: • market • limit • fill or kill • all or none • execute and eliminate • iceberg • multiple fills	3.2
4.3.3	understand the operation, purpose, benefits and limitations of using a central counterparty	3.3
4.3.4	understand the concept of stamp duties and other transaction taxes and costs on securities trades and the potential for their variation between types of security	3.4
4.4	**Indices** On completion, the candidate should:	
4.4.1	understand how different indices are created and their purpose: • types of index • purpose of weighted indices • purpose of unweighted indices • sector versus national indices • price return, total return and net total return indices • the implications of free float on market capitalisation	4
4.5	**Government Bonds** On completion, the candidate should:	
4.5.1	know the functions, obligations and benefits of the following in relation to government bonds: • primary dealers • broker-dealers • inter-dealer brokers • government issuing authorities	5

Syllabus Unit/ Element		Chapter/ Section
4.6	**Corporate Bond Markets** On completion, the candidate should:	
4.6.1	understand the characteristics of corporate bond markets: • decentralised dealer markets and dealer provision of liquidity • the impact of default risk on prices • the differences between bond and equity markets • dealers rather than market makers • bond pools of liquidity versus centralised equity exchange • relevance of the retail bond market	6.1
4.7	**Dealing Methods** On completion, the candidate should:	
4.7.1	know the different trading methods for bonds: • OTC inter-dealer voice trading • inter-dealer electronic market • OTC customer-to-dealer voice trading • customer-to-dealer electronic market • on-exchange trading	7

4.7.2	understand the different trends between trading methods:
	• characteristics of electronic trading:
	    ○ OTC
	    ○ exchange-traded
	• price-driven via inter-dealer brokers (IDBs) – dealer-to-dealer
	• request for quote (RFQ) – customer-to-dealer
		7.2

4.7.3	know the factors that influence bond pricing:
	• issuer factors:
	    ○ yield to maturity
	    ○ seniority
	    ○ structure
	    ○ technical factors
	    ○ credit rating
	• market factors
	• benchmark bonds
	• liquidity premiums for highly traded bond issues
	• indicative pricing versus firm two-way quotes
	• availability of a liquid repo market and the difficulty in offering illiquid bonds
	• inability to borrow or cover shorts
		7.3

Element 5	Corporate Actions	Chapter 5
5.1	**Income Events** On completion, the candidate should:	
5.1.1	understand the main types of dividends and bond coupon payments: • characteristics • benefits to the investor • benefits to the issuing company	1

Syllabus Unit/ Element		Chapter/ Section
5.2	**Capital Events** On completion, the candidate should:	
5.2.1	know the main types of bond repayment events: • bullet maturities • callable and puttable bonds • sinking funds	2.1
5.2.2	understand the characteristics and rationale for capital restructuring events and the effect on the company's accounts: • bonus issues • stock splits • reverse stock splits	2.2
5.2.3	be able to calculate the impact of bonus issues, stock splits and reverse stock splits on the share price	2.3
5.3	**Capital Raising Events** On completion, the candidate should:	
5.3.1	understand the main features and purpose of open offers and placings	3.2
5.3.2	understand the characteristics of rights issues: • reasons for a rights issue • structure of rights issue • stages of rights issue • pre-emptive rights • trading nil paid	3.1
5.3.3	be able to calculate the impact of a rights issue on the share price	3.1.2
5.3.4	be able to calculate the maximum nil paid rights to be sold to take up the balance at nil cost	3.1.4
5.3.5	be able to calculate the value of nil paid rights	3.1.3
5.4	**Share Capital and Changes to Share Ownership** On completion, the candidate should:	

5.4.1	understand why share buybacks are undertaken:
	• governing regulation:
	   ○ resolution at AGM
	   ○ limits on percentage of shares and price
	   ○ use of company's own money
	• key aspects of share buybacks – criteria to comply with
	• different structures regarding block trades
	• accelerated book build – best efforts basis
	• accelerated book build – back stop price
	• bought deal
		4.1

5.4.2	understand how and why stake building is used:
	• strategic versus acquisition
	• direct versus indirect:
	   ○ direct – outright purchase, ie, dawn raid
	   ○ indirect – CFDs
	• disclosure thresholds, including mandatory takeover threshold
		4.2

Syllabus Unit/ Element		Chapter/ Section
5.4.3	know the characteristics of takeovers and mergers	4.3

Element 6	Clearing and Settlement	Chapter 6
6.1	**Activities** On completion, the candidate should:	
6.1.1	understand the main stages of clearing and settlement	1
6.1.2	understand the concept of DvP and the main differences between DvP models 1 to 3 as defined by the BIS	2
6.1.3	know the concept of custody and the roles of the different types of custodian: • global • regional • local • sub-custodian	3
6.1.4	understand the implications of registered title: • registered title versus unregistered (bearer) • legal title • beneficial interest • voting rights • right to participate in corporate actions	4
6.1.5	understand the basics of designated and pooled nominee accounts and their uses, and the concept of corporate nominees: • designated nominee accounts • pooled nominee accounts • details in share register • function of corporate nominees • legal ownership • beneficial ownership • effect on shareholder rights of using a nominee	5
6.1.6	understand the concepts, requirements, benefits and disadvantages of deals executed cum, ex, special cum and special ex: • timetable • effect of deals on the underlying right • effect on the share price before and after a dividend • the meaning of 'books closed', 'ex-div' and 'cum div', cum and ex-rights • effect of late registration • benefits that may be achieved • disadvantages/risks • when dealing is permitted	6
6.1.7	understand what continuous linked settlement (CLS) is and its purpose: • the settlement of currencies across time zones • receiving and matching instructions • advantages • how it reduces settlement risk (Herstatt risk)	7

Syllabus Unit/ Element		Chapter/ Section
6.2	**Stock Borrowing and Lending** On completion, the candidate should:	
6.2.1	know the uses of, requirements and implications of stock lending: • what is stock lending • stock lending versus repo • purpose for the borrower • purpose for the lender • risk	8
6.2.2	understand the function of stock borrowing and lending intermediaries (SBLIs), including: • use of custodian banks • administration, including collateral • regulation • effect on the lender's rights • lender retains the right to sell	8

Element 7	Accounting Analysis	Chapter 7
7.1	**Basic principles** On completion, the candidate should:	
7.1.1	understand the purpose of financial statements	1.1
7.1.2	understand the requirements for companies and groups to prepare accounts in accordance with applicable accounting standards and the difficulties encountered when comparing companies using different standards: • accounting principles • International Financial Reporting Standards • International Accounting Standards	1.2
7.1.3	understand the differences between group accounts and company accounts and why companies are required to prepare group accounts (candidates should understand the concept of goodwill and minority interests but will not be required to calculate them)	1.3
7.2	**Statements of Financial Position** On completion, the candidate should:	
7.2.1	know the purpose of the statement of financial position, its format and main contents	2.1
7.2.2	understand the concept of depreciation and amortisation	2.3
7.2.3	understand the difference between share capital, capital reserves and revenue reserves	2.4
7.2.4	know how loans and indebtedness are included within a statement of financial position	2.5
7.3	**Income Statement** On completion, the candidate should:	
7.3.1	know the purpose of the income statement, its format and main contents	3.1
7.3.2	understand the difference between capital and revenue expenditure	3.2

Syllabus Unit/ Element		Chapter/ Section
7.4	**Cash Flow Statement** On completion, the candidate should:	
7.4.1	know the purpose of the cash flow statement, its format as set out in IAS 7	4.1
7.4.2	understand the difference between profit and cash and their impact on the long-term future of the business	4.2
7.4.3	understand the purpose of free cash flow and the difference between enterprise cash flow and equity cash flow	4.3
7.5	**Financial Statements Analysis** On completion, the candidate should:	
7.5.1	understand the purpose of ratio analysis and its limitations	5.1
7.5.2	understand the following key ratios: • profitability ratios (gross profit and operating profit margins) • return on capital employed	5.2
7.5.3	understand the following financial gearing ratios: • investors' debt to equity ratio • net debt to equity ratio • interest cover	5.3
7.5.4	understand the following investors' ratios: • enterprise value to EBIT • enterprise value to EBITDA • earnings per share • diluted earnings per share	5.4
7.5.5	be able to calculate the following investors' ratios: • earnings per share • price earnings ratio (both historic and prospective) • gross dividend yield • gross dividend cover	5.4

Element 8	Risk and Reward	Chapter 8
8.1	**Investment Management** On completion, the candidate should:	
8.1.1	know the basics of risk and reward: • assessment of returns • types of risk • quantifying risk	1.1
8.1.2	understand the risk and reward of investment in equities: • risk profile • effect of longer term • can offer income and capital appreciation • purpose and use of dividends	1.2
8.1.3	understand the risk and reward of investment in money market instruments: • risk profile • use as short-term investment	1.3

Syllabus Unit/ Element		Chapter/ Section
8.1.4	understand the risk/reward of investments in debt (fixed-interest, floating-rate and index-linked): • compared to equities • effect of holding to maturity • can combine low risk and certain return • can provide a fixed income • inflation risk • interest rate risk • default risk	1.4
8.1.5	understand risk profile of investment in overseas shares and debt: • country risk • exchange rate risk	1.5
8.1.6	understand the risks facing the investor: • specific/unsystematic • market/systematic • interest rate risk • inflation risk	1.6
8.1.7	understand how to optimise the risk/reward relationship through the use of: • correlation • diversification • use of different asset classes	1.7
8.1.8	understand active investment management methodologies and strategies, and their advantages and disadvantages	1.8
8.1.9	understand passive investment management methodologies and strategies and their advantages and disadvantages	1.9
8.1.10	know the role of hedging in the management of investment risk and how to achieve it: • futures • options • CFDs	1.10
8.1.11	understand the general concept of ranking in respect of shares and corporate bonds in the event of a company's liquidation	1.11
8.2	**Institutional Investment Advice** On completion, the candidate should:	
8.2.1	know the differences between institutional client profiles including: • pension funds • life and general insurance funds • hedge funds • regulated mutual funds • banks	2.1

Syllabus Unit/ Element		Chapter/ Section

8.2.2	understand the need for the publication of regulatory information and financial communications and the types of entity through which publication is achieved:
	• PIPs:
	  ○ RNS
	• SIPs:
	  ○ Bloomberg
	  ○ Reuters
	• analyst research
		2.2

Examination Specification

Each examination paper is constructed from a specification that determines the weightings that will be given to each element. The specification is given below.

It is important to note that the numbers quoted may vary slightly from examination to examination as there is some flexibility to ensure that each examination has a consistent level of difficulty. However, the number of questions tested in each element should not change by more than plus or minus 2.

Element Number	Element	Questions
1	The Financial Services Profession	3
2	Asset Classes	24
3	Primary Markets	16
4	Secondary Markets	14
5	Corporate Actions	9
6	Clearing and Settlement	9
7	Accounting Analysis	13
8	Risk and Reward	12
Total		**100**

CISI Associate (ACSI) Membership can work for you...

Studying for a CISI qualification is hard work and we're sure you're putting in plenty of hours, but don't lose sight of your goal!

This is just the first step in your career; there is much more to achieve!

The securities and investments sector attracts ambitious and driven individuals. You're probably one yourself and that's great, but on the other hand you're almost certainly surrounded by lots of other people with similar ambitions.

So how can you stay one step ahead during these uncertain times?

Entry Criteria:
Pass in either:
- Investment Operations Certificate (IOC), IFQ, ICWIM, Capital Markets in, eg, Securities, Derivatives, Advanced Certificates; or
- one CISI Diploma/Masters in Wealth Management paper

Joining Fee: £25 or free if applying via prefilled application form   **Annual Subscription (pro rata):** £125

Using your new CISI qualification* to become an Associate (ACSI) member of the Chartered Institute for Securities & Investment could well be the next important career move you make this year, and help you maintain your competence.

Join our global network of over 40,000 financial services professionals and start enjoying both the professional and personal benefits that CISI membership offers. Once you become a member you can use the prestigious ACSI designation after your name and even work towards becoming personally chartered.

* ie, Investment Operations Certificate (IOC), IFQ, ICWIM, Capital Markets

Benefits in Summary...
- Use of the CISI CPD Scheme
- Unlimited free CPD seminars, webcasts, podcasts and online training tools
- Highly recognised designatory letters
- Unlimited free attendance at CISI Professional Forums
- CISI publications including *The Review* and *Change – The Regulatory Update*
- 20% discount on all CISI conferences and training courses
- Invitation to the CISI Annual Lecture
- Select benefits – our exclusive personal benefits portfolio

The ACSI designation will provide you with access to a range of member benefits, including Professional Refresher where there are currently over 100 modules available on subjects including Anti-Money Laundering, Information Security & Data Protection, Integrity & Ethics, and the UK Bribery Act. CISI TV is also available to members, allowing you to catch up on the latest CISI events, whilst earning valuable CPD.

Plus many other networking opportunities which could be invaluable for your career.

Professional Refresher

Self-testing elearning modules to refresh your knowledge, meet regulatory and firm requirements, and earn CPD.

Professional Refresher is a training solution to help you remain up-to-date with industry developments, maintain regulatory compliance and demonstrate continuing learning.

This popular online learning tool allows self-administered refresher testing on a variety of topics, including the latest regulatory changes.

There are currently over 100 modules available which address UK and international issues. Modules are reviewed by practitioners frequently and new topics are added to the suite on a regular basis.

Benefits to firms:
- Learning and testing can form part of business T&C programme
- Learning and testing kept up-to-date and accurate by the CISI
- Relevant and useful – devised by industry practitioners
- Access to individual results available as part of management overview facility, 'Super User'
- Records of staff training can be produced for internal use and external audits
- Cost-effective – no additional charge for CISI members
- Available to non-members

Benefits to individuals:
- Comprehensive selection of topics across sectors
- Modules are regularly reviewed and updated by industry experts
- New topics added regularly
- Free for members
- Successfully passed modules are recorded in your CPD log as active learning
- Counts as structured learning for RDR purposes
- On completion of a module, a certificate can be printed out for your own records

The full suite of Professional Refresher modules is free to CISI members, or £250 for non-members. Modules are also available individually. To view a full list of Professional Refresher modules visit:

cisi.org/refresher

If you or your firm would like to find out more, contact our Client Relationship Management team:

+ 44 20 7645 0670
crm@cisi.org

For more information on our elearning products, contact our Customer Support Centre on +44 20 7645 0777, or visit our website at cisi.org/refresher

er

Professional Refresher

Top 5

SCORM COMPLIANT

Integrity & Ethics
- High-Level View
- Ethical Behaviour
- An Ethical Approach
- Compliance vs Ethics

Anti-Money Laundering
- Introduction to Money Laundering
- UK Legislation and Regulation
- Money Laundering Regulations 2017
- Proceeds of Crime Act 2002
- Terrorist Financing
- Suspicious Activity Reporting
- Money Laundering Reporting Officer
- Sanctions

General Data Protection Regulation (GDPR)
- Understanding the Terminology
- The Six Data Protection Principles
- Data Subject Rights
- Technical and Organisational Measures

Information Security and Data Protection
- Cyber-Security
- The Regulators

UK Bribery Act
- Background to the Act
- The Offences
- What the Offences Cover
- When Has an Offence Been Committed?
- The Defences Against Charges of Bribery
- The Penalties

Latest

Cryptocurrencies
- Bitcoin
- Altcoins
- Central Bank Digital Currency and Cryptofiat
- Trading Cryptocurrencies
- The Impact of Cryptocurrencies

Change Management
- Types of Change
- Change Theories
- The Complexities of Change
- Leading Change
- Key Skills and Competencies

Regulatory Update
- General Regulatory Changes
- Sector Changes

Common Reporting Standard (CRS)
- What is the CRS?
- Implementation and Compliance
- Practical Issues
- The Global Perspective

Cross-Border Investment Services
- The UK System
- Overseas Regulation
- Applicability
- Face-to-Face Meetings
- Distance Communications
- Brexit Implications
- Gifts and Entertainment
- Tax Evasion, Money Laundering, and Terrorist Financing

Operations

Best Execution
- What Is Best Execution?
- Achieving Best Execution
- Order Execution Policies
- Information to Clients & Client Consent
- Monitoring, the Rules, and Instructions
- Best Execution for Specific Types of Firms

Approved Persons Regime
- The Basis of the Regime
- Fitness and Propriety
- The Controlled Functions
- Principles for Approved Persons
- The Code of Practice for Approved Persons

Corporate Actions
- Corporate Structure and Finance
- Life Cycle of an Event
- Mandatory Events
- Voluntary Events

Wealth

Client Assets and Client Money
- Protecting Client Assets and Client Money
- Segregation and Holding
- Due Diligence of Custodians and Banks
- Reconciliations
- Records and Accounts
- CASS Oversight

Investment Principles and Risk
- Diversification
- Factfind and Risk Profiling
- Investment Management
- Modern Portfolio Theory and Investing Styles
- Direct and Indirect Investments
- Socially Responsible Investment
- Collective Investments
- Investment Trusts
- Dealing in Debt Securities and Equities

Banking Standards
- Introduction and Background
- Strengthening Individual Accountability
- Reforming Corporate Governance
- Securing Better Outcomes for Consumers
- Enhancing Financial Stability

Suitability of Client Investments
- Assessing Suitability
- Risk Profiling
- Establishing Risk Appetite
- Obtaining Customer Information
- Suitable Questions and Answers
- Making Suitable Investment Selections
- Guidance, Reports and Record Keeping

International

Foreign Account Tax Compliance Act (FATCA)
- Foreign Financial Institutions
- Due Diligence Requirements
- Reporting
- Compliance

MiFID II
- The Organisations Covered by MiFID II
- The Products Subject to MiFID II
- The Origins of MiFID II
- The Impact of MiFID II
- The Products Covered by MiFID II
- Cross-Border Business Under MiFID II

UCITS
- The Original UCITS Directive
- UCITS III
- UCITS IV
- Non-UCITS Funds
- Latest Developments

cisi.org/refresher

Feedback to the CISI

Have you found this workbook to be a valuable aid to your studies? We would like your views, so please email us at learningresources@cisi.org with any thoughts, ideas or comments.

Accredited Training Partners

Support for exam students studying for the Chartered Institute for Securities & Investment (CISI) qualifications is provided by several Accredited Training Partners (ATPs), including Fitch Learning and BPP. The CISI's ATPs offer a range of face-to-face training courses, distance learning programmes, their own learning resources and study packs which have been accredited by the CISI. The CISI works in close collaboration with its ATPs to ensure they are kept informed of changes to CISI exams so they can build them into their own courses and study packs.

CISI Workbook Specialists Wanted

Workbook Authors

Experienced freelance authors with finance experience, and who have published work in their area of specialism, are sought. Responsibilities include:
- Updating workbooks in line with new syllabuses and any industry developments
- Ensuring that the syllabus is fully covered

Workbook Reviewers

Individuals with a high-level knowledge of the subject area are sought. Responsibilities include:
- Highlighting any inconsistencies against the syllabus
- Assessing the author's interpretation of the workbook

Workbook Technical Reviewers

Technical reviewers to provide a detailed review of the workbook and bring the review comments to the panel. Responsibilities include:
- Cross-checking the workbook against the syllabus
- Ensuring sufficient coverage of each learning objective

Workbook Proofreaders

Proofreaders are needed to proof workbooks both grammatically and also in terms of the format and layout. Responsibilities include:
- Checking for spelling and grammar mistakes
- Checking for formatting inconsistencies

If you are interested in becoming a CISI external specialist call:
+44 20 7645 0609

or email:
externalspecialists@cisi.org

For bookings, orders, membership and general enquiries please contact our Customer Support Centre on +44 20 7645 0777, or visit our website at cisi.org